GET WHAT'S YOURS

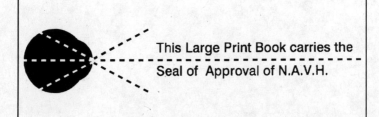

This Large Print Book carries the
Seal of Approval of N.A.V.H.

GET WHAT'S YOURS

THE SECRETS TO MAXING OUT YOUR SOCIAL SECURITY

LAURENCE J. KOTLIKOFF, PHILIP MOELLER, AND PAUL SOLMAN

THORNDIKE PRESS
A part of Gale, Cengage Learning

GALE
CENGAGE Learning®

Farmington Hills, Mich • San Francisco • New York • Waterville, Maine
Meriden, Conn • Mason, Ohio • Chicago

GALE
CENGAGE Learning

LIBRARY OF CONGRESS CATALOGING-IN-PUBLICATION DATA

Kotlikoff, Laurence J.
  Get what's yours : the secrets to maxing out your social security / by Laurence J. Kotlikoff, Philip Moeller, and Paul Solman. — Large print edition.
    pages cm. — (Thorndike Press large print lifestyles)
    ISBN 978-1-4104-8073-6 (hardcover) — ISBN 1-4104-8073-9 (hardcover)
    1. Social security—United States. 2. Retirement income—United States.
I. Moeller, Philip. II. Solman, Paul. III. Title.
HD7125.K65 2015b
368.4'300973—dc23   2015010651

Published in 2015 by arrangement with Simon & Schuster, Inc.

Printed in Mexico
1 2 3 4 5 6 7 19 18 17 16 15

I dedicate this book to the flower of my life — Bridget Jourgensen.
— LAURENCE KOTLIKOFF

To Cheryl and the joy of seeing you every day.
— PHILIP MOELLER

To my grandchildren: Bella, Joe, Will, Finn, Bridget, Anderson, and Hadley.
— PAUL SOLMAN

CONTENTS

1
GETTING PAUL NEARLY
$50,000 IN EXTRA BENEFITS
OVER TENNIS

This book was born of a simple question —
How old are Paul and his wife?

Larry and Paul were taking a break from
what they call tennis, shooting the breeze,
since talking is easier than running after er-
rant shots. Larry launched into a harangue,
as he often does; this one was about Social
Security's impossible complexity. Paul was
listening, as usual, with his skeptical journalist's ear. Or, maybe, since it was Larry, just
half-listening.

Then Larry asked, How old were Paul and
his wife and when were they planning to
take their Social Security benefits?

Proudly, Paul told Larry not to worry: he
and his wife had it all figured out. They
would both wait until 70, when Paul would
get something like $40,000 a year instead of
the $30,000 or so if he took his benefits at
66, his *"full"* — but not *"maximum"* — retirement age, which was coming right up. Paul

had been reading and saving those annual green statements from the Social Security Administration for years with their "Estimated Benefits." He'd been reading his wife's, too. As the family's financial planner, he knew just how much they were entitled to.

But how old are you and Jan? Larry asked.

What difference does it make? said Paul. Like I say, we're both waiting until 70.

It makes a big difference, said Larry.

Okay, Paul's wife would soon turn 66; he, 65.

Here's what you do, said Larry, never at a loss when it comes to speaking in the imperative. Jan should apply for her Social Security retirement benefit when she turned 66, but then "suspend" it. That is, she would make herself eligible for the benefit but wouldn't take it.

Then, said Larry, when you (Paul) turn 66, you apply *just* for a *spousal* benefit. When you each hit 70, you do as originally planned — you each take your own retirement benefits, at which point they will start at their highest possible values.

Or, Larry continued, clearly thinking aloud, *you* apply and suspend at 66 and *Jan* begins taking the spousal benefit, since you earned more than she did, didn't you?

Paul can be quite dismissive of what he considers Larry's flights of fantasy, Larry being the epitome of "often overstated, but never in doubt." Yet Paul had begun to pay close attention. Having reported on business and economics on public television for decades, Paul understood the intricacies of business, finance, and economics better than most Americans (though admittedly, that may not be saying much). The exceptions, however, were the professional economists he'd befriended in the course of his career. Larry was one of them, and among the most deeply versed in financial planning.

Spousal benefits? Paul had vaguely heard of them. He had, however, never imagined he or his wife were eligible for any, though, had you asked him why not, he couldn't have told you.

Spousal benefits for four years. That should be almost $50,000, Larry quickly estimated.

An aside is in order here. Larry is a world-famous scold or, he will tell you, a dead-on Cassandra, with respect to Social Security's insolvency. Advising people like Paul to take extra benefits from the system while himself decrying the system's funding shortfall was not what Paul expected to hear. (More on

11

that in Chapter 18.) But Larry believes it's not fair that some beneficiaries get more than others simply because they *know* the system's rules. And Paul and Phil agree with him.

Fifty thousand dollars? Explain, Paul said.

Well, if Jan's Social Security full retirement benefit were, say, $24,000, you'd be eligible to get half that as a spousal benefit: about $12,000 a year. And if you get $12,000 a year from age 66 to age 70, that's $48,000. If, on the other hand, Jan takes the spousal benefit on *your* Social Security earnings record, she'll get more per year but for only three years instead of four, because she'll be 67 by the time you become eligible, only three years from 70. But still, that would mean . . . etc.

However number-laden the trees, the forest was plain to see: there seemed to be an unambiguous strategy for maximizing benefits that Paul and Jan were eligible to collect, having contributed for decades, but had been entirely unaware of.

If this is true, said Paul, I'm buying you dinner. Anywhere in the world.

Boston will do, said Larry, who also lives there. But there are dozens of really important details like this one. What we should really do (we're compressing here) is write a book. And we should include Phil Moeller, a retirement expert who's already spoken with me about such a project. He's been a financial journalist for years, and has written article after article for *U.S. News & World Report* and *Money* about retirees who collectively leave tens of *billions* of dollars in Social Security benefits on the table by failing to claim everything to which they are entitled. Plus, Phil loves the Red Sox (although not as much as the Baltimore Orioles) and the New England Patriots.

Fast-forward. Paul's wife came of age (66). She filed and suspended — by phone. The person she talked to couldn't have been nicer. *Paul* came of age. He filed for a spousal benefit. The Social Security woman on the phone had never heard of file-and-suspend, checked with her supervisor, and came back on the line to thank him for enlightening her about a strategy she could now share with everyone who called. When they hit 70, both Paul and his wife called again, were again reprocessed — graciously, competently, and within minutes, though his wife was nonplussed when asked if she'd ever been a nun. And Paul has since taken Larry to dinner, and a pretty good dinner at that.

GET WHAT'S YOURS — AND YOU DON'T EVEN HAVE TO BUY LARRY A MEAL

We've written this book to help people maximize the Social Security benefits they have earned and therefore, we believe, deserve to get. We three authors — Boston University economist Laurence Kotlikoff, journalist and aging expert Phil Moeller, and *PBS NewsHour* economics correspondent Paul Solman — have spent years studying the system and making it intelligible to the public.

Why have we bothered to write this book?

Because Social Security is, far and away,

14

Americans' most important retirement asset. And that's not only true for people of modest means. Middle-income and upper-income households actually have the most to gain, in total amounts, from getting Social Security right. Toting up lifetime benefits, even low-earning couples may be Social Security millionaires. And except for the Bill Gateses and Warren Buffetts of the world — whose percentage of the population was exceedingly modest last we checked — Social Security is a *very* meaningful income source.

So, this book is for nearly every one of you who's ever earned a paycheck and wants every Social Security benefit dollar to which you are entitled — entitled because you paid for it. You earned it. It's yours. It can even be yours if you never contributed a penny to the system but have or had a spouse, living or dead, who did. It may even be yours if you spent some of all of your career working for employers who did not have to participate in Social Security.

Perhaps you wondered, when you got your first paycheck, what the huge deduction for that four-letter word "FICA" referenced. If you learned that it stood for the Federal Insurance Contributions Act, you might have been none too pleased at first, but then assuaged by hearing that these "contributions" — week after week, month after month, year after year, out of each and every paycheck (up to a limit) — would lead to higher retirement benefits.

Even those of us who aren't superrich, but have earned and saved a lot, view Social Security as a critical lifeline. We realize, after the Crash of 2008, that no assets — not our homes, not our bonds, and certainly not our stocks — are safe from life-altering declines. We realize that even our private pensions, if we have them, may hinge on our former employer staying in business and inflation not eroding the pension's purchasing power. (It's the rare private-sector pension that boosts payments to protect against inflation.) We also know that we could, with plausible breakthrough medical discoveries, live to 100 or longer.

But isn't Social Security a bigger deal for the poor? Actually, it's not. To be sure, Social Security benefits are a crucial lifeline for lower-income beneficiaries. And, yes, Social Security benefits rise less for higher earners than do their FICA tax contributions. But benefits do rise with both time and earnings and they involve *very* big sums.

Take, for example, a 60-year-old couple, who both stop working at that age, each partner having earned Social Security's taxable FICA limit — the maximum taxable amount, starting at age 25. That maximum was $22,900 in wage income in 1979, when they began working; it's $118,500 for 2015, going up every year in lockstep with the nation's average wage increases. Running coauthor Larry's maximizemysocialsecurity.com software, a 60-year-old couple who earned at or above the payroll tax ceiling their entire lives would get $31,972 each or $63,944 a year collectively if they began taking benefits at 66, which is their Full Retirement Age (FRA). (We will have more to say about the FRA and other official Social Security terms in Chapter 3, and key terms like this one also are explained in the Glossary at the end of the book.) If they deferred benefits until age 70, they'd get $42,203 ($84,406), which is 32 percent higher than their age 66 benefits, because for every year you wait, Social Security pays you a benefit that's *8 percent higher* than the year before, even before its annual inflation adjustment.

For such a couple, collecting Social Security at 62 represents a $1.2 million asset. In other words, you'd need a nest egg of $1.2 million to produce the same amount of annual income that you'll get from Social Security, assuming you could safely earn 2 percent a year above inflation on your investments.

Now, $1.2 million is more than many upper-middle-income retirees have saved by retirement age. The net worth of a typical household headed by someone aged 65 to 69 is only a fourth of this amount and much of it is in the value of their home. And all you have to do is stay alive and those Social Security payments will keep coming each and every month — payments guaranteed by the United States government and protected against inflation. That's because every January, you get, by law, annual benefit raises that equal the prior year's rate of inflation.[1]

Moreover, there is a huge amount of money at stake in *maximizing* one's Social Security benefits. The $1.2 million valuation, large as it is, actually assumes our 60-year-old couple makes the *wrong* Social Security benefit collection decisions. It assumes they take their retirement benefits as early as possible and forgo cashing in on what are, to them, free spousal benefits like the one Paul took. If they make the right decisions, they can increase the value of their lifetime Social Security "asset" by more than $400,000, to $1.6 million!

This 33 percent increase may sound hard

to believe, but it's true. The couple just needs to apply for the right benefits at the right time, as Larry advised Paul and Jan to do. Simple enough. But figuring out what to apply for and when to do it is not simple. Indeed, Social Security is the most complicated "simple" program you're ever likely to encounter.

One more story, just to drive home the point of complexity. It comes from our Technical Expert, Jerry Lutz.

One day, while Jerry still worked for Social Security, a claims representative approached him with a question. A new claimant's husband had died of a heart attack while they were having sex. They had been married for less than 9 months, the threshold for receiving survivor's benefits from Social Security. But one of the exceptions to the 9-month duration of marriage rule involves "accidental death." Up until then, Jerry had considered "accidental" to mean something like a car wreck. But his job was to research tough cases like this one. So he searched the vast Social Security rule book and found POMS GN 00305.105, which describes an accidental death in part as follows:

A "bodily injury" occurs whenever the outside force or cause affects the body sufficiently to interfere with its normal function.

The cause of the bodily injury is:

"External" if it originated outside the body. An external force can include an injury suffered due to weather conditions or exertion.

NOTE: By exertion we mean an activity that involves at least moderate effort for the average person. Routine activities, e.g., standing, do not constitute exertion for purposes of finding accidental death. Circumstances which more readily lend themselves to a favorable finding of accidental death include:

- an unexpected heart attack occurs during moderate exertion;
- an unforeseen event negates the voluntary nature of an activity, e.g., an exercise machine breaks down while exercising;
- some unintended, unexpected, and unforeseen result occurs during exertion, e.g., a fall or slip while running; or
- a crisis or sudden peril requires strenuous exertion.

"Moderate exertion"? Arguably. "Unintended" and "unexpected"? Indubitably. And so, based on the claimant's testimony and her husband's death certificate, widow's benefits were eventually conferred, but the determination was anything but simple.

There are 10,000 baby boomers reaching retirement age every day. Each of them needs to know precisely how to get Social Security's best deal. But Paul's best moves — or Larry's or Phil's, for that matter — aren't necessarily yours. The Social Security system has 2,728 core rules and thousands upon thousands of additional codicils in its Program Operating Manual, which supposedly clarify those rules. In the case of married couples alone, the formula for each spouse's benefit comprises 10 complex mathematical functions, one of which is in four dimensions.

This book contains minimal math, excepting the "simple" formula presented in this endnote.[2] Rather, it explains in the simplest possible terms the traps to avoid and basic strategies to employ in maximizing a household's Social Security retirement, spousal, child, mother/father, survivor, divorcee, and disability benefits. That covers a whole lot of ground, which is why this book is about Social Security and nothing else. And why it's not as succinct as we (and you) might like.

We will point out Social Security's windfalls and pitfalls — explain obscure benefits and more obscure penalties; benefit collection strategies like *file and suspend* (applying for benefits, but not taking them) and *start, stop, start* (starting benefits, stopping them, and restarting them), which we bet most of you have never heard of. We'll also get into the details of Social Security's *deeming* rules (being forced, in some cases, to take certain benefits early at a very big cost) and related gotchas that can handicap you financially for the rest of your life.

We'll walk you through Social Security's significant incentives to get divorced, to get married, or to live in sin depending on your circumstances. Do you know about Social Security's hidden payoff to working late in life? About the Earnings Test (loss of benefits at certain ages from earning too much) that may not really be a test at all? How about the Family Maximum Benefit (the limit to the benefits your family can collect based on your work record)? It's actually not a maximum. It's also unfairly low for poor, disabled workers.

Throughout, we'll emphasize the often huge payoff from waiting to collect benefits.

But we'll also explain lots of situations where it's best *not* to wait. We'll even throw in the mythical man with four ex-wives who could theoretically collect divorce or widower benefits on each of them. The ever-surprising and often frustrating Social Security Sudoku puzzle goes on and on. We're here to solve it.

We're also relieved that you came to us to learn about Social Security and aren't relying solely on Social Security's advice. Frankly, Social Security is not the first place we'd send you to learn how to maximize your lifetime benefits. With the exception of the system's small number of Technical Experts (including former Technical Expert Jerry Lutz, who reviewed this book for accuracy), many of Social Security's official or phone support staff are insufficiently trained or too beleaguered to dispense information or advice about the system's ins and outs. And they aren't supposed to give advice anyway. We're going to provide specific examples of people losing lots of money by believing or following what the well-meaning folks at Social Security told them. Unfortunately, the local Social Security office is single-stop shopping for most retirees making their benefit decisions. And many of them are waiting pretty late in the game before even thinking about managing what for most retirees is their largest financial asset.

At the surface level, Social Security is complex because it has so many seemingly crazy rules. At a deeper level, its complexity reflects social policy that, when translated into practice, produces results that often defy common sense. An example is paying survivor benefits, based on the work records of ex-spouses, to divorcees who remarry, but only if they remarry after reaching age 60. Get remarried at 59 and 364 days and you're out of luck. Another perversity is paying benefits to mothers (or fathers) of young children if their spouse is collecting retirement benefits, *but only if the parents are married.* If the parents are divorced, too bad.

The result is a government retirement system that few if any can decipher without the kind of help provided here. And yet, for most people, Social Security is their *only* retirement option. Moreover, given the virtual disappearance of company pensions, except for those grandparented under old plans, and the failure of most Americans either to contribute or contribute fully to 401(k), IRA, and other retirement accounts, Social Security is, well, pretty much it for pretty much all of us.

Our book will be organized around general lessons, supporting examples, specific game plans tailored to your situation, and answers to actual questions posed to Larry in his enormously popular "Ask Larry" column, which appears weekly on Paul's *PBS News-Hour* Making Sen$e Business Desk (http://www.pbs.org/newshour/making-sense/).

A warning that we'll issue up front and reiterate throughout the book: we will often repeat ourselves. The worst that can happen, we figure, is that you'll simply skim and skip ahead. Much worse would be your forgetting some of your key options and thus nullifying, at least for yourself, the whole point of *Get What's Yours*. And for those of you who might think the repetitions betray a lack of confidence in our readers, know that we authors ourselves still check our notes on these items when we hit the key age milestones, despite having written about Social Security for years.

PAUL AND JAN GOT WHAT'S THEIRS. TIME TO GET WHAT'S YOURS.

This book was born of Paul's first Social Security encounter with Larry. We wrote it to help people like you, who don't happen to know Larry, get every last penny Social

Security owes you. We've spent a huge amount of time trying to come up with clear, correct answers to questions we all face so you don't have to.

Finally, we think it's more than legitimate for you to feel *entitled* to these benefits, a feeling deeply rooted in all those years of FICA payments, buttressed by the annual Social Security statements itemizing your past contributions and projecting your future benefits, and guaranteed by our politicians' unwavering promises to defend the system and what it owes you. You have been forking over payroll taxes your entire working life; you deserve to get what you paid for; and it's the law.

2
Life's Biggest Danger Isn't Dying, It's Living

As a prospective retiree, what should you be most afraid of? Golf elbow? Dr. Phil fatigue? Driving your spouse to drink? Dementia? Death?

We apologize for such brutal candor, but from this book's point of view, none of the above. We think your greatest fear should be *immortality.* Or, failing that, an epically long life. That's because — if you're the typical American who has saved less than $10,000 on average by the time you're 10 years from retiring — the longer you live, the greater the danger of your "golden" years turning to lead, weighed down by penury and its attendant anxieties.

You will face rejections by doctors who disdain Medicare. Your children may face crippling debt to buy you a long-shot cure that no insurance — public or private — will cover. You won't leave the house without a companion for fear of falling, yet won't be able to afford one, or even a cab (or Uber).

In other words, the greatest danger you may face is *outliving your savings,* which brings us quickly to this chapter's punch line: the best way to mitigate that fate, in terms of Social Security, is a strategy we'll be emphasizing throughout this book: be *patient* in taking certain benefits because they can be bigger — *much* bigger — if you wait.

We realize that many baby boomers have *already* outlived their savings and therefore exist more or less hand-to-mouth. If you fit this description, you may have no option but to take whatever you can get from Social Security as soon as possible. Ditto if your health or luck or gene-pool draw rules out a long life. We know there are many special circumstances that support early claiming of benefits.

But for the rest of you, we counsel patience. And for those of you who took retirement benefits early and think it's now too late, we're here to tell you that you retain the option of suspending your benefits at Full Retirement Age (66 for current retirees) and starting them up again at or before age 70. Even for those of you cursed with a supposedly fatal disease who might feel you should take whatever you can while you're still alive and kicking, we suggest thinking twice; medical breakthroughs are always possible. And, as we'll explain, collecting early can cost your current and ex-spouses big bucks in lower widow/er benefits.

A FEW WORDS OF WARNING TO EARLY CLAIMANTS

Most of you will have a clear and obvious choice. And if you aren't waiting until 66 or 70 to take at least one benefit that will be much higher, adjusted for inflation, than the amount of that benefit available at an earlier age, you are, in our opinion, imprudent, if not nuts. Moreover, this isn't just about *you*. Not surprisingly, the benefits of your "dependents" — spouse, ex-spouse, surviving spouse, and children — *depend* on your work record. And in the case of survivor benefits available to family members when you die, these benefits depend on precisely when you decided to collect your own retirement benefit.

Amazingly, however, at least to us, this is not what happens. Take a gander at this nifty little table, pulled from an annual Social Security report (the Social Security Administration, or SSA, issues nearly as many reports as it has beneficiaries):

MEN									
Year	Number	62	63	64	65	66	DI*	67–69	70+
2009	1,454,000	44	7	7	12	15	12	2	1
2010	1,384,000	43	8	7	11	16	13	2	1
2011	1,345,000	41	7	8	10	17	14	2	1
2012	1,362,000	38	6	7	12	18	16	2	1
WOMEN									
2009	1,279,000	50	6	7	10	11	12	2	2
2010	1,245,000	48	8	7	10	11	12	2	2
2011	1,243,000	47	7	8	10	12	12	2	2
2012	1,269,000	43	7	7	12	12	15	2	2

CLAIMING AGES. *Percentages (rounded to nearest percent). *DI = Disability payments are automatically converted to retirement payments at Full Retirement Age.*

The three of us were taken aback by how few people are on the far right-hand side of this table. One to 2 percent of people wait until 70 to take their Social Security? How can that be?

The big reason, as just mentioned, is that lots of people need whatever money they can get as soon as they can get it. Rainy day funds are pretty much nonexistent for most Americans. So when a storm hits, our finances are swamped and we begin bailing. After the Great Recession, more people claimed Social Security early. That was true for retirement benefits, but applications for

Social Security Disability Insurance also spiked. As the economy has slowly improved, early claiming percentages have declined to longer-term trend levels. Unfortunately, better financial planning and rainy day funds aren't part of the recovery story.

Regardless of the overall health of the economy, people who lose their jobs in their early 60s tend to file early for Social Security to replace their lost income. So do people who work in physically demanding jobs. They also tend to file early, often because they're worn out, their jobs have become too demanding, and they don't think they'll last very long. And people who began work when they were young also tend to file early, for obvious reasons: enough is enough. "I've paid for years and years for these benefits. I finally want to see them in my hands." Finally, it turns out, early filers also are more likely to have traditional pensions than those who don't file early. Maybe they feel they can better afford reduced Social Security benefits, as strange as that sounds.

But it also turns out that the when-to-file decision can be shaped by how it's explained to you. To abbreviate lots of research, people who frame their Social Security benefits decision from the vantage point of being 62 are greatly influenced by the fear of losing four years of benefits if they wait until age 66. Framing the decision from a 66-year-old's perspective, however, will cause more people to wait to that age or something close to it. A similar behavioral wild card is whether the advice people receive about filing for Social Security emphasizes how much money they could *lose* by not filing early versus the possible *gains* they would see if they delayed filing. Also, "The use of 'break-even analysis' has the very strong effect of encouraging individuals to claim early," according to a recent study by top economists on how behavioral framing affects claiming decisions.[1]

We'll explain shortly why this sort of "break-even analysis" may seem appropriate, but isn't. For now, though, we simply note what behavioral economists have long known: that while we humans do like to make money, our fear of *losing it* is an even more powerful driver of our decisions.

Last, but hardly least, the Social Security Administration routinely nudged people toward early claiming. Until several years ago, the agency discussed the claiming decision as a "break-even" calculation, a simple version of which might go like this. Your benefit at age 66 is projected to be $1,000. If you begin taking benefits at 62, they will be only $750 a month. By waiting until 66, you'll have passed up $36,000 in benefits (48 months at $750 a month). Your benefit at 66 will net you an extra $250 a month for the rest of your life. But it will take you 12 years, until age 78, before you'll make up the $36,000 you passed up by not filing at age 62. That is, your extra $250 a month will bring you $3,000 more a year; 12 years later, you'll have made up the full $36,000. You will have "broken even." But, as we will stress shortly, calculating your benefit collection options this way is miles off base. Yet approaching it this way caused people to claim benefits 12 to 15 months sooner than if people were told that Social Security had determined that it will cost the program the same amount of money regardless of when people claim benefits. The break-even lingo tended to make people worry that delaying benefits was a gamble. The agency has since shifted its communication approach to providing a value-neutral perspective.

But just to come full circle here, the SSA maintains that claiming age makes no difference in overall program spending. However, while that may be the case when considering benefits for everyone and average mortality statistics, there are significant exceptions when it comes to individual longevity, keyed mostly to education and income levels. And some experts even dispute that the system as a whole is neutral to claiming dates. A 2012 study by economists John B. Shoven and Sita Nataraj Slavov found the system was not actuarially fair or balanced but tilted in favor of people who delayed taking benefits.[2]

Now, maybe we're naïve, but it is hard to accept that more than 83 percent of American men and 85 percent of the nation's retirement-age women were so financially strapped that they *had to* claim benefits before reaching their Full Retirement Ages (let alone age 70). Recent research agrees. One study concluded that nearly 40 percent of those who claimed benefits early came to regret their decisions later.[3]

Can we overcome this bias? Yes, but doing so may require us to delve into a deeper, darker explanation of how we make decisions. Psychologists might loosely call it economic multiple personality disorder, best dealt with if understood. Here's the argument.

How Many People Are You, Anyway?

We tend to think of ourselves as being one person — one unitary self. But Hamlet was of two minds. The eighteenth-century Scottish philosopher David Hume wrote: "I cannot compare the soul more properly to anything than to a republic or common-wealth, in which the several members are united by the reciprocal ties of government and subordination." The nineteenth-century poet Walt Whitman famously noted: "I contain multitudes."

It's by now a commonplace in psychology that multiple selves contend over one body and its consciousness. Think of your last sudden bout of "road rage." Who *is* that person controlling your behavior in such an outlandish way? Recall the New Year's resolutions routinely broken by Groundhog Day. Or, more dramatically, picture the alcoholic whose long-term morning self takes a dose of Antabuse so that s/he will vomit when the impulsive "alcoholic" self takes over and tries to knock down a stiff drink in the afternoon.

What is the relevance of multiple selves to the timing of Social Security benefits? It's the difficulty of exercising impulse control — of delaying gratification. The classic example is a Stanford experiment in which psychologists put one marshmallow in front of young children to eat and offered them a choice: they could eat it now or wait a few minutes and get a second one.

You know the problem as well as we do. If the self of the moment can't be coaxed to care enough about your future self (or selves), "you" will overindulge in the here and now.

And so it is with Social Security. Your multiple selves duke it out inside your brain to protect their own living standards, using their own very different time horizons.

BE THE BEST SELF YOU CAN BE
But let's be clear: this book is written for only one of those selves — the reflective, rational long-term thinker, the one who reads books about Social Security, who realizes the organism it inhabits may live to 100 or beyond. This "adult" self is located in the youngest part of the brain — the prefrontal cortex that evolved after the parts we share with reptiles. Our reptilian self rules our reflex emotions while the prefrontal "you" tries not to drive while tipsy, or smoke, or hang glide. And, unless the organism formerly known as you is in dire need or facing imminent and sure demise, it doesn't automatically take Social Security retirement benefits early. Because to do so would be to ignore that self's fiduciary responsibility to, well, all your future selves.

Admittedly, there's a philosophical problem here. You might say: "Why should I care about any of my future selves? What have

37

they ever done for *me*?" If that's your attitude, this chapter has little to offer.

But, in moments of reflective repose, as you presumably are at this very moment, you might feel as protective about your doddering, weak-kneed, ever-feebler future self or selves as the authors of this book do about *theirs.* If this is the case, you will not want to let him, her, or "them" suffer the fate of outliving "your" savings.

Such discussion inevitably leads to a next question: how long might the bunch of you's live? Social Security has its own actuaries to estimate such probabilities and posts an Actuarial Life Table. Here's a summary:

	MEN		WOMEN	
	Death	Years	Death	Years
Age	Odds*	Left	Odds*	Left
40	0.22%	38.23	0.13%	42.24
50	0.53%	29.35	0.33%	33.02
60	1.10%	21.27	0.67%	24.3
70	2.45%	14.03	1.64%	16.33
80	6.16%	8.1	4.39%	9.65
90	16.84%	4.02	13.11%	4.85

*Probability of dying within one year.

We reproduce, in the Notes, an expanded

table.[4] If you consult it, you will see that a 60-year-old woman faces odds of only two-thirds of a percent that she will die in the next 12 months. On average, she has another 24.3 years to live, or until she is past age 84. Remember that these are averages, so by definition many people will live longer and some of them much longer. For a 65-year-old couple, the odds are 50 percent that at least one spouse will live to 94 and 25 percent that he or she will live to the age of 98![5] And never forget Jeanne Calment, the Frenchwoman who lived to a documented age of 122. (Some say it was the red wine.)

RED WINE AND OTHER
LONGEVITY MIRACLES

Note that if you believe these 2009 Social Security projections, your "break-even" for waiting to collect until 70, even if you're thinking only of the benefits for yourself, is somewhere in the low 80s. (And no, you don't have to factor in inflation, since all Social Security benefits are adjusted for the cost of living.) To make the point in simple arithmetic, if you were to start drawing your "full" retirement benefit of, say, $20,000 a year at age 66, you'd have taken a cumulative sum of $80,000 by age 70. But your "maximum" benefit, earned by waiting until 70, figures to be about $26,000 a year. (It might be even higher if you keep working at age 66 and raise your Social Security earnings base.) So at a minimum, you'd be getting an extra $6,000 a year. But even at "only" $6,000 a year extra, you can see that in barely 13 years, you'd have earned back the $80,000 you passed up in years 66–70.

"But wait," you might be thinking; "I would be earning money on that $80,000 if I socked it away. That's worth something, isn't it? Shouldn't I be calculating the break-even point, based on a reasonable expectation of returns I can get on that money if I invested it?"

In a word, no.

Unfortunately, we've come across many, indeed, far too many people who are absolutely convinced that the break-even period is relevant for thinking about when to take Social Security benefits. Many software programs, including "leading" commercial ones (but not Larry's, he is quick to note), display break-even analysis. And as recently as 2008, the Social Security Administration told its public claims representatives to use a break-even framework to help potential retirees decide when to begin taking benefits, as we mentioned earlier.[6]

WHY BREAKING EVEN
IS BREAKING BAD

Associated with the focus on break-even is the notion that "I can take my Social Security benefits early and invest them in stocks and make more money than I'll get from SS." And yet a third proposition is that we should run Monte Carlo computer simulations to see the chances of doing better on the stock market by taking our benefits now.

Viewing Social Security as an investment rather than as an insurance policy encourages thinking about it in terms of break-even approaches. Our advice: *Don't do it!*

If you insist on evaluating an insurance policy as an investment, based on break-even analysis, consider your house. Think about whether it makes sense to buy home-owner's insurance on a break-even basis. How? Compare the money it costs you in premiums to buy the insurance with the cost if your house burns down, multiplied by the vanishingly small chance that it will. If this so-called "expected value" of the policy is less than the premium, the insurance "investment" fails the break-even test.

Now, we guarantee that the expected payoff from "investing" in your home-owner's policy is less than the premium the insurance company charges you, meaning that you can't break even buying home-owner's insurance. The reason is that the insurance companies charge "loads" to cover administrative and other underwriting costs. Thanks to these loads, the total payoffs from homeowner's insurance, life insurance, car insurance, health insurance, etc., are always less than the premiums charged. Therefore, if you focus solely on the break-even, you should never buy any insurance at all.

But that would be crazy. You don't analyze standard insurance this way because you are focusing, properly so, on the worst-case scenario — your house burns down, your car is totaled, you get cancer.

Very few of us can afford to play the odds of catastrophe. And you're in no better position when it comes to Social Security longevity insurance.

In the longevity sphere, the worst-case scenario is, to reiterate, living too long — living to your maximum possible age of life, and, as a result, outliving your savings and income. Social Security provides insurance against this worst-case scenario. This insurance is safe against inflation and against default. It's also dirt cheap. There is no close substitute for it in the market.

OUR EARNEST EFFORT TO HELP
YOU KEEP MORE OF WHAT'S YOURS

Now, after this plea, if you're still stubbornly tempted to take Social Security benefits at age 62 and invest them on your own, please consider that you're not liable to beat its rate of return anyway.

Let's assume you're the average investor since, on average, those of you reading this probably *are*. Well, over the 20 years from 1991 to 2011, the average American investor actually *lost money,* after accounting for all costs and inflation. The reason would seem to be following the crowd — buying when stocks and bonds are flying high, and selling when they tank and sink to new lows. This, of course, is exactly the opposite of investing's Golden Rule: Buy low, sell high. But on average, we cannot be trusted to do so.

The average American's rate of annual loss is only −0.4 percent, however, so you shouldn't *subtract* anything from that $80,000 you'd have been paid by Social Security for waiting four years. But unless you're sure you can beat the average investor, which probably means you're illegally trading on insider information, you shouldn't *add* anything, either.

Still tempted? Then let us remind you of

the discoveries of behavioral economics over the past several decades, which help explain the fact mentioned earlier: that individual investors, on average, *lose money,* after you adjust returns for inflation.

The main message of behavioral economics, which is really a branch of psychology: Human beings consistently overestimate their own powers. This bias even has a name: "illusory superiority" or, on public radio, "the Lake Wobegon effect," after Garrison Keillor's famous description of the imaginary Minnesota town of Lake Wobegon, where "all the women are strong, all the men are good-looking, and *all the children are above average.*"

Documented examples abound.

In a survey of faculty at the University of Nebraska, two-thirds rated themselves in the top 25 percent for teaching ability. Nearly 90 percent of MBA students at Stanford University rated their academic performance in the top half of the class.

Nor is this a new phenomenon. Back in 1976, 70 percent of students taking the annual SATs thought they were in the top half of their peers with respect to leadership ability. Getting along with others? A full 85 percent put themselves above the median, and — we love this — 25 percent rated themselves in the top 1 percent.

And while "illusory superiority" is a worldwide phenomenon, it's especially acute for those of you contemplating the investment of Social Security money — Americans, that is. A famous survey of drivers half a century ago found that 69 percent of Swedes considered themselves above average in driving skill. Americans? *Ninety-three* percent! Safe driving? Seventy-seven percent of the Swedes called themselves above average; 88 percent of the Americans.

Twenty-five years later, American self-delusion had hardly budged. Asked to rate themselves by eight different measures, including skill and safety, only one driver in five thought themselves *below* average.

Applied to the world of investing, the widespread recognition of the consequences of illusory superiority can be expressed in only two words: mutual funds! Mutual fund investment managers — and these are the highly paid "experts" of investing, remember — regularly fall short of where they think they will end up. The results of their actively managed investment funds routinely fail to match even market averages. As a result, low-cost index funds sprang up to purchase large numbers of securities whose performance will match market averages.

They do not actively manage their holdings and have no illusions about their superiority. But they have become the dominant standard for retirement plan holdings! If so many of the experts have thrown in the towel on coming out ahead, why should anyone expect Social Security recipients to fare better?

DON'T OVERESTIMATE YOUR ABILITY TO MAKE FINANCIALLY SAVVY DECISIONS

This evidence on overoptimism may come as no surprise, but it should give us pause. To repeat, Social Security's Delayed Retirement Credit adds 8 percent a year to lifetime benefits between the ages of 66 and 70 — *after inflation,* though with no compounding. Even if you love taking risks and therefore ignore our point about insurance, you should protect yourself against self-delusion.

Finally, speaking of risk, we are obliged to report that as your brain ages, the decision-making part — the prefrontal cortex, home to the previously rational self — starts to deteriorate at age 50 or so. Not quickly, we should add, but inexorably. Here's an excerpt from an interview Paul did with brain researcher Dr. Jordan Grafman at the

National Institutes of Health some years ago:

DR. JORDAN GRAFMAN: I think the way people have to make decisions when they get older is to be much more cautious about new ventures. And that's where they might need to work with other people, to collaborate, to take the advice of other family members or advisors.

Therefore, said Grafman, when it comes to investing, we should all do it more conservatively as we age, "because since the prefrontal cortex is probably not functioning as effectively as it did when you were younger, you're going to be more prone to impulsive decision making."

That, of course, is precisely what Social Security protects us from.

So look again at the longevity table in the Notes at the end of the book and observe that if you made it to age 66 as a man in 2009, your life expectancy was about 83; as a woman, more like 86. But think about this: these are *averages* — half or so will die before these ages and the rest later. So the critical question is: can you afford to take the chance that you'll be among those who outlive your actuarial life expectancy?

Or would you rather take out old-age insurance against that eventuality, which is just what waiting until 70 to take higher Social Security *is:* extra old-age insurance. Moreover, these averages have risen every year since 2009, especially among more educated and affluent groups.

ARE WE NEAR A TIPPING POINT FOR LONGEVITY?

Consider the longevity forecast of Ray Kurzweil, the fabled techno-whiz who invented at age 28 the first machine that could speak what it read, vastly enhancing the lives of blind Americans like Stevie Wonder who could afford it and eventually benefiting us all. As a 60-something adult, he now takes 150 pills a day, has written, among other books, *The 10% Solution for a Healthy Life, Fantastic Voyage: Live Long Enough to Live Forever,* and *Transcend: Nine Steps to Living Well Forever.*

His goal, he told Paul in 2011, "is to get to a point in the future where the progress is so rapid that we're adding more time to life — your remaining life expectancy — than is going by. That will be a point where the sands of time are running in rather than running out — a tipping point. And that's only 15 years away by my calculations."

Speaking for our own frontal lobes, we three authors are planning to live to at least 100. Larry's conservative ESPlanner financial software defaults to age 100 for planning purposes. And when another of us — Paul — uses the software to determine the adequacy of his and his wife's accumulated savings, he plugs in 110, just to be safe. As for Phil, his trim physique speaks volumes, and he also swears that after an hour on the elliptical, he knows exactly what being 100 feels like.

We're not suggesting you plan on living forever or even to 110. But waiting for your maximum benefit at 70 instead of grabbing your earliest available benefit at 62 will be worth 76 percent more in benefits every year right through eternity if you and Uncle Sam make it that far, due to the 8 percent a year Social Security pays you to wait.

Say you're the typical Social Security recipient who would take the average yearly benefit of $15,936 for Americans in 2015, according to the Social Security Administration website. That amount would account for about 40 percent of your pre-retirement income. Waiting until 70 would then be worth about $5,000 a year after break-even at age 83. That adds another 13 percent to your pre-retirement income. Every year. For life. So now imagine you live until 90. That's an extra $35,000 in constant (inflation-adjusted) dollars ($500 a year × 7 years). Live till 100 and it's $85,000 in present dollars. Live till 110: $135,000. Jeanne Calment (122): $195,000.

And if, instead of the *average* benefit, we consider the *maximum,* we're talking about a difference of $10,142 a year, in which case, *double* all the totals in the previous paragraph.

WHAT YOU CAN DO TO ENFRANCHISE THE "LIFE PRESERVER" SELF

We have embraced a model of human behavior based upon a competition among various internal "selves." So our advice is to enfranchise one of them — the adult within; the long-term planner; the *life preserver* self. Keep reminding yourself: You are the guardian of your future self.

3

SOCIAL SECURITY — FROM A TO ZZZZZZZ

Getting yours — *all* of what's yours — requires understanding not just general facts but also a slew of specific details about Social Security and its benefits. To do this we will need to suspend what Phil calls the "just-tell-me-what-to-do" syndrome, which he encounters again and again in public speeches about Social Security. Yes, we live in a busy and complex world, we're pressed for time, and we may have become so used to getting communications in short bursts that even Twitter's 140 characters seem gabby.

Unfortunately, with Social Security, the initial answer to nearly every significant benefit question is "It depends." Later chapters will provide details about various claiming decisions, given your own particular circumstances. But first, we're going to describe the basics, as well as provide some essential details. We are aware that Social

Security's basic rules are less engrossing than, say, *How Harry Potter Profited from the Crash of 2015* or *Fifty Shades of Hot Pink*. But the rewards are likely to be more enduring. And for memory-challenged recidivists, there is a Glossary with key terms at the back of the book. For those already in the know, jumping ahead to Chapter 4 will not get you expelled from our book and will introduce you to our three key Social Security rules for getting what's yours.

SOCIAL SECURITY HAS LOTS OF DIFFERENT BENEFITS

Here is a list of different benefits, one or more of which almost surely apply to *you*:

- retirement benefits;
- spousal benefits (how Paul got his in Chapter 1);
- spousal benefits for those caring for an eligible child or children;
- child benefits for the young kids of retirees;
- child benefits for disabled children of retirees, regardless of the child's age;
- divorcee spousal benefits.

We're not done and neither, perhaps, are the benefits to which you're entitled. There are also widow/widower survivor benefits, divorcee widow/widower survivor benefits, survivor benefits to young children, survivor benefits to disabled children regardless of age, parental benefits, and disability benefits.

YOUR WORK RECORD CAN GENERATE BENEFITS FOR BOTH YOU AND OTHERS

The first thing you need to know is how to qualify for Social Security. The answer is simple: to be eligible for benefits on your own work record, you need to have worked for 40 quarters of a year — 10 years in total. Those quarters don't have to be consecutive. You can work, trek Nepal for 15 months (or 15 years, for that matter), return home, and start racking up more quarters. But they have to be in "covered" employment — jobs where Social Security payroll taxes, aka "FICA contributions," are deducted.

A key point here: once *you* qualify for benefits, so might your current spouse, your ex-spouse(s), your young children, your disabled children, and even your parents. Any and all of these people may be eligible to receive benefits based on your work record. Moreover, if and when you die, your work record can continue to provide benefits — known as *survivor* benefits — to your loved ones, or even not-so-loved ones.

There's a flip side to this coin. You *yourself* can receive spousal benefits, divorcee spousal benefits, survivor benefits, and divorcee survivor benefits based on the work records of *your* current or former spouses. You also may be able to collect parent benefits if you've been financially supported by a child and he or she dies.

Clearly, then, a lot is riding on your covered earnings record. If you don't know it, you can and should get it from Your Social Security Statement. Go to this Web address — http://socialsecurity.gov/myaccount/ — which the agency calls "my Social Security." You will need your Social Security number and must have a valid email address, a U.S. mailing address, and be at least 18 years old. You'll also need to enter personal information that only you know, so when you use your online account, Social Security will ask you some security questions that only you can answer. The agency is sensitive to hacking and other security concerns, so you may need to spend some time figuring out what's called a "strong" — in encryption terms — password. You also can sign up for an additional level of account security but it will take extra time and also involve text messages to your cell phone.

Once you've set up your account, either download or print out the current copy of Your Social Security Statement. It features Social Security's year-by-year record of the wage earnings on which you (and your employers) have paid Social Security payroll taxes. Not only will you then know your contribution record but you'll also get a good idea of the Social Security benefits to which you're entitled. And if there are mistakes in the record, which can happen for a host of reasons, you should take steps to correct them.[1]

A WORD ABOUT
SOCIAL SECURITY LINGO

Social Security uses elaborate and, we think, often confusing terms to describe its benefits and how they're calculated. Still, this language may be crucial to getting your best mix of benefits. For example, you might not think there is much practical difference between the words "eligible" and "entitled." Hah! No soup for you! The agency uses "eligible" to mean that you are qualified due to age or other circumstances to file for and collect benefits. "Entitled" means you have actually done so and are collecting benefits.

It is easy to confuse these meanings but there are circumstances where doing so could cost you.

We are going to adopt the agency's terms for this book, not because we like them but because their plain-language equivalents are often foreign to agency representatives. Arming you with indispensable rules of thumb won't do you much good if Social Security doesn't know what you're talking about and immediately dispenses with them (and you). So we will be providing a commonsense grounding of the system, but in *Social Securitese* as well as English.

AIME IS NEVER HAVING TO SAY YOU'RE SORRY

The first of these terms is your AIME. It stands not for "love" in French, but your Average Indexed Monthly Earnings. (Social Security's penchant for capital letters can be especially governmental and mind-numbing). Average Indexed Monthly Earnings may be a mouthful, but all it really means is your "earnings base" (sometimes just called "base") — your covered wages and self-employment income subject to Social Security FICA taxation — the ones itemized on Your Social Security Statement.

You may not realize it — and if you earn

the median U.S. wage income of just over $40,000 a year, why would you? — but the Social Security or FICA or "payroll" tax only applies to wage plus self-employment income up to a certain limit, sometimes called the "tax max" by Social Security. For 2015, the maximum or ceiling on Social Security's taxable earnings is $118,500. Social Security looks at your covered earnings each year, forms a special average of these earnings — that's your earnings base or AIME — and plugs this base into a formula to figure out your full retirement benefit.

How exactly is the AIME arrived at? Social Security takes each of your past years' covered earnings and adjusts them — "indexes" them — to reflect the rise in average wages each year — from the year you first earned them to the year you turn age 60. Indexing keeps average benefits more closely aligned with average real wage levels and avoids harming people who earned more money earlier in their careers.

So, for example, say you made $20,000 a year in 1980 when you were only 25 years old. This year, at age 60, you expect to make $80,000. That's four times as much in unadjusted terms, but wages have gone up a lot during the past 35 years. Indexing evens out the value of wages you earned earlier in life so that they are credited with their fair share of the lifetime earnings on which your Social Security benefits are based.

Indexing, in this case, will blow up the $20,000 by 3.5 times to $70,000 before these and other indexed years of earnings are ranked to find the largest 35. The 35 are then averaged to determine Average Indexed Monthly Earnings. Without this indexing, people who earned more when young would be penalized relative to those who earned more when old. That's because those who earned more when old did so when wages in general were higher.

But your covered earnings are adjusted — the official word is "indexed" — only *until* age 60. Covered earnings *after* age 60 aren't adjusted for wage growth. (As we'll explain later, the fact that post-60 earnings are not indexed can be a big incentive to continuing to work past normal retirement age.)

What next? Social Security then ranks, from highest to lowest, all these yearly earnings — both indexed and *unindexed.* Finally, the agency adds up the largest 35 annual amounts, takes an annual average (dividing the total by 35), and then divides again by 12 to produce your *monthly* earnings base — your AIME.

But what, you might ask, if you don't *have* 35 years of covered earnings? Suppose, for example, you only have 20 years of covered earnings? In this case, Social Security will say you have 15 years of zero earnings and include those zeroes in its average. This means that working more years, up to 35, can make a huge difference. If, for example, you have just 10 years of covered earnings and add only one more, you'll raise your base by 10 percent and increase your lifetime Social Security benefits dramatically!

SOCIAL SECURITY VERBATIM
BE REALLY NICE TO YOUR KIDS

"If you are a minor convicted of intentionally causing your parent's death, you *may* [our emphasis] be denied survivor benefits on the earnings record of your parent."

ALL QUOTES FROM OFFICIAL
SOCIAL SECURITY RULES

PIA: WE DARE YOU TO GUESS WHAT THOSE LETTERS STAND FOR

The next acronym of note is your Primary Insurance Amount, or PIA. That's your basic benefit itself, based on your work record of covered earnings. The PIA is also equal to what's called your full retirement benefit, the retirement benefit you receive when you start collecting Social Security at what the law defines as your Full Retirement Age (FRA).

A few words here about the age of eligibility. While for Social Security it begins at age 62 or even earlier, depending on specific benefits and when you choose to take them, for almost all of you, FRA will be at least 66. For anyone born before 1943, the FRA was 65. For those born between 1943 and 1954, including much of the baby boom, it's 66. And for people born in 1955 and later, the FRA will start rising in 2021 by two months every year until it reaches 67 for anyone born in 1960 or later. Here's the full table, as it appears on the Social Security website.

FULL RETIREMENT AGE

Year of Birth	Age
1937 and prior	65
1938	65 and 2 months
1939	65 and 4 months
1940	65 and 6 months
1941	65 and 8 months

Year of Birth	Age
1942	65 and 10 months
1943–54	66
1955	66 and 2 months
1956	66 and 4 months
1957	66 and 6 months
1958	66 and 8 months
1959	66 and 10 months
1960 and later	67

Source: Social Security Administration.

THE PIA BENEFIT FORMULA IS HIGHLY PROGRESSIVE

The formula that determines your full retirement benefit or PIA, based on your lifetime earnings base or AIME, is progressive. This means it gives lower-wage workers — those with low earnings bases — a disproportionately better deal. In 2015, for example, the full retirement benefit formula is 90 percent of the first $826 of your monthly earnings base, plus a much lower 32 percent of the base above $826 through $4,980, plus a mere 15 percent of the earnings base over $4,980. These different percentages are applied at what the agency calls "bend points," which are adjusted each year based on the growth in economy-wide average earnings.

If you're like most people looking at a

string of seemingly random numbers like these, your eyes may have started to cross. But if you're not sure you believe that the Social Security benefit formula is progressive, here's an example. Say you begin taking your full retirement benefit at age 66. If your base in 2015 was exactly $826, your full retirement benefit thus is $743: 90 percent of your base covered income of about $10,000 a year.

Now imagine your brother's base was twice as big: $1,652 or about $20,000 a year. *His* full retirement benefit would be $1,008; about $12,000 a year, less than two-thirds of *his* base. And if you had a Wall Street cousin with the largest base possible — meaning she'd earned at or above the annual payroll tax ceiling for at least 35 years — *her* monthly base would be a whopping $8,891 in 2014 or more than $106,000, nearly 11 times larger than your $826 and $10,000. But *her* full retirement benefit would amount to only $2,659 a month — an annual PIA or "full" Social Security retirement benefit of $31,912. Now, this may sound substantial, but would represent a mere 30 percent of her base. Put it another way: she would have earned 11 times more than you did and contributed 11 times more in taxes to Social Security than you did, yet her full retirement benefit would be barely three times larger than yours.

To make things even more complicated, adding a touch of what one might call gallows math, Social Security calculates your PIA differently if you happen to have died before age 62. Indeed, if you leave behind a surviving spouse or ex-spouse, it will make two different calculations and give your survivor the higher of the two resulting death-related PIAs. You, let's assume, won't be able to much care about this, but members of your family and even ex-family might, for very good reason. By the way, the two calculations are trying to respond to the fact that if you *are* dead, you've potentially had a shorter covered earnings history, which could make the standard full benefit measure uncomfortably and perhaps unfairly low for dependents, past or present.

A GREAT BENEFIT OF SOCIAL SECURITY BENEFITS: THEY'RE INFLATION-PROOF (PRETTY MUCH)

Starting January 1 of each year, Social Security raises all the benefits it's paying out by the rate of inflation that occurred between the prior two Octobers, as measured by a widely used version of the consumer price index. There have been proposals to use a different price index to set this annual Cost of Living Adjustment, or COLA, which would lower the COLA adjustment by a modest amount each year. There was a huge hue and cry, however, because even small changes in the COLA will have a meaningful impact on retiree benefits over time.

But none of the proposed benefit adjustments changes the fact that Social Security does a good job of maintaining the real buying power of the dollars it pays out. And this is a big, big deal.

SOCIAL SECURITY'S FULL RETIREMENT BENEFIT FORMULA IS INDEXED TO ECONOMY-WIDE WAGE GROWTH

To further ensure that Social Security benefits grow through time in proportion to workers' wages, Social Security annually raises the dollar bracket amounts in its PIA formula — the $826 and $4,980 thresholds mentioned earlier — by each year's growth in economy-wide average wages.

Incidentally, since the system also indexes Social Security's taxable earnings ceiling to growth in economy-wide average wages, as wages have become more unequally distributed across the workforce in recent years, a larger share of total wages has moved above the ceiling — from 10 percent in 1983, according to Social Security, to 15 percent today.[2]

This is putting even more pressure on Social Security's long-term finances, which we'll discuss in Chapter 18. But this book is about getting what's yours, not fixing the system or bemoaning its fate. And so we press on.

EARLY BENEFIT REDUCTIONS

If you take retirement, spousal, or survivor benefits early (before Full Retirement Age) they will be subject to an Early Retirement Reduction for every month you do so. The reduction is hefty. For example, taking your own retirement benefit at 62 rather than at FRA currently entails a 25 percent lower monthly payment. Taking your *spousal* benefit at 62 entails a 30 percent reduction. And taking your *survivor* benefit at 60, instead of waiting until FRA, currently means a 28.5 percent reduction.

For those born after 1960, which includes all our kids, the hits for taking their own retirement benefits or spousal benefits at age 62 are larger: 30 percent and 35 percent.

This is because the FRA for these folks will be 67, not today's 66. That adds another 12 months of benefit reduction to the respective hits, because the early benefits age will remain 62. In the case of survivor benefits, things are different. The hit is fixed through time. The monthly reduction factor is adjusted over time to ensure that it never exceeds 28.5 percent.

DELAYED RETIREMENT CREDITS

Through its Delayed Retirement Credit (DRC), Social Security raises your personal retirement benefit for *each month* you wait to claim beyond Full Retirement Age (FRA) and the raises continue right through to age 70. Remember, the FRA is 66 for those born between 1943 and 1954. The DRC is 8 percent a year, or .67 percent a month, until you turn 70.

To put both rules in round numbers, if you were due a monthly $1,000 retirement benefit at age 66, it would be reduced 25 percent to $750 if you claimed benefits at age 62. It would rise 32 percent (four times the 8 percent annual increase) to $1,320 if you deferred benefits until age 70. The difference between $750 and $1,320? A whopping 76 percent!

To put it in monetary terms and plugging

in pretend numbers just to make the point, suppose you are now 62 and are eligible for a reduced early retirement benefit of $20,000 a year starting immediately. If you wait until 70 to start collecting, you'll get an extra $15,200 a year — just for being patient and thinking long-term. The new patience-earned benefit will be $26,667 a year starting at age 66; $35,200 starting at age 70. You might think about it this way: if you manage to live to 100, God willing, that would be $15,200 a year more after age 70 than had you started at age 62 — an extra $456,000 in today's dollars (since the benefits will be inflation adjusted) for waiting past 62, in return for giving up eight years' worth of benefits at $20,000 a year: $160,000 in total.[3]

In 2012, the last year for which data are available, an astounding (to us) 38 percent of men and 42 percent of women filed for Social Security benefits at age 62; *another* 25 percent of men and 26 percent of women filed before reaching their FRA of 66. And to our near disbelief, only 1.1 percent of men and 1.7 percent of women waited until age 70 to file. That is, almost *none* of your and our fellow Americans.

And, to gild this lily a bit more, waiting, as we've already pointed out, might also significantly swell lifetime benefits not only for you but quite possibly for current and former family members who depend on you. And, should you pass on, to eligible survivors.

Increasing the FRA to 67 will also have an effect on DRCs — Delayed Retirement Credits. They will apply to a maximum of only three years from their current four years. So, the maximum value of the DRCs will be reduced to 24 percent from 32 percent.

WITHDRAWING YOUR RETIREMENT BENEFIT

Your timing of retirement benefits is crucial — both for the size of your own payments and those you might collect on the earnings record of a current or ex-spouse, dead or alive. Because of its importance in everything that follows, keep in mind that Social Security gives you a year from the time you file for a retirement benefit to say, "Yikes. I made a mistake. I want to pay back what I received so far and be treated as if I never applied for a retirement benefit." Unfortunately — and this is something most people don't know or ignore at their peril — what you'll need to pay back includes any Medicare Part B premiums or tax withholdings that were deducted from ur Social Security payments.

Disabled workers should pay special attention to the withdrawal option. The reason is that Social Security doesn't wait for disabled workers to file for retirement benefits on their own. It automatically files for them when they reach RA. In so doing, it transforms their disability benefit into a retirement benefit. But taking a retirement benefit at FRA may not be est in terms of maximizing lifetime benefit And the way — indeed the only way - for disabled workers to avoid being forced into a possibly bad collection strategy is to withdraw their retirement benefit upon reaching FRA.

SUSPENDING YOUR
RETIREMENT BENEFIT

When you *withdraw* your retirement benefit, as we've just outlined, you te Social Security to treat you as never having filed for a retirement benefit. When you *suspend* your benefit, however, you tell Social Security to treat you as having filed for your retirement benefits, but to put them on hold until you restart them. This has two advantages. First, formally filing for a retirement benefit, even if you suspend it, can let your spouse and children collect spousal and child benefits on your work recd. Second, it lets you accumulate Delayd Retirement Credits so that when you start your benefits, they will be higher. Suspending your retirement benefit (you cat suspend any other type of benefit) is onpermitted between FRA and 70. These arelso the years when Delayed Retirement Cdits kick in.

Suspending our benefit has one nice final feature. You d decide at any time to cancel your suspensn. In this case, Social Security will pay you, a single lump sum, all the suspended hefits less the value of any Delayed Retiment Credits you picked up. There can b a big downside to filing for your retiremet benefit even if you suspend it, however. Iwill eliminate your ability to take a benet linked to a spouse's work record (curmt, former or deceased) by itself, while etting your own retirement benefit grow.

In Despair Because You've Already Left Money on the Table? All Is Not Lost.

In the course of reading this book, you may well come across a benefit to which you were already entitled, but have not applied for. Thanks to "retroactivity," you can apply today and receive six months' worth of that benefit *retroactively,* in the form of a lump sum. We explain this — with an example — in Chapter 16, "Secret #16."

SOCIAL SECURITY VERBATIM
THE CASE OF THE MISSING
CORPSE

"In a disappearance case where the body is not recovered, you must clearly prove the death of the missing person. Submit all available evidence, including: statements of persons having knowledge of the situation; letters or notes left by the missing person that have a bearing on the case."

ALL QUOTES FROM OFFICIAL
SOCIAL SECURITY RULES

THE FULL MONTY ON YOUR FULL RETIREMENT AGE

Later chapters will discuss further the significance of your FRA. The agency also calls this, on occasion, your *normal* retirement age. But for many of us contemplating the end of work, this age is neither full nor normal. Not anymore. By the time you reach 66, your life expectancy is about 83.

Nearly a third of people aged 65 through 69 were still in the labor force in 2012, up from 26 percent in 2002 and 21 percent in 1992. More to our point, perhaps, 20 percent of Americans aged 70 to 74 were still in the labor force in 2012. We could go on, buffeting you with statistics. But for now, please just keep in mind that taking benefits before, at, or after your FRA can have an enormous impact on your lifetime benefits.

As we've said, taking benefits *before* full retirement age reduces them, while waiting past this age *increases* them. But taking benefits before FRA may also trigger other unappealing events.

Reaching FRA also changes the nature of how continued employment income might affect your Social Security benefits. FRA, to repeat, is an important pivot point for many Social Security benefit decisions.

BEWARE OF THE DEMON KNOWN AS DEEMING

Depending on your household's specific circumstances, Social Security may force you to take your retirement benefit early (before FRA) if you happen to take a spousal or divorced spousal benefit early. It can also force you to take a spousal or divorced spousal benefit early if you take your retirement benefit early.

So what's wrong with taking two benefits at once?

When Social Security deems you to have filed for two benefits at the same time, it won't give you the full value of both benefits. Instead, it will give you the larger of the two (or nearly so). If you file carefully, Social Security will let you collect two different benefits at two different *times* without forcing you to take the larger of the two. But you can't do this if you've been deemed to be taking them simultaneously. So you'll forever lose out on the opportunity to collect the maximum total of both benefits.

Fortunately, deeming does not affect survivor benefits. And there is no deeming once you reach Full Retirement Age without yet collecting.

SPOUSAL AND WIDOW/WIDOWER BENEFITS: HOW ARE THEY CALCULATED? FIRST, SPOUSES

Spousal benefits — a core part of *Get What's Yours* — can be half of your spouse's full retirement benefit. Or they can be a lot less. Understanding how to maximize these benefits is thus a very big deal.

And deeming can play a major role here.

Spousal benefits can be reduced because of deeming. But if you wait until Full Retirement Age, when deeming is no longer a factor, and this benefit is the only one you take, it will equal one-half of your spouse's full retirement benefit. (Reminder: your spouse has to have filed for her or his own retirement benefit for you to take a spousal benefit. Also, your spouse's full retirement benefit isn't necesarily the actual retirement benefit they'll collect if they collect early or late.) Getting 50 percent of your spouse's benefit is also true for *divorced* spouses, with the relevant full retirement benefit being that of your ex. But in all cases — spouse, ex-spouse, or survivor — if you're taking your own benefits, things change, and can change drastically, as we will explain.

NEXT, SURVIVOR'S BENEFITS

What's the actual amount a widow or widower, including a divorced widow(er), might get in survivor benefits? We're not glad you asked, because it depends on a whole bunch of things.

Thing 1 is when your spouse dies. If he dies before age 60, Social Security calculates his PIA, on which widow benefits are based, in two different ways and uses the larger of the two numbers.

Thing 2 is whether your deceased spouse or deceased ex-spouse took his retirement benefit early (and, with apologies for repetition, by early we mean before FRA). If he did, this can lower your widow's benefits, which are calculated based on a special formula. It's called the RIB-LIM, which stands for Retirement Insurance Benefit Limit. (The formula is about widow[er]'s benefits, but the acronym refers to retirement benefits. Go figure.)

The RIB-LIM formula seems to have been designed to drive us crazy. It's the smaller of two numbers, one of which is the larger of two numbers.[4] We kid you not.

If you're in RIB-LIM world, your own benefit will depend on whether you *yourself* take your widow's benefit early and also *how* early. If you take it as early as possible — at 60 — you'll get 71.5 percent of your former spouse's PIA. If you take it closer to Full Retirement Age, you'll get the larger of the reduced retirement benefit your spouse was collecting or 82.5 percent of your spouse's PIA.

Now for thing 3, which occurs if your spouse died having *not* taken his retirement benefit early. In this case, your widow's benefit (before any reduction due to you yourself taking this benefit early) equals your dead spouse or ex-spouse's PIA if he died before FRA. If he died after FRA, your widow's benefit is the actual benefit, inclusive of Delayed Retirement Credits, he was receiving when he died or would have received had he applied for benefits the day he died. The same holds true if your spouse is or was a woman.

Yes, applying for benefits the day you die can be a challenge. But it may be easier than mastering the RIB-LIM formula. And if you don't make it to the local office before you check out, Social Security will pretend you did. (See Chapter 12 for more on RIB-LIM.)

Do You Know about Child-in-Care Spousal Benefits?

Surviving spouses with young children can collect child-in-care benefits. They amount to 75 percent of their deceased spouse's PIA, and there is no reduction penalty for collecting them early. In some cases, it may be better to take this benefit and defer your own retirement benefit. In other cases, it may be greater than your own retirement benefit, even at age 70. If the child in question was disabled before the age of 22, this child-in-care benefit could continue as long as the child remains unmarried and disabled. Indeed, a disabled child could be 90 and still collect a child survivor benefit.

If a spouse has a child in care who is under age 16 or disabled (having being disabled before age 22) and the worker is alive and has filed for retirement, the child-in-care spousal benefit is 50 percent of the worker's PIA, and the spouse can receive it at any age. The child is also eligible to receive benefits on the worker's earnings record. The benefits also will be 50 percent of the worker's PIA, subject to the Family Maximum Benefit. If the worker dies, the child-in-care spousal benefit would become a mother benefit if she still has a child in care, and it would increase to 75 percent. If the spouse is aged 60 or older, she has the choice of receiving the larger of either the mother or the widow benefit. The widow benefit could equal what her late husband was collecting — if he had filed for retirement benefits — or what he would have been entitled to collect if he had not filed for benefits at the time of his death. (Note: the overwhelming percentage of parent and widow[er] benefits involve women, so we will often assume the person involved is a woman.)

Are your children, or any you know,

eligible for benefits through their retired, disabled, or deceased parents? If they are, the basic rules specify half of the parent's primary amount; if the parent is deceased, the benefit is larger: 75 percent. More complicated provisions kick in for situations where both parents' benefits may be the basis of the claim, and for multiple-child households. Lastly, unlike normal spousal benefits, child-in-care spousal benefits don't trigger deeming.

EVER HEARD OF PARENT BENEFITS?

Our guess is no. Well, if you were paying for more than half of, say, your mom's support and you pass away, she can collect a parent benefit equal to 82.5 percent of your PIA. If she is collecting benefits on her own, she will, however, receive only the larger of the two benefits.

BE AWARE OF THE FAMILY MAXIMUM BENEFIT

As we've noted, there is usually a "however" with Social Security's rules, and there's *a huge* one here: the Family Maximum Benefit (FMB). Child, ex-spouse, and survivorship benefits could cause overall Social Security payments to exceed this ceiling. If that happens, payments to all beneficiaries would be reduced to bring total family payments under the ceiling.

We'll note another twist here. Your primary insurance amount (PIA) is calculated by plugging your average earnings (AIME) into what is a decidedly progressive formula. The Family Maximum Benefit is pretty much the opposite. Surprisingly, it's calculated by plugging your primary benefit amount into a formula that is *re*gressive — one that treats high earners disproportionately better than low ones. If your primary benefit is very low, your total Family Maximum Benefit will be only 150 percent of that amount. With a somewhat larger PIA, however, the maximum rises to 187 percent. It then ebbs, ending up at 175 percent of your primary benefit. But even a 175 percent family maximum for those with the highest full retirement benefit for themselves is considerably more than the 150 percent for workers with the lowest personal benefits.

The way this benefit is calculated doesn't make sense to us. But while there is nothing you can do about it, the application of this maximum can affect your optimal Social Security claiming decisions.

Also, if you're disabled, there's a different, potentially far more restrictive FMB, which we'll tell you about later. For very low earners who become disabled, this FMB is *zero,* apart from what the disabled worker herself receives. We feel this is even more unfair than the low-income FMB.

ALSO BE AWARE OF
THE EARNINGS TEST

If you are collecting retirement benefits and have not yet reached your FRA, your Social Security benefits may be reduced if you also have outside wage earnings (investment and pension income does not count).

Now, don't get too worked up here. In most cases (and we will explain the exceptions), this is just a cash flow issue since Social Security will, over time, restore these reductions starting when you reach FRA.

That said, there are two trigger levels — one for the years before you reach FRA and a second for the year in which you reach it. For someone whose FRA is 66, their Social Security benefit would be reduced by $1 for every $2 in earnings (including earnings in non-covered employment) that exceeded $15,720 while they were aged 62 to 65. During the year they turn 66, their benefit would be reduced by $1 for every $3 in earnings that exceeded $41,880, and only those earnings accrued in the months before reaching FRA are counted. These are 2015 trigger levels; the levels are changed every year to reflect national wage trends.

The Earnings Test may also affect your spousal benefits if your outside earnings exceed the trigger levels. Those benefits also will be reduced if your spouse is collecting retirement benefits, has not reached FRA, and earns more than the trigger levels.

Benefit reductions are not prorated during the year but front-loaded. This can play havoc with your budget. For example, if your outside earnings reduced your $18,000 annual benefit to $12,000, your $1,500 monthly payment would not be reduced to $1,000 for an entire year. Instead, you would get *no* Social Security payment for 4 months and then the $1,500 payment for 8 months.

However (remember that there always seems to be a however with Social Security), spousal benefits and survivor benefits received by people because they have minor or disabled children in their care will *not* be restored if they are reduced because of the Earnings Test. Equally important, and perhaps even more confusing, if you are collecting one type of benefit before FRA and switch to spousal or widow(er) benefits after FRA, you won't necessarily recoup the retirement benefits you lost due to the Earnings Test.

A Year of Grace Notes for the Earnings Test

If you file for your retirement benefits early and are hit by the Earnings Test, Social Security's grace year rule helps you — during your first year only of collecting benefits — by not counting any earnings you made in the months before you began collecting benefits. For the months after you began collecting, the rule permits the Earnings Test to be applied on a monthly and not annual basis (meaning that the annual earnings limits would be divided by 12 and compared with your monthly earnings). To illustrate, assume you began collecting benefits early in July, had made $50,000 in the first half of that year, and had no outside earnings the second half of the year. Under grace year provisions, you would not be hit with Earnings Test benefits reductions.

'Cause I'm the Taxman, Yeah, I'm the Taxman

Federal taxes may be due on up to half of your Social Security benefits if what's called your "combined income" is more than $25,000 a year ($32,000 for joint filers). If you make between $25,000 and $34,000 ($32,000 and $44,000 for joint returns), you may owe federal taxes on up to 85 percent of your benefits. You will never pay federal income taxes on more than 85 percent of your benefits. These combined income thresholds are not adjusted for inflation, so over time more and more people have seen their Social Security benefits subjected to federal income taxes. Combined income is defined as the total of your adjusted gross income plus any nontaxable interest you receive (from, say, municipal bonds) plus *half* of your Social Security benefits.

Social Security will withhold federal income taxes from your benefit payments. The agency will let you select one of four percentage withholding amounts — 7, 10, 15, or 25 percent. You can request withholding when you apply for benefits and can change this amount later by filing IRS Form W-4V (available at http://www.irs.gov/pub/irs-pdf/fw4v.pdf).

YOUR BENEFITS — WITH STRINGS ATTACHED

When Social Security says you can get a benefit, there are always strings attached. Here are some examples.

- **Retirement Benefits** — you have to be 62 or over to collect.
- **Spousal Benefits** — you have to be 62 or over to collect and your spouse has to have filed for his or her retirement or disability benefit. You need to have been married at least a year to qualify for spousal benefits on a new spouse's work history.
- **Divorcee Spousal Benefits** — you have to be 62 or over to collect, as does the spouse on whose benefits you're collecting, unless he/she is collecting disability benefits. You also have to have been married for at least 10 years, not be currently remarried, and you must be divorced for at least 2 years if your ex is not himself or herself collecting their own retirement or disability benefit.
- **Widow/Widower Survivor Benefits** — you have to be 60 to collect, but only 50 if you are a disabled widow or widower and didn't remarry before age 60 (50 if disabled). And, apart from death caused by accident, you need to have been married for at least 9 months. Depending on your year of birth, the FRA used in calculating your survivor benefits can be 4 months

earlier than the FRA used in calculating your retirement and spousal benefits.

- **Divorcee Widow/Widower Survivor Benefits** — you have to be 60 or over (50 or over if you are disabled) to collect on a deceased ex to whom you were married for at least 10 years provided you didn't remarry before 60 (50 if disabled).
- **Spousal Benefits If You Have a Child of the Retired Worker in Your Care** — you can be any age and collect a spousal benefit if your spouse has filed for a retirement or disability benefit and you are caring for his or her children who are under age 16 or disabled. If one or more is disabled, then you may collect regardless of their age(s) provided the disability began before age 22.
- **Mother/Father Benefits If You Have a Child of Your Deceased Spouse in Your Care** — you can be any age and collect this survivor benefit based on your former spouse's work record if you are caring for his or her children who are under age 16 or disabled (regardless of their age provided the disability began before age 22). But to

be eligible, you cannot currently be remarried. On the other hand, you need be married only one nanosecond (not the standard 9 months for widow-[er]'s benefits) to qualify for this benefit.

- **Divorcee Spousal Benefits If You Have a Child of the Retired Social Security–Eligible Spouse in Your Care** — you have to be 62 or older to collect, provided you were married for 10 or more years, are not remarried, your ex is 62 or older or is entitled to disability benefits, and you are caring for his or her child or children who are under age 16 or disabled (regardless of their age provided the disability began before age 22).

- **Child Benefits for Children of Retired or Deceased Workers** — if your parent has filed for a retirement benefit or is deceased, you are eligible if you are either under age 18 (19 if you are still in elementary or secondary school) or are disabled (provided your disability began prior to 22).

As the above list indicates, the Social Security stars often have to be carefully aligned for you to collect certain benefits.

If, for example, you're 62 and your husband is 22, you'll be 102 before you can collect a spousal benefit based on his work record unless he becomes entitled to disability benefits. That's because your husband has to file for a retirement or disability benefit before *you* can collect a spousal benefit and your husband has to be at least 62 (which is 40 years from now) to file for a retirement benefit.

This chapter lays out the contours of the system. But it doesn't tell you how to *Get What's Yours* — maximizing your family's lifetime Social Security benefits. The next chapter gives you three basic rules we've developed to guide your decisions. If you follow them, you shouldn't go wrong. Easier said than done, as you now know.

SOCIAL SECURITY CLAIMING BASICS

Before people make a decision, it is natural to want to know what others have done. Product reviews and rankings abound. Social media have made crowdsourcing a near-obligatory act for growing numbers of us before we actually sign on the dotted line or, more likely, open an app that will sign on our behalf. And while the three of us sometimes feel we would like to take Social Security out to the woodshed, the program does a thorough job of measuring what people do and building an extensive statistical record of how Americans actually use Social Security.[5] (For a look at the numbers of people getting Social Security and their benefit levels see the end of the Glossary.)

SOCIAL SECURITY IS NOT A RETURN OF YOUR TAX DOLLARS

You can pay Social Security taxes on every penny you earn and end up with no more benefits than someone who never worked a lick. Thanks to Social Security's spousal and survivor benefits, spouses who don't work and never did can receive benefits — reasonably large ones, even — based purely on their living or dead or ex-spouse's earnings record. Yet if you're a spouse who *did* work and paid Social Security taxes year after year, you may end up with no extra benefits than had you never worked at all. That's because, if you're simultaneously collecting a spousal or survivor benefit based on your mate's earnings record as well as your own retirement benefit, Social Security will give you the *larger* of your own retirement benefits or those that come via your spouse.

Curiously — some might say "deviously" — Social Security hides the fact that if you get only your spousal or survivor benefits, you aren't really getting anything back for all your *own* contributions. Say your spousal or survivor benefit is $1,000 a month and your own retirement benefit is $800 a month. Social Security will give you the $1,000, but they will tell you you're getting your own $800 benefit plus a $200 redefined spousal or survivor benefit.

Now, with all this information behind us, let's examine three rules you should follow to maximize your Social Security benefits.

4

THREE GENERAL RULES TO MAXIMIZE YOUR LIFETIME BENEFITS

Social Security's thousands of rules and thousands upon thousands of explanations of its rules can lead to despair, if not defeatism. This book is designed to revive your spirits by helping you navigate the maze, suggesting strategies for the more common — and some decidedly *un*common — situations that beneficiaries encounter.

But first, to simplify things, we're going to suggest three general rules that millions of Americans ignore at enormous cost. They may already be obvious to you from what we've explained thus far, but they bear emphasis, and repetition. If you take away nothing else from this book, take away these.

THE THREE GENERAL RULES

Rule 1 Be Patient: Take Social Security's best deal by waiting to collect for as long as possible — taking much higher benefits over somewhat fewer years.

Rule 2 Get ALL of What's Yours: Take all the benefits available to you based on the work history of your current spouse, your ex-spouse(s), your deceased spouse(s), and your deceased ex-spouse(s).

Rule 3 Get the Timing Right: Since you can't collect two benefits at once, collect one benefit early while letting the other benefit grow.

Let's explain.

RULE 1 IS LIKE THE MORAL OF AN AESOP FABLE: PATIENCE PAYS

Here's why taking much higher benefits over a few fewer years makes sense.

Social Security reduces benefits if taken early — "early" meaning before age 66 these days — and increases them significantly if taken *after* age 66. Or, to put it another way, taking your benefits earlier than you absolutely need to is inordinately expensive. The raw numbers:

- Retirement benefits starting at 70 are 76 percent higher than those starting at 62.

- Spousal benefits are 43 percent higher at Full Retirement Age than at 62.[1]
- Survivor benefits are 40 percent higher at FRA than at 60.

And, to repeat, when we're talking about higher Social Security benefits, we're talking about *real* benefit increases — increases over and above inflation.

REWARDING PATIENCE, BUT ONLY UP TO A POINT

In the case of your own retirement benefit, which you can start to take as early as age 62 (and about 40 percent of Americans do), Social Security's ever-greater reward for waiting to collect ends at 70. If you wait beyond age 70 to take your retirement benefit, it won't be any higher. So whatever you do, don't wait to contact Social Security until after your 70th birthday. We know that readers, like customers, are always right. But unless you're intent on doing your bit to lower our national debt and deficit, delaying benefits past the age of 70 would be, to understate the case, unwise.

Another reason to be patient, though only up to a point, involves *spousal* benefits. These benefits are such a secret to so many Americans that we explained them in detail

in the last chapter as one of our key A to
Zzzzzzzz.

The limitation on patience applies here
because deferred spousal benefits rise in
value between age 62 and FRA but they do
not rise beyond that point. So holding out
any longer won't hike your spousal benefits
one red cent, save for the annual inflation
adjustment.

As for survivor benefits, which are available as early as age 60 (age 50 for widow-
[er]s of disabled workers), the reward for
patience also ends at FRA.

RULE 2: TAKE ALL THE BENEFITS
YOU CAN GET

Rule 2 — availing yourself of all eligible
benefits — is a no-brainer. More is more. If
you can get extra benefits for yourself or
your family members at no cost in terms of
your own retirement benefit, go for it. As
we keep emphasizing, it's in the contract:
you paid for it; you earned it.

But the reason we make this into its own
rule is that, as we related earlier in the story
of Larry and Paul, you can be a very smart,
sophisticated person (or at least pretend to
be one), yet be completely oblivious to
what's due you. That can make you feel
pretty dumb. But it shouldn't. Not knowing

about Social Security's *auxiliary benefits* is a very common affliction, in part for one very understandable reason: the government hasn't gone out of its way to tell you about them.

Here's what the government might tell every American, perhaps in the notice the Social Security Administration sends every year about our *own* retirement benefit:

The FICA taxes you pay are meant to provide more than just retirement benefits. They may also provide extra financial support to your current and former spouses and to your young children and disabled children, to your surviving spouses and children, and even your parents. There are a lot of conditions that must be met for these benefits to be paid out, but they may apply to you.

So don't ignore these auxiliary benefits. And don't forget that if you are or were married, you may be able to collect benefits on your current or former spouses' earnings history.

Last we looked, there was no such notice. As a consequence, an unknown number of Americans are surely leaving substantial sums on the table — hundreds of thousands of dollars in some cases.

RULE 3: TIMING . . . IS EVERYTHING

At any given moment, many of you are eligible for more than one benefit: your own retirement benefit and an *auxiliary* one. But, to repeat, if you try to collect both benefits at the same time, Social Security won't give them to you. Instead, you are entitled to take only one at a time. But if and when you do, the other benefit effectively vanishes. So the question is: *which* to apply for, and when?

This potential for one benefit to wipe out another of greater long-run value may be the nastiest of the 25 Social Security gotchas we catalog in Chapter 17. You can check them out anytime you want, along with the 50 good-news secrets we've assembled, presented in Chapter 16.

Rule 3 and timing issues are factors in many of our gotchas and secrets. This rule pertains to those who are married, were married, or may get married. That's pretty much everyone. Even priests, nuns, and monks should read about Rule 3. They may have married, divorced, or widowed relatives, friends, or parishioners who need advice. Or they could wind up in extra-clerical arrangements themselves. This also applies to the devoutly secular single: confirmed bachelors and their female counterparts.

Rule 3 pertains to serial brides as well as grooms who marry more than once. But things are more complicated for such folks, in their personal lives, perhaps, and surely when it comes to Social Security. We'll elaborate in due course.

Multiple benefits come in two flavors: spousal and survivor. So there can be either a) retirement and *spousal* benefits, including divorce spousal benefits, or b) retirement and *survivor* benefits, including survivor benefits for those who are divorced. It's easy enough to get confused by the fact that retirement benefits are based on your *own* earnings record, whereas spousal and survivor benefits are based on your *spouse's* earnings, whether the spouse is deceased or ex. But the vexing complexity of the system goes well beyond this.

ON WHICH TWO BENEFITS SHOULD YOU FOCUS?

The first question you need to answer before timing the benefits for which you may be eligible is: Which two benefits pertain to you?

Here's a short guide to the answer:

If you've been married for at least a year and your spouse is alive, the two benefits at issue are your retirement benefit and your spousal benefit. Thus the revelation that spawned this book: Larry informing Paul that he could collect on either his own covered earnings record or that of his wife, Jan.

Fortunately, Paul was not in a position to

97

be confounded by a second category: that if you were married for at least 9 months and your spouse is deceased, the two benefits are your retirement benefit and your survivor benefit.

Nor did Paul have to worry about a third situation: having been divorced after at least 10 years of marriage with an ex still alive, in which case, the relevant benefits would be regular retirement and divorced spousal.

Finally, if someone is divorced after at least 10 years of marriage and the divorced ex has died, the benefits in question are the retirement benefit and the divorced survivor benefit.

In considering where you fit on the grid, bear in mind the old phrase "hitched today, gone tomorrow." That is, you may be married when you first consult the grid and divorced not long after. Or you may be ex'd at the moment and knotted within days. Or, sad to say, widowed. Or, though we mean no hex, God knows, *about to be* widowed. The point is that it may be relevant to imagine yourself in each of these situations because it's possible that one or more of them will happen to you.

IMPLEMENTING THE TIMING RULE — AN INITIAL SURVIVORSHIP EXAMPLE

Rule 3 will come up in several chapters but it's important enough to warrant an extended example up front. So let's imagine a hypothetical widow named Edith, living in Vermont. Her case may not apply to you now, or ever. But it's a simple way to make the timing rule's complications concrete, instead of just stating them in the abstract.

Our Edith is 62 and has spent her life as a cook at a fast-food restaurant. She was married to hypothetical husband Bert, a veterinarian, until last night, when, ironically, he drove into a moose near Montpelier. The moose walked away. Bert did not.

Because she's over 60, Edith would now be eligible to collect a survivor benefit. But because today happens to be her 62nd birthday, she's also freshly eligible to collect her own retirement benefit. (A cautionary reminder: both her survivor and retirement benefits will be reduced if taken before 66, Edith's Full Retirement Age.)

Bert earned more than Edith. Once she has recovered from Bert's moose mishap, she rushes to her local Social Security office and asks to get all the benefits she can. They comply by giving her both her retirement benefit plus her "excess" widow benefit.

Edith has just #$%$ herself royally because she has violated Rule 3: her timing has wiped out one of her benefits.

A lengthy aside here to make a point especially close to Larry's heart. If Edith asks Social Security what happened to her own retirement benefit, they'll tell her something we find highly misleading. Rather than tell Edith that her retirement benefit has been wiped out by her survivor benefit, they'll instead tell her she *is* getting her retirement benefit plus a smaller, redefined survivor benefit equal to the *difference,* or excess, between her survivor benefit and her retirement benefit.

So if we suppose Edith's monthly survivor benefit is $2,000 and her monthly retirement benefit is, say, $1,800, Social Security will send Edith $2,000 — $ 1,800 on her record plus $200 on Bert's record, combined into one opaque payment.

Edith worked her entire life, slinging burgers on the midnight shift at McDonald's. Her earnings record would confirm that she and the company contributed every year for 40 years to Social Security: 12.4 percent of her total earnings. Nonetheless, she would end up getting nothing whatsoever of her own retirement benefits despite all those years of FICA taxes, even though

Social Security would pretend that she is.

And even if Edith's own retirement benefit were not $1,800, but $1,999, her monthly $2,000 payment would not change by one red cent. Why? Because her survivor benefit would *still* be larger than her retirement benefit. Again, no matter how Social Security describes things, *if you are eligible for two benefits at once, you just get one, and it can wipe out the other.*

EDITH GETS AT LEAST SOME OF WHAT'S HERS

But now here's the value of this book, and the reason we've written it, in the hope that the Ediths of America will read it. Watch what happens if Edith applies *just* for her own retirement benefit at 62 and waits until her FRA, age 66, to file for her survivor benefit.

In this case, Edith will actually get her retirement benefit for four years. It will, as we've explained, be smaller because she starts it early, at age 62, rather than waiting until as late as age 70. But it won't be wiped out by her survivor benefit for those four years. That's because of one simple tactic: she doesn't *file* for her survivor benefit until age 66.

The beauty of this strategy is that Edith,

who we imagine is in robust health, loses nothing by waiting to collect her survivor benefit until age 66. True, she will collect only $1,800 a month for four years as her own benefit instead of $2,000 as husband Bert's widow and if that $200 a month is the difference between comfort and penury, she may have no choice but to collect. But were she to wait until her FRA of 66 to collect her *survivor* benefit, it would then not be $2,000, but $2,469, adjusted for inflation. That's a 23 percent higher real benefit, year in and year out, from age 66 to her death, or from here to *eternity,* if science manages to arrest or reverse the process of aging before Edith's passage. And unlike retirement benefits, survivor benefits do not increase past FRA, so there's no reason for Edith to wait.

Some of you may now quickly ask the break-even question: how long before Edith makes back the $200 a month she will forfeit between ages 62 and 66? We think this is the wrong way to look at the decision. But even you break-eveners will easily compute that it would take Edith less than two years to make back the $200 a month she would have left on the table — 20 1/2 months, to be almost exact. That's because she would be getting an extra $469 every month as soon as she reached 66.

Now take a look at Edith's scorecard in terms of following the three rules around which this chapter is built. First, by waiting to get higher benefits, Edith would be following Rule 1. Second, by waiting, she would also able to follow Rule 2 and avail herself of more than one benefit. And third, she would be following Rule 3 by getting her timing right — taking one benefit early and letting the other grow before taking it when it's reached its maximum value.

By contrast, if Edith had tried the initial strategy — claiming both her benefits at age 62 — she would have left serious money on the table: an extra $469 a month from age 66 until her death. Twenty more years is a fair estimate of her life expectancy, so that's an extra $5,628 a year for 20 years, or $112,560 in today's dollars. (Just for kicks, since this is all hypothetical, we've also computed the total were she, however improbably, to reach Jeanne Calment's record age of 122: $315,168, inflation adjusted.) As noted earlier, Americans' retirement readiness is so lacking that even $112,000 dwarfs the average retirement nest egg.

OR, EDITH COULD TAKE HER SURVIVOR BENEFIT FIRST

There is a simple variation on the Edith strategy. Imagine that she had earned *more* than husband Bert: she the vet; he the short-order cook. In that case, we would advise her, if she can afford it, to start collecting her *survivor* benefit on her 62nd birthday and hold off collecting her *own* retirement benefit for as long as possible — until age 70, when it would be at its highest possible value, 76 percent larger than at age 62. Again, she would be following all three rules: patience; multiple benefits; timing.

LEAVING MONEY ON THE TABLE: NOT FROM US ALONE

We make no claim to be investigative reporters who have discovered these strategies on our own. The Center for Retirement Research at Boston College, run by economist Alicia Munnell, did a study of spousal claiming behavior. It found that people were forgoing nearly $10 billion in annual Social Security spousal benefits merely by failing to optimize the "greater of the two" benefit strategies we've been discussing here. That 2009 research was based on 2006 data, so just imagine how much is going unclaimed today, nearly a decade and millions of baby boomer retirements later.

THE THREE GENERAL RULES —
ONCE MORE, WITH FEELING

"Tell them what you'll tell them, tell them, and then tell them what you told them" is the time-worn formula for good teaching, essay writing, and anything you want people to remember. But with Social Security's bewildering maze of rules, elaborated in mind-numbing legalese, we're worried that your memory may reject our earnest efforts at repetition. So let's fall back on pedagogy's fail-safe method for imprinting lasting knowledge — terrorizing the student.

If you're an average American — and even modestly *above* average — you are facing a retirement you almost surely cannot afford, or cannot afford without a major lowering of expectations and standard of living. There is, these days, a fair chance that you will be forced to stop working sooner than you supposed due to a clear-the-decks boss, a hair-trigger economy, or a fickle physiology; that you will, as a consequence, find yourself involuntarily retired with far less savings than you had anticipated; and/or that you will live far longer than you had planned. You may therefore become dependent on Social Security to an extent you never imagined. If this were to happen — and to many of you it absolutely *will* — navigating the system deftly could be a matter of (comfortable) life versus a kind death, as in "I'd rather be dead" because you're incapacitated, yet can't afford the help to so much as get out of bed. That's the risk if you aren't careful and take the wrong benefit advice about what to do or not to do.

Unfortunately, much of the confusion emanates from Social Security itself. Not in what it says, but rather in what it doesn't say or doesn't say clearly enough about what you can't do or must do. For married and divorced couples, for example, Social Security's deeming provisions, which we mentioned and will discuss in detail in the next chapter, are a leading example. If you ignore them, you do so at your peril.

5

STRATEGIES TO FOLLOW THE THREE RULES

You know the Social Security goal we share with you — Get What's Yours. You know the three rules. Now here are some guidelines for following those rules and examples to illustrate, including one involving a brilliant economist for whom Larry "earned" more than twice what he had for Paul.

A warning: the strategies laid out here won't work in all situations. We've emphasized this before. And we have often thought during the past two years that maybe this should have been our fourth rule: "It Depends."

STRATEGY: AVOID DEEMING

Social Security, whether intentionally or not, has set traps that can keep you from getting what's yours. As we said in Chapter 3, the worst, in Larry's view, is *deeming,* which can force you to take both retirement and spousal (or divorced spousal) benefits early, that is, at a reduced level, and leave you with only the larger of the two. This is at odds with Rule 3, which says take one benefit first, while letting the other grow. So, *Avoid Deeming* is our first practical strategy.

STRATEGY: DON'T FILE FOR EARLY SPOUSAL BENEFITS

The only way to avoid early retirement benefit deeming is simply not to apply for an early spousal benefit. And if you are worried about having to take a permanently reduced retirement benefit (which you should be), this means your retirement benefit is likely to be meaningful, which means your excess spousal benefit (the amount greater than your retirement benefit) is likely to be small or zero, which means applying for an early spousal benefit will produce nothing or very little anyway.

STRATEGY: IF MARRIED, COORDINATE BENEFIT COLLECTION WITH YOUR SPOUSE

We have tried to explain that what one spouse does can impact what the other spouse can do, and vice versa. Specifically, in order for one spouse to collect a spousal benefit, whether it's a full spousal benefit or an excess spousal benefit, the other has to have filed for a retirement benefit, as Paul's wife, Jan, did to enable Paul to collect as her spouse.

Hence, besides all the other bedeviling coordination problems facing married couples — from bills to kids, from travel hassles to connubial bliss — there is the need to coordinate their *benefit collection* in order to maximize their lifetime benefits.

So, how *do* you coordinate your benefits?

The answer is make sure both of you have read and understood what we've explained thus far, or that one of you has, and preached the gospel to the other.

We next suggest you sit down and talk about what each of you wants to do and how that will impact the other. Admittedly, this can get sticky in cases where couples don't pool their incomes and thus don't make spending decisions based on the total pot of money. In such cases, you may need to make special arrangements about how you will be spending your *combined* Social Security payments.

Figuring out successful ways of getting spouses to communicate is beyond our pay grade. Surveys repeatedly find that couples often don't communicate effectively and that talking about money is especially hard for them to do. We'd humbly suggest that it can make sense to involve a financial counselor or other trusted third party.

Fortunately, Social Security has a provision called *file and suspend*, which helps married couples overcome some of their potential filing conflicts.

STRATEGY: FILE AND SUSPEND

Suppose you and your spouse have both reached Full Retirement Age: 66. You have never worked. You want to start receiving a spousal benefit. Your partner, however, wants to wait until 70 to collect her largest possible retirement benefit.

You have read that once you reach your own FRA, there is no advantage to waiting even a day longer to collect a spousal benefit, for one simple reason: you won't get anything extra for doing so. But for you to collect any spousal benefit at all, your *spouse* needs to have filed for *her* retirement benefit. And we just got through haranguing you that he or she should wait until age 70 to do this.

You've been to marriage and financial counselors and are still at each other's throats about this decision, probably because the counselors knew nothing about file and suspend. Here's what you should do — file and suspend. This is the strategy that Paul and Jan used in Chapter 1.

The wife can file for a retirement benefit, but then immediately suspend its collection and restart the benefit at or before age 70, during which time she will earn Delayed Retirement Credits of 8 percent a year. But filing for her own retirement benefit permits her spouse to file a *restricted application* just for his spousal benefit. He could collect this benefit for 4 years and then begin collecting his own retirement benefit at age 70 (assuming it was larger than his spousal benefit). This was Larry's revelation to Paul with regard to wife, Jan, which eventuated in a total benefit, spread over ages 66 to 70, equal to a year's tuition at a pricey college, a C-Class Mercedes sport sedan, or a sizable wedding for a child.

HOW TO VOLUNTARILY SUSPEND

Voluntary suspension of benefits for people reaching FRA has been permitted only since 2000 and was enabled under terms of a law known as the Senior Citizens' Freedom to Work Act of 2000. There is no special form to complete and your signature on the request is not required. With advance apologies for automated-response calling delays and hassles, call Social Security (1-800-772-1213 [TTY 1-800-325-0778]), or visit a local Social Security office, and tell them you want to suspend benefits.

The agency is supposed to provide you a notice that says:

We have received your request to stop your benefits to earn special credits that will increase the benefits you will receive at age 70. We will reinstate your benefits at age 70, adding the special credits to your benefit amount.

You also can file the request in writing. Submitting a written request is not necessarily better than a phone call, but it does create a written record, which might help you should there be any subsequent problem with your request. And putting it in writing means you don't need to depend on the notes taken over the phone or in person by a Social Security customer representative. If you do write, here is the gist of what should be included:

TO: Social Security Administration
FROM: John Doe (Social Security
    #123-45-6789; Birthdate
    xx-xx-xxxx)
RE: Request to file and suspend
    retirement benefit

I am writing to "file and suspend" my benefits effective as of Month Day, Year, when I will be AB years and CD months old.
    Please confirm your receipt and ap-

proval of this request via email or letter.

> Sincerely,
> John Doe
> Email address
> Home Address

Send this letter to the location corresponding to your home zip code, using the Social Security Office Locator at https://secure.ssa.gov/ICON/main.jsp.

If you are receiving Medicare and were receiving Social Security benefits when you suspended them, your Medicare payments can no longer be paid automatically and deducted from your Social Security payments. You will need to pay your Medicare premiums out of your own pocket. Don't forget this, as failure to do so can mess up your benefit suspension.

(Also, voluntary suspensions only apply to your retirement benefits. If you are receiving a dual benefit, the excess amount payable on the nonretirement benefit will continue. For example, if you were entitled to a retirement benefit of $1,300 a month and, as a widow or widower, were already receiving a survivorship payment of $1,500 a month based on your late spouse's earnings record, you could suspend your retirement benefit and still receive $200 a month as the excess survivorship benefit.)

Social Security assumes that people who file and suspend upon reaching their FRAs will continue to suspend until they turn 70. Its rules state that the agency will automatically resume retirement benefits when the recipient turns 70. If you want to resume benefits earlier, just tell the agency you want your retirement benefit reinstated. You can communicate this just as you did your desire to file and suspend in the first place.

If you want to see more on this topic, check out the agency's general information page on suspended benefits at http://www.ssa.gov/retire2/suspend.htm. And if you are truly into the details, check out the often impenetrable Program Operations Manual System, or POMS. The key provisions involving file-and-suspend begin at https://secure.ssa.gov/apps10/poms.nsf/lnx/0202409100.

STRATEGY: DIVORCED SPOUSES CAN ALSO FILE RESTRICTED APPLICATIONS

Now let's suppose you're divorced. You have reached your FRA and have not yet filed for your own retirement benefit. Just like a spouse still married, you too can file a restricted application for a spousal benefit and let your own retirement benefit keep growing.

There are, however, four significant *if-and-only-ifs* in this case:

1. you have to have been married to the spouse on whose record you're claiming a spousal benefit for a full 10 years and not a day less;
2. you are not currently remarried;
3. your ex is 62 or over;
4. you've been divorced for 2 or more years, or your ex has filed for their retirement benefit.

STRATEGY: START, STOP, START

Social Security lets you suspend your retirement benefit at any time after FRA and before age 70, regardless of when you started it. This means that you can, for example, start your retirement benefit at age 62, suspend it at FRA, and start it up again at age 70.

When you restart your benefit, it will be increased from the level it was at when you suspended it. So taking benefits early still comes at a cost in terms of post-age-70 benefits. For example, someone who just turned 62 and can receive a $2,000 monthly retirement benefit starting immediately would receive a 76 percent larger benefit of $3,520 by waiting to start until age 70. In contrast, if the person starts the $2,000 benefit now, stops it at 66 (FRA) and starts it again at 70, the benefit from age 70 on will be just 32 percent larger, or $2,640 per month.

But why do that?

Three reasons.

First, you may have some income, such as a private pension, that doesn't kick in until you reach full retirement or thereabouts and you need money to live on till then. But once that other income comes on line, you'd like to take advantage of the Delayed Retirement Credit.

Second, by filing early you can let an older (but still under age 70) spouse collect just his or her spousal benefit based on your earnings history.

Third, you may have children under 16 or disabled children who can collect child benefits once you file for your retirement benefit. And if you do have such children and if you do so file, you may also be able to provide child-in-care spousal or child-in-care divorced spousal benefits to your current or ex-spouse.

Does this pay?

In some cases it does. Suppose, for example, that you are an age-62 wife and your husband is age 66. You've been the low earner. You also are convinced you're not going to live beyond age 85. If you start your benefit at 62, stop it at 66, and start it at 70, you'll permit your husband to get a spousal benefit from 66 to 70. This spousal benefit amounts to four years of half of your full retirement benefit. Yes, taking your benefit early violates Rule 1 — *Be Patient* — but patience, in your case, doesn't provide as much of a payoff because of your relatively short maximum age of life. As a single person, you might have been indifferent between taking your retirement benefit at 62 and starting it at 70. But being married and able to get your husband what amounts to four years of a free spousal benefit makes start, stop, start the best strategy in terms of maximizing lifetime benefits.

Even if you've taken benefits early and later regretted doing so, you can stop them at FRA and restart them later to earn Delayed Retirement Credits and at least get more of what's yours.

STRATEGY: TAKE YOUR SURVIVOR BENEFIT AS EARLY AS POSSIBLE AND YOUR RETIREMENT BENEFIT AT 70

Glenn Loury is one of the world's premier economists and has constructed incisive mathematical models covering topics as diverse as the intergenerational transmission of inequality, the process of technological innovation, and the creation and propagation of racial stereotypes. But Glenn, a chaired professor at Brown University, knew very little about Social Security's survivor benefits. Well, nothing really.

And, tragically, survivor benefits were relevant to Glenn. His wife, Linda, had passed away the year before. Linda was also an esteemed economist, with a long and well-paid career at Tufts University.

Glenn and Larry had just finished dinner at a restaurant when Glenn mentioned he was thinking about selling his house and moving into a smaller place. Age 65, he said that he (like Paul) expected to keep working until at least 70 and take his Social Security then.

"Glenn," said Larry, "have you thought about taking survivor benefits?"

"You mean from Linda?"

"Yes."

"No. I earned a lot more than Linda."

"And so you're sure that disqualifies you from survivor benefits?"

"Yes."

"Are you really sure?"

Glenn laughed. "No, I'm not *really* sure. Am I missing something?"

"How does this sound? I make you, let me see, about $120,000 in the next two minutes and you pay for dinner." (Larry was getting used to the gravy train.)

"I'm in," said Glenn.

Larry then explained to Glenn that in a year, when he turned 66 and reached FRA, he could apply just for a survivor benefit based on Linda's earnings record. Linda had passed away at age 58, but the survivor benefit is equal to what her full retirement benefit *would have been* had she lived until 66 — $30,000 per year.

"But," Glenn asked, "how can I collect benefits if I'm the higher earner?"

"Good question," said Larry. "Even though you're the higher earner, you're not going to take your own retirement benefit until 70. Yes, once you start taking your own retirement benefit, you'll get only the larger of the two benefits — your retirement and survivor benefits. But between 66 and 70, that won't happen.

"And the beauty of this is the part that

you already knew — by waiting four years until age 70 to collect *your* retirement benefit, it will rise a lot." Then Larry repeated the familiar 32 percent increase refrain. "So you get a lot more money in retirement benefits by waiting, and you also get the survivor benefits for four years, well, for *free!*"

"But," objected Glenn, "I'll still be working. Isn't there an Earnings Test whereby I lose benefits if I earn too much money?"

"Yes, but it ends when you reach 66, which is your Full Retirement Age."

Yet another friend would be picking up the tab.

Let's expand on this case study just a bit, because of course most people aren't going to be in Glenn's shoes.

Glenn wasn't able to benefit from taking a survivor benefit before FRA because he was still working, and at his relatively lofty income, the earnings test would have wiped out any benefits (survivor or retirement) that he could have taken before FRA.

Yes, he'd get the money back. But the Earnings Test money is returned to you in incrementally higher benefits over the years of your actuarial life expectancy. Since Glenn would be taking the survivor benefit only until age 70, however, he wouldn't recoup most of the deferred money.

But if there was another person in this situation who was at least 60 and not working, taking his survivor benefit right away would be his best option.

Yes, taking a survivor benefit as early as age 60 means a big early survivor benefit reduction, specifically, 28.5 percent. The choice was whether to begin taking the reduced survivor benefit at age 60 or wait until a later year, when he'd get a higher benefit. We calculated all possible scenarios — wait until age 61, until age 62, etc. — and it turned out that even with the steep reduction, waiting past age 60 to collect a survivor benefit never made sense.

STRATEGY: TAKE YOUR RETIREMENT BENEFIT AS EARLY AS POSSIBLE AND YOUR SURVIVOR BENEFIT AT FULL RETIREMENT AGE

If your unreduced survivor benefit (your survivor benefit at FRA) is larger than your retirement benefit would be if you take it at age 70, it's best to take your retirement benefit starting at the earliest possible date that it's not wiped out by the Earnings Test. This way you can get your retirement benefit, while you let your survivor benefit grow to its highest value at FRA and then switch to taking it.

At FRA, it's best to take your survivor benefit, since it will then beat its largest possible value. You'll receive just your survivor benefit starting at FRA, but it will be described as the sum of your own reduced retirement benefit plus your excess survivor benefit (your survivor benefit less your own reduced retirement benefit).

STRATEGY: GET MARRIED, GET DIVORCED, LIVE IN SIN

Social Security has incentives for some people to marry, for others to divorce, for others to wait to get married, for others to wait to divorce, and for others to live in sin.

We'll give you one example here, involving Richie Rich — a single, 65-year-old, very high-paid lawyer who marries 65-year-old Bessie, a lovely Romanian gal who just received her citizenship. Bessie was an investment banker back in Romania, but hasn't been employed since landing in the States a decade ago.

Richie and Bessie met on Match.com and fell instantly in love with the idea of getting married for money. This they do after Richie has Bessie sign a prenuptial agreement. When they both reach FRA (66), Richie files and suspends and Bessie begins collecting half of Richie's $32,000 full retirement benefit. Bessie sends Richie $8,000 a year from roughly a thousand miles away because, well, they choose not to live together and they don't have to.

These strategies don't exist in isolation or a vacuum. They comprise the road network, if you will, of the Social Security system. How these roads intersect and where you want to drive on them depends on your age, financial situation, health, and other variables that only you know. And not just you. The same variables are involved for your spouse and your family.

It can be very hard even to know what choices are out there without spending a lot of time learning about Social Security and listening to the questions and problems encountered by real people struggling to understand the system and get what's theirs. The good news is that we've been doing this for a long time, and we've boiled down what we've learned here. The bad news is that one of the most important things we've discovered about understanding Social Security is that you can't trust a lot of what other people say about it, beginning with the folks who work for Social Security.

STRATEGY: WAITING TO COLLECT YOUR RETIREMENT BENEFIT MAY BE THE WRONG MOVE

Why would you violate our Rule 1 and start your retirement benefit early if by waiting until age 70, you will collect up to 76 percent more, forever, on an inflation-adjusted basis?

Let's rehearse the four reasons in a little more detail:

1. You may need the money. There are eight years between 62 and 70. They are eight *short* years once you've lived them, but they can be eight *long* years if you have too little income and/or savings. A dear friend of Paul's got laid off at the financially challenged *PBS News-Hour* at age 67. Nobody's fault. But she had fully intended to work until 70 and was delaying her benefits until they would reach their peak. Now she can't. "That will cost me $600 a month for the rest of my life," she said. "But I can no longer afford to wait."

2. A medical condition arises that you believe will dramatically reduce your life expectancy. A terminal

diagnosis would be reason enough to start taking benefits right away if a) you aren't married, so your spouse's widow's benefit doesn't come into play or, b) if your potential widow isn't in a position to collect a widow's benefit due to the Government Pension Offset (see Glossary) or having taken a retirement benefit that exceeds her widow's benefit. But you can now buy a genetic screening test at very low cost that provides your likelihood of getting any number of diseases. We're not aware of a company offering refined projections of life expectancy from DNA data. But if there isn't one yet, there soon will be.

3. Applying for your own retirement benefit early may be advantageous in order to make an older spouse eligible for a spousal benefit on your earnings record. Say, for example, that you're a high-earning woman who reaches 62 when your spouse hits 66 — the current FRA. By filing at 62, you entitle your spouse to collect a full spousal benefit equal to half of your full retirement ben-

efit between 66 and 70, provided he doesn't file for his own retirement benefit during these years.

4. Another big reason to file early is to enable a young or disabled child to begin collecting a child benefit. Once this happens, your spouse may be able to collect a child-in-care spousal benefit. We say *may* because the spouse may be working and thus lose the benefit due to the Earnings Test (see Chapter 3 or the Glossary). Also, if a disabled child is involved and is living in an institution, the child-in-care benefit may be disallowed.

5. And, as we said earlier, you may be widowed. In this case, taking your retirement benefit early and waiting until FRA to take your survivor benefit *may* maximize your lifetime benefits.

6

BE CAREFUL TAKING
SOCIAL SECURITY'S ADVICE

Social Security began handing out regular monthly benefits in 1940, five years after the program was created to bolster a Depression-wracked nation. It was a big change for a laissez-faire country, though it provided a safety net that would seem skimpy today: the typical Social Security payment was $17.50 a month in 1940, or roughly $300 in today's dollars.

What began as a Model T Ford program, however — one size fits all — has been expanded, amended, reformed, and socially engineered into a fully loaded Rube Goldbergmobile. It has a driver's manual a mile thick that we'd bet most of Social Security's own representatives can't follow.

Consider the story of John, one of the many Americans who email or call Larry regularly for help on their Social Security claims. (As we've written, Larry answers as many questions as he can every Monday on

Paul's PBS Making Sen$e Web page.) It would be nice if John was an outlier, but he's not.

John is 66 (or was when he wrote in); his wife had just turned 62. He and his wife are fairly well-off and John was still working. So they didn't need to take Social Security right away. John called Social Security and asked the person on the phone if he could file for his retirement benefit and suspend its collection so that his wife could get a spousal benefit right away.

John told the Social Security representative that he'd been the higher earner. According to John, the Social Security rep told him that he could and should file and suspend and that his wife would then get a spousal benefit. John's wife had earned more than $60,000 a year until the last 10 years, but not much of late. John and the rep figured her own retirement benefits would be very low. But they were wrong. Social Security's benefit formula is so progressive that the couple's respective benefits actually will be similar.

And if John had filed for his retirement benefit, and his wife had then filed for her spousal benefit, she would have been deemed to also be filing for her retirement benefit because she would have been filing before reaching her FRA. She'd get something close to the larger of the two benefits, which, in her case, would likely have been her retirement benefit — *not* her spousal benefit. And it would have been reduced forever because she supposedly filed for it early!

Further, by having John file and suspend, the Social Security rep was throwing away *John's* option to collect a spousal benefit through age 70 on his wife's earnings record, and wait until 70 to collect his largest possible retirement benefit. All she had to do was file for her retirement benefit at 62, in which case John would get a reduced spousal benefit for four years. She could then, at her FRA, a) file for her own excess-spousal benefit (which would surely be zero) or b) suspend her own retirement benefit until she turned 70.

The happy ending here is that John contacted Making Sen$e and a real nightmare became just a bad dream. Had he not, he and his wife could well have headed to the local Social Security office and made a huge financial mistake.

SOCIAL SECURITY DOESN'T HAVE THE RESOURCES TO GET YOU WHAT'S YOURS

The agency is overwhelmed with requests for advice, benefit calculations, and requests. It's hard to believe, but the agency gets 3 million requests for information every week.

Social Security services more Americans than any other agency of government, including the Internal Revenue Service. And yet it does so with shrinking staff and resources.

How big is the job? In 2013, roughly 163 million people had Social Security payroll taxes withheld from their paychecks. According to the program's 2014 annual trustees' report, Social Security provided payments to 40.8 million retirees and their dependents, 6.2 million survivors of deceased workers, and 11 million disabled workers and their dependents.

In total, the agency provided more than $812 billion in benefits, including $672 billion in retirement and survivor benefits and $140 billion in disability payments. And yet the program's administrative expenses were less than 1 percent of the money it handled.

Consider the howls from health insurance companies when Obamacare required them to pay out at least 85 percent of their revenues in benefits. How, they lamented, are we going to run our organizations, pay our employees, and reward our owners retaining only 15 percent of our revenues?

And in the allegedly efficient *private* financial sector, the fees — in order just to *manage* your money — are often far higher.

Yes, some financial companies, like Vanguard, operate with very low overhead. Their management fees on some funds average less than a *fifth* of 1 percent. But Vanguard isn't taking in money from 160 million people and almost as many businesses a month and sending out 57 million checks. Nor is it besieged daily by millions of people asking questions and making requests.

Given its importance, you'd think the agency would be given ample resources to do its job, but the opposite is true. The Social Security Administration is under a fiscal siege thanks to congressional budget cuts. In late 2012 the agency was forced to cut operating hours at more than 1,200 field offices and began closing them at noon each Wednesday. At the time, more than *180,000 people a day* were visiting those offices and the agency was handling 450,000 phone calls. Every single day. The numbers, swelled by baby boomer retirements, have likely increased since. And yet agency employment is down by more than 11,000 — to about 75,000 in recent years. In the five years ending in mid-2014, the agency had closed 64 field offices, 5 percent of its total. Wait times have increased. And employment losses have been weighted toward the agency's most experienced staffers. Yes, SSA has developed a growing ability to conduct business online. But most people want (and need) a *human being* to help them make fateful, once-in-a-lifetime financial decisions.

SSA regularly surveys consumers about their perceptions of the quality of its services. Based on its 2013 surveys, public satisfaction rates were 74 percent for 800 calls, 79 percent for field office calls, and 91 percent for field office visits.

One way to look at it: the glass is three-quarters full when it comes to electronic encounters, *nine-tenths* full when the contact is human to human, face-to-face. The more journalistic appraisal, however, would be that fully one-quarter of all customers are *dis*satisfied online or by phone, and a tenth of them even after going to the Social Security office.

But more to the point, how can the public know if it *should be* satisfied? If beneficiaries and would-be beneficiaries don't get a second opinion, how are they to know whether they're getting good information or being disastrously misled, even if by a very well-meaning person? The simple fact is that the SSA representative on the phone, or across from you at the table, is often overworked and undertrained.

2013 PUBLIC SATISFACTION WITH SOCIAL SECURITY SERVICES

SERVICE	PEOPLE SERVED	SERVICE RATINGS (%)	
		Satisfied	Excellent
800 Callers	56,000,000	70	22
Field Office Caller	46,000,000	78	36
Field Office Visitor	44,000,000	93	42
Card Center Visitor	1,000,000	92	36
Hearing Office Visitor	500,000	92	31
Internet Benefit Applications	3,000,000	90	28
Internet Change Address/Direct Deposit	900,000	95	41
Internet Disability Reports	800,000	84	24
Internet Requests	4,000,000	90	34
TOTAL ALL SERVICES	156,200,000	80	33

"INFORMATION," NOT "ADVICE"? TAKE IT WITH A SHAKER (OR MAYBE A MINE) OF SALT

Social Security claims that its representatives do not give *advice* to consumers. Instead, they say, they provide *information.* This would surely come as news to most of the people who ask it for help.

Moreover, what seems like the simplest Social Security question can require considerable thought by even the most knowledgeable personnel and a lengthy explanation to the questioner. Their recourse, then, is to provide one-size-fits-all answers. This is especially true in the online world, where the agency has been making much of its new public service effort.

Further, and this is very important, Social Security claiming decisions are often irreversible.

Go into nearly any retail store in this land, buy a product in error, and you will be able to later return it. But that's often not the case with mistaken Social Security claiming decisions, even if prompted by the agency's own representatives. Thus the agency's information could wind up being the most costly "advice" you ever get.

A final red flag. In the words of Social Security itself, "The fact that we determine that a claimant meets the requirements for entitlement does not preclude us from making another determination that the claimant no longer meets those requirements at some subsequent date," according to the agency's vast Program Operations Manual System, or POMS. A reasonable inference to draw:

135

even *correct* information from Social Security may be, in the lingo of Wall Street money managers, no guarantee of future returns.

**SOCIAL SECURITY VERBATIM
JUST THE FACTS, MA'AM**

Social Security representatives are instructed to explain that "individual employees who administer the program are not at liberty to substitute their own judgment or opinion for rulings, regulations, or the law. . . . Do not attempt to explain the rationale for any particular operational guidelines, nor go to any great lengths to justify them."

*ALL QUOTES FROM OFFICIAL
SOCIAL SECURITY RULES*

ESTIMATES OF YOUR FUTURE BENEFITS: WHICH SHOULD YOU TRUST?

You might think that online calculators, including the ones that are provided for free, will give you the right strategy for maximizing your lifetime benefits. Some will, some won't. This is particularly true if your situation differs from the average.

There are two ways online calculators can go badly wrong. They can take in the wrong inputs, and they can make the wrong calculations with those inputs. Social Security calculators geared to be quick don't take in enough information "above the hood" — in their user interfaces — to make the right calculations "under the hood" — in their computation engines. So even if a quick calculator's computation engine is correctly programmed — *a very big if* — it can't produce accurate results.

Another way that online calculators provide "quick and dirty" answers is in presenting their results. Some just tell you what to do without showing you any details of their underlying calculations. Others simply add up all future Social Security benefits that you'll receive over your remaining lifetime. This violates Economics 101, which says benefits received in the future aren't worth as much as benefits received today for the simple reason that you have to wait to collect them.

SOCIAL SECURITY'S OWN CALCULATORS

Depending on which Social Security source you use, you may receive different answers to your request for an estimate of future benefits. Social Security has various estimation techniques. We're all for freedom of choice but think these sources should agree with one another. It turns out they don't.

Your choices include:

- SSA's official annual statement with benefit estimates;
- An over-the-phone Social Security staff estimate;
- An in-person estimate at a local office;
- Four different online benefit calculators, each of which gives you a number.

But if the numbers vary among these seven estimate options — and they very likely will — you won't immediately know why, or which to believe, though the calculators do say that the numbers provided are estimates and that there are many reasons they might differ from your actual benefits.

Let's take a look at perhaps the most familiar of these estimates — that provided in the annual earnings statement, which Social Security calls Your Social Security

Statement. It itemizes your earnings history and lays out its assumptions about your future earnings. But in presenting the retirement benefits you can collect, starting at different ages, the statement doesn't say whether the amounts are shown in today's dollars, adjusted for inflation, or in dollars of the year in which you start collecting. Nor does it say whether the benefit estimates take into account America's projected real-wage growth between the year of the statement and the year benefits collection might begin. Yet, until age 60, your benefits are indexed to this very number: the overall wage growth of American workers. And afterward, they're adjusted yearly for the cost of living.

In fact, the benefit estimates on your earnings statement assume no growth in Social Security's Average Wage Index (AWI) as well as no future inflation *whatsoever*! And this despite the fact that, since 1952, the AWI has grown in all but one year and prices have risen in all but two years.

Likewise, if you call or visit your Social Security office, they will give you benefit estimates, but won't necessarily tell you what dollars they are quoting your benefits in, or whether they are *assuming* economy-wide wage growth. And they may not know to tell you since they too are relying on calculators and reports whose underlying assumptions aren't immediately apparent.

Moreover, if you are requesting a benefit quote for when you pass age 65, they may quote your benefit net of Medicare's Part B premium payment, since this is backed out of the payment you would actually get each month. It may also be quoted net of withholding for federal income taxes.

Okay, those are the problems with Your Social Security Statement and personal advice from Social Security, either by phone or in person. But what about the four online calculators?

We went to the main Social Security calculator page (http://www.ssa.gov/planners/benefitcalculators.htm) and took each of them out for a spin.

First we followed the advice provided in Chapter 3 and created an online account at *my Social Security* (http://www.ssa.gov/myaccount/). We were then able to use the agency's own record of our Social Security earnings history (we used only one coauthor's actual earnings history). Here's how the calculators stacked up against one another:

Quick Calculator
(http://www.ssa.gov/OACT/quickcalc/index.html)

It was quick indeed and it also showed results in both today's dollars (unadjusted for inflation) and in *future* dollars (adjusted to reflect the rising cost of living). We entered in $80,000 a year in covered earnings up until the year we would begin claiming benefits. This calculator said our retirement benefit at age 70 would be $2,622 in current dollars and that benefits would be $1,905 for a spouse, plus $1,429 to a qualifying child, with a Family Maximum Benefit of $3,348. The problem is, if we didn't know better, we might well have stopped there.

Online Calculator
(http://www.ssa.gov/retire2/AnypiaApplet.html)

This was a lot of work, as it asked for earnings for every year since our first in the labor force. Fortunately, we were able to plug in the details from our version of Your Social Security Statement. We used the same $80,000 a year in estimated future covered earnings as before.

But here's the punch line. This nonquick calculator said our monthly retirement benefit at 70 would be $3,249! That's 24 percent more than what the Quick Calculator generated: $627 a month, *for the rest of our life.* And our spousal, child, and family benefits all would be comparably higher as well.

Detailed Calculator
(http://www.ssa.gov/OACT/anypia/anypia.html)
This is the most time-consuming tool to use. It requires you to download software to your computer and to enter your year-by-year earnings history again. But the software has been updated with the latest benefit computations, including the most recent annual Cost of Living Adjustment (COLA). It also was the only tool that calculated our Primary Insurance Amount, or PIA. According to the Detailed Calculator, our retirement benefit at age 70 would be $3,198 a month — an estimate not far from the Online Calculator's $3,249.

Retirement Estimator
(http://www.socialsecurity.gov/estimator/)
This calculator provides benefit estimates based on your actual Social Security earnings history. It does so by asking you for identifying information, including your Social Security number. It then pulls your actual earnings history from agency computers and produces an estimate. Once

142

you've entered this information and answered a couple of other questions, you get a result quickly. So, it's much easier to use than the Online Calculator or the Detailed Calculator. And it's accurate as well. It said our retirement benefit at age 70 would be $3,249 a month — identical to the Online Calculator.

For one last comparison, we went online to consult our current Your Social Security Statement. It said our retirement benefit at age 70 would be $3,205 a month. That was lower than the other detailed calculators. But in looking at the reason, it turns out the agency was assuming our future earnings would be smaller than our own estimates.

TAKING A TEST DRIVE
OF THE AARP CALCULATOR

There are scads of free calculators out there. We're going to take a deep look into the one provided by AARP. Odds are, it's one of, if not the most heavily used (roughly 750,000 times a year, AARP says). Also, the questions we pose about it are valid considerations in using other calculators. And the greatest shortcoming of all of them (or at least all of them we've seen, and that's a lot) is their focus on being easy to use. But as we've seen, when it comes to Social Security, simplicity is the enemy of accuracy.

AARP, as you probably know, used to be shorthand for the American Association of Retired Persons. With some 37 million members ages 50 and above, AARP pays a lot of attention to Social Security. Simple doesn't necessarily mean off base. But it could be the case here, as careful readers of Chapter 3 will see.

Jean Setzfand, AARP's vice president of financial security, stresses that simplicity and ease of use were important considerations in designing AARP's calculator. She is a fan of more sophisticated calculators, which often charge fees. "Many of them are terrific," she said in an interview with us. "But they are more for a financial advisory audience. We're not targeting sophisticated investors. . . . [The AARP tool] is really for individuals who have a basic understanding of their finances."

AARP's tool gives you two ways to provide your PIA, which, of course, is the building block for calculating all the benefits you and yours can get on your earnings record.

Method 1 entails entering your earnings and letting the calculator figure out your PIA. If the tool solicited your exact earnings history, it would be able to calculate your PIA precisely. But instead it asks you to enter your average earnings.

But what's the meaning of "average earnings"? The instructions say, "If your earnings have gone up and down over the years, enter an average salary, even if it's different than your current salary." Okay, but is this an average salary measured in today's dollars or is it an average of the actual dollars you earned each year in the past? The website doesn't say. But it can make a huge difference to the calculated PIA. And even if you knew whether to enter your past average earnings in actual dollars or today's dollars, that doesn't suffice to determine your PIA. Indeed, if you didn't work for 40 quarters in covered employment, your PIA will be zero because you won't be eligible for any benefits, period. If you do have 40 quarters under your belt and *if* you enter your average past covered earnings correctly, your PIA may still be miles off. The reason is that the accurate calculation of your PIA is based on your Average Indexed Monthly Earnings (AIME), which, in turn, is based on each year's separate level of earnings. In other words, when you made your earnings can matter — *a lot*!

Moreover, the AIME calculation only uses past *covered* earnings, not your total earnings. But the AARP calculator doesn't tell you to enter your average past *covered* earnings. It just tells you to enter your average earnings, which users will likely take to mean their total, not their covered earnings.

To understand how bad just this mistake could be with respect to getting a benefit estimate from AARP, we ran a single person — call him Dan — twice through a software program (Larry's Maximize My Social Security) that incorporates precise earnings histories. In each case, the person's average nominal earnings are $50,000. But in one case, Dan earns exactly $50,000 each year for 40 years. In the other case, Dan earns $100,000 each year for 20 years and zero otherwise. Although Dan's average earnings are the same, his benefits in the first case are one-third larger than in the second case!

Setzfand noted that possible inaccuracies with letting people calculate their own average earnings were one reason AARP recommends that people get their actual earnings history from Social Security and plug this number into the AARP calculator. This sounds fine. But what number, we would ask, should they use?

How long will you continue to work? The AARP calculator must assume you'll work through FRA, but it doesn't say. And if you are only going to work for two more years and FRA is eight years away, well, that's yet another potential decent-size mistake entering into your PIA calculation. This is particularly the case for workers who earn above the taxable maximum after age 60. For such workers, their AIME is guaranteed to go up for each year they work after age 60 because each extra year's worth of covered earnings thrown into the pot will always be larger than the other ones in the pot.

Furthermore, without exactly correct data on your past covered earnings, it's impossible for an online calculator to properly figure out how much your benefits will rise due to your continued earnings after age 60. (This process, known as Social Security's Recomputation of Benefits, is explained in the next chapter.) It's also impossible to properly calculate Social Security's Windfall Elimination Provision, which we will cover in detail in Chapter 15.

Understanding these problems with AARP's first way to use its calculator might lead you to say, "fuhgeddaboudit," and proceed to AARP's second way. But the second way to use the calculator assumes you won't work at all in the future. It also takes you to one of Social Security's online calculators, which will provide a PIA estimate that is guaranteed, if you're under 60, to come back with the wrong estimate of your PIA (as we just explained).

Since the AARP calculator is taking in, in this case, a Social Security–produced PIA estimate that is likely to be wrong, the question is whether the calculator's underlying code is fixing the problem with the PIA so entered. Setzfand said there is no adjustment to the number received from Social Security. This might not be a material problem. But it could be and, of course, you won't know.

The AARP calculator pays a lot of attention to combined benefits of married couples, and this is a good thing. It also gets a gold star from us for comparing benefit estimates with spending trends among retired persons, providing a useful view of budgeting realities tied to Social Security income. However, for married spouses where one partner's optimal strategy depends on what the other does and vice versa, starting off with off-base PIAs can easily undermine the calculation of what's best for the couple to do jointly.

If you ask for your retirement benefit, the good folks at Social Security may quote your benefit in dollars of the year you will reach full retirement. That could screw up the AARP calculator. Or they may quote you not your full retirement benefit, but your *reduced* retirement benefit if you start talking to them about taking benefits early. This too will screw up the AARP calculator, since it's looking for the full retirement benefit. Then there's the issue of your Medicare Part B premiums and automatic federal income tax withholdings. You may be given a "benefit amount" that's net of one or both of these things. Finally, if you are eligible for an excess spousal or an excess survivor benefit, it's possible you'll be quoted a benefit amount that's inclusive of these auxiliary benefits, which will also cause the AARP's calculator to produce misleading benefit estimates.

FINANCIAL ENGINES
REVS UP ITS CALCULATOR

Financial Engines is a 401(k) advisory firm founded by Nobel laureate economist William Sharpe. Its clients provided retirement services to about 9 million employees in mid-2014, which is also when it began to offer a free Social Security calculator. Many of the assumptions in its calculator reflect limitations similar to those noted in the AARP and other quick-and-easy calculators. However, in explaining the rationale behind Financial Engines' work, the company's chief investment officer, Christopher Jones, covered some crucial realities about Social Security that we'd like to share.

First off, Jones said, the need for a quick calculator that can be used in five minutes or less is a necessity, not a marketing gimmick. Otherwise, people will hit what he called a behavioral "blocking condition" and simply will not proceed. There is some sacrifice to accuracy in this calculator, perhaps, but it's not large. And he said the calculator is particularly accurate for those people nearing retirement and thus facing Social Security claiming decisions.

Second, Jones said, the fate of surviving spouses is key to making optimal claiming decisions. Yet many people — and many calculators — fail to consider spousal benefits or consider them accurately. Financial Engines uses longevity odds that include the probabilities for both spouses. On average, he said, the surviving spouse will live another 11 years after losing their mate. This is a much bigger gap than indicated by mortality tables. But this figure is built into the company's calculator when it spits out claiming advice.

Financial Engines also interviewed hundreds of people near retirement before launching its calculator. What it found is that people dread burning though their nest eggs, particularly during their early retirement years. In terms of Social Security, then, they would tend to favor taking benefits earlier to avoid spending down their savings.

So, where the lifetime values of different Social Security claiming options are similar (and Jones said this is often the case), Financial Engines will "tilt" toward recommending that people take benefits earlier.

Jones himself acknowledged the irony of this approach. For, while there is some risk that people who do not take benefits might die early, deferring Social Security benefits is, in his view, the best financial option available today. Delayed Retirement Credits allow Social Security benefits to rise by 8 percent a year, plus the rate of inflation. And the payments are guaranteed by the federal government. "That's a screamingly good deal," he said, while agreeing that "in general, the population is very poorly informed with respect to the benefits of delaying Social Security."

"The deferral strategies do better 90 to 95 percent of the time," he said. "The only situation where starting early makes sense is where you *and* your spouse both die early."

DECODING "YOUR SOCIAL SECURITY STATEMENT"

Your Social Security Statement is the agency's annually updated record of your actual earnings and projected benefits. Typically, the latest one would arrive in the mail annually and include a year-by-year record of what is called your covered wage employment — each year's earnings, ever since you began working, up to the amount of that year's wage ceiling for payroll taxes. (The statement never explained the wage ceiling, so when some people reviewed their "earnings record," they couldn't figure out why their yearly amounts were lower than what they had actually been paid.)

Despite its idiosyncrasies, Your Social

Security Statement was long the single most authoritative look at your Social Security benefits. Besides reflecting your earnings history and, thus, your projected retirement benefits (with the flaws we've already noted), Your Social Security Statement was (and remains) the only easily accessible record of how much money you earned every year. After 30 or 40 years in the workforce, try rounding up this information on your own. With an average of 10,000 baby boomers turning 66 every day from 2011 to about 2030, more and more people need this information. But a couple of years ago, the SSA, its budget pressed, announced that it would stop sending out printed statements. The agency later said it would create the ability to provide the statements online. Still later, it said anyone who asked for an old-fashioned printed statement could get one in the mail. And, more recently, it developed plans to automatically send paper statements to people once every five years — at 25, 30, 35, 40, 45, 50, 55, and 60.

The number of people who have signed up for the online version of their annual statement is, by now, in the millions. But this big number remains a small percentage of the number of people who used to be mailed the annual statement. (The cost of this mailing, by the way, was something like 80 cents apiece.)

One problem, of course, is that if you don't see your statement, you won't be able to take a look at your official earnings record and related benefits projections. More to our point here, you also won't be able to see if the agency has made any mistakes in calculating your earnings record. And, guess what? Mistakes are made all the time. The most frequent cause of errors involves people who overpay their Social Security taxes because they are working at multiple jobs that take out payroll taxes from both salaries. Not often, but often enough, the agency fails to receive the correct information or to properly track these multiple jobs and, as a result, undercounts your payroll taxes and future Social Security benefits.

You can fix these mistakes. But only if you see them, and then go through an SSA dispute resolution process.

THE PRIVACY PROBLEM: HOW TO UNCOVER YOUR EX-SPOUSAL AND SURVIVORSHIP BENEFITS

Spousal benefits are hugely important in many people's Social Security claiming decisions. So are benefits for divorced spouses and benefits for surviving spouses of deceased Social Security benefits. Here, our beef is not only with the agency's confusing rules and often inconsistent advice. We're also perplexed by the agency's privacy rules, which won't permit the divorced access to their ex-spouses' earnings records or automatically let widows and widowers have access to their late spouses' earnings records. Optimal claiming decisions are hard enough even when you know all the numbers. They become impossible when you can't get the information you need.

Given Social Security's benefit formulas, ex-spouses have a legal claim to benefits based on their former spouses' earnings records. But if they can't get access to these records, they can't properly decide when to retire, or how much to save for retirement, or in which order to take their spousal, retirement, and survivor benefits, or when to start taking one or more benefit.

Yes, once ex-spouses are close to the time of being able to collect benefits on their ex- or deceased husbands or wives, they can find out from Social Security what these benefits will be. But that's *very late* in the day. And yes, if they are really knowledgeable about the system, they can roughly infer what their spouses must have made and then run through the potentially thousands of combinations of benefit collection dates to figure out which one is optimal. But this is not something we recommend anyone try on their own.

As for learning whether your ex is collecting benefits, don't expect Social Security to notify you. The Social Security Administration doesn't know who is or was married to whom. You need to establish you are or were married by providing a copy of your marriage certificate or your final divorce decree. But to collect divorced spousal benefits, you need to have been married at least 10 years, have an ex who is at least age 62, and have been divorced for two or more years *or have an ex who has filed for his or her retirement benefit.* Because of those requirements, knowing whether your ex has filed matters a great deal if you were divorced less than two years ago. But the only way to know if your ex has filed is to ask him or her. We think people deserve a better way to get access to benefits to which they are legally entitled.

7
THE BENEFITS OF
NOT RETIRING

If you're sick and tired of your job, you can't stand your boss, and you can't wait to retire, please stop and think it over. This is a huge financial decision. You need to get it right.

Idyllic retirements are more the stuff of movies than real life. Your golf game may be lousy; your bowling, worse. You may already go to as many book clubs and yoga sessions as you can stand. You could drive your partner nuts hanging around 24/7, and you could live, well, forever. There are mice who now live three times as long as they are meant to thanks to scientists injecting them with special gene therapies. Yes, they are mice and you are men (or women). But don't forget that Jeanne Calment made it to 122 without any PEDs (performance-enhancing drugs). Do you really want to be retired and living on peanuts for more than half a century?

Beyond the issues raised by greater longevity, the Great Recession made retirement impossible for millions. The need to continue earning money for current needs, let alone rebuilding nest eggs, replaced notions of beachfront cabanas.

The very concept of retirement has gotten a makeover in recent years. The aforementioned recession created a cottage industry of advice about whether retirement was an outmoded concept. It also highlighted our widespread financial unpreparedness for retirement. As we told you in the beginning of *Get What's Yours,* the amount of money that most Americans — even those in middle age — have saved for their later years falls far short of anything resembling a sufficient retirement nest egg. The lesson for millions of us has been to settle for a meager existence in our later years. Or to keep working.

WORKING CAN BE GOOD FOR YOUR HEALTH

But the point of this chapter is to demonstrate that the financial benefits of staying on the job can be enormous in terms of the Social Security benefits for you and even for others who may be at least somewhat dependent on them.

First of all, each year of continued work

means a year of not having to tap retirement savings. Those savings can actually grow, both from a year of investment gains on one's savings and, if the job includes an employer-supported 401(k) or other retirement benefits, a year of new plan contributions. Last, but hardly least, the length of your actual retirement will have been shortened by a year. You will, in sum, wind up with more money to fund a shorter retirement. And, to once again pound the drum we've been incessantly (if not headache-inducingly) beating, should this extra year of work allow you to also delay taking Social Security for a year, your benefit will grow by about 8 percent plus the rate of inflation (although not compounded) until age 70.

Beyond dollars, it turns out that continuing to work also may bring you better health and even a longer life — not bad for whatever passes these days for punching a time clock. Retirement, it turns out, may be hazardous to your health. Studies have found that being in a workplace setting can provide social connections, a sense of accomplishment, and other forms of mental and physical stimulation. Not working can lead to isolation, boredom, and stress.

A French study released in 2013 even found a solid link between continued work and avoidance of dementia. That government study of nearly 430,000 retirees found their risk of being diagnosed with dementia declined by more than 3 percent for each extra year they worked before retiring. Thus, someone who retired at, say, 65, had nearly a 15 percent lower risk of getting dementia than someone who retired at age 60.

Generalizations can be misleading. For example, people with dementia may tend to retire earlier. But there is certainly evidence that work is good for us on many fronts. One of those fronts, as we said at the outset, is Social Security, and the roles it plays in shaping retirement plans.

WORKING CAN BE GOOD FOR YOUR WALLET, TOO

Back in Chapter 3, we talked about Average Indexed Monthly Earnings (AIME) and explained how they were used to calculate your Primary Insurance Amount (PIA). This is the amount of money you would receive in retirement benefits if you filed for them at your Full Retirement Age (FRA). We also emphasized that the PIA is a key figure in determining many other Social Security benefits.

As it turns out, the decision to continue working in later life also may have an impact on your AIME and thus on your PIA and . . . the thighbone's connected to the hipbone, and so on. In short, this is another potentially big deal, and we hope that explaining it in detail will be time well spent.

Every year that you work at jobs where you pay Social Security taxes, your earnings can become one of the years used to calculate your AIME. Recall that there are up to 35 earnings years included in the AIME. If you have more than 35 years, then Social Security uses the *highest* 35 years to compute your AIME. You need to keep this in mind because it could play a role in your decision about continuing to work.

Social Security calculates your AIME by "indexing" your past earnings — adjusting them for subsequent economic growth, just as you'd adjust amounts from the past — wages, prices, and so on — to put them in terms of today's dollars. Social Security does this by multiplying your past earnings by an index that reflects the annual changes in average national earnings for every year since you began making money until you turn 60. It includes what it calls net compensation — wages, tips, and other compensation subject to federal income taxes and reported on your annual W-2. Since 1991, it also has included contributions to deferred compensation plans, excluding certain distributions from plans that are reported as taxable compensation.

(If you're interested in a tangent — and *we* were — in 2012, net compensation in the United States totaled $6.53 trillion — $6.3 trillion in compensation and $230 billion in net deferred compensation. There were more than 153.6 million wage earners that year. Dividing $6.53 trillion by 153.6 million produced an average wage of $42,498.21. But of course the average includes your favorite hedge fund manager and that CEO whose compensation is soaring even as his company's stock is tanking. So, the *average* wage was much higher than the median or midpoint of wages, where half the people made more and half less. The national median wage was $27,519 in 2012. If this were a book about the startling and, in our mind, menacing increase in wage inequality in this country, we would point out that in 1991, the median national wage was nearly 72.1 percent of the average, but that it has fallen steadily since then and was less than two-thirds of the average in 2012.)

Tangents aside, wage indexing stops at age 60. By the time a person qualifies for early retirement benefits at age 62, their earnings history through age 60 would have been calculated, and the Social Security system would have the information it needs to calculate their PIA and any early retirement reductions that would apply to their benefit should they begin claiming before FRA.

However, for purposes of evaluating the appeal of continuing to work in your 60s and even 70s, *the end of wage indexing at age 60 could be a very, very big deal.* Remember when we said that your AIME is based on your 35 years of *highest* indexed earnings? Well, stopping indexing at age 60 means that each subsequent year's earnings have a good chance of *becoming* one of your new top 35 earnings years. And if this happens, this new top-35 year will replace the lowest year of the 35, and Social Security will *automatically recompute* your AIME and all the retirement benefits tied to it.

The reason a new top-35 year is likely past age 60 is that your covered earnings in the year you turn 61 — and every subsequent year no matter how old you are — are counted at their actual or nominal value. What might this mean?

Here are three scenarios:

1. Say your earnings rise by about 3 percent in your 61st year and that

this is in line with the national wage base. Your nominal earnings will be 3 percent greater than the previous year. Your previous top 35 years of indexed earnings, by contrast, won't change at all. They've already been locked in place — indexed as of age 60 and fixed forever. So, if your compensation at 61 is even only 3 percent higher than at 60, the odds are pretty good it will become a new top-35 year.[1]

2. If you earn above the annual ceiling for payroll taxes, the benefits of continuing to work past 60 are nearly guaranteed. That's because any increase in the Average Wage Index will also increase the ceiling on payroll taxes. So, more of your earnings will be included and they will almost certainly represent a new top-35 earnings year for you. An exception might occur if the national wage index declined. But since 1951, this has only happened once (and when it did, the tax ceiling did not decline but stayed the same as the previous year).

3. The rate of inflation kicks up and your unindexed wages jump from

the prior year. No matter how virulent the inflation, you get full credit for that higher wage in terms of your Social Security benefit. In fact, a horrible bout of inflation just might put you on Social Security easy street. The agency's Recomputation of Benefits will be very kind to you, and Social Security's annual Cost of Living Adjustment (COLA) will ensure that inflation does not erode the purchasing power of your benefit.

CASE STUDY: A HIGHER EARNER WORKS MORE AND COLLECTS MORE

Now let's consider a higher earner whose record we know with absolute certainty: Larry.

Larry did the math for his own benefits. He calculated the value today of all his lifetime benefits, reducing future benefits for the effects of assumed inflation. Larry was 62 when these calculations were done. If he had stopped working at that age and waited 8 years to collect Social Security, his lifetime benefits to age 100 would have been $774,210.

But here's the epiphany relevant to this chapter: Given that he has a tenured professorship at an august institution — Boston University — and various other interests of note, Larry has every incentive to *work* until 70 as well. And were he to do so — health permitting — his lifetime benefits, assuming he makes it to 100 and future inflation is 3 percent a year, would rise *another* $80,312 to $854,522. And, if still of sound mind and body, why stop at 70? If he worked till 80, his benefit would rise another $88,154 to $942,676.

In other words, working to age 80 would raise Larry's lifetime Social Security benefits by 22 percent ($942,676 divided by $774,210 equals 1.22). And this only has to do with the Recomputation of Benefits because in each scenario, he is waiting to collect his retirement benefit until 70 and taking full advantage of the Delayed Retirement Credit (DRC) that increases your benefits if you start them from FRA until 70. (There is no additional DRC once you reach age 70.)

Much of the bump in Larry's case comes from the fact that he didn't really start contributing much to Social Security until he was 29. He was in grad school before then and on a postdoctoral fellowship after grad school. So he has low-earning years among the 35 Social Security uses as his base. Given that he now earns well above the covered earnings ceiling, his base will rise every year in which he earns more, in nominal dollars, than he did in a low-earning year of his youth, even though it's been adjusted through age 60 for U.S. wage growth.

In Larry's case, working *up to* age 70 will kick out all the low-earnings ages from his Social Security record. But what seems remarkable is that working from 70 to 80 would generate an even larger increase in lifetime benefits.

The reason is that he's above Social Security's earnings ceiling and thus will enjoy the benefits we noted above in Scenario #2. The essence of what's going on is that the AIME formula doesn't properly adjust for inflation and this failure to do so confers a Social Security benefit advantage to people who continue to work, especially those earning at or above the payroll tax ceiling. But even people earning below the ceiling are likely to benefit, especially if their current earnings are relatively high and grow relatively rapidly in the future.

Working After Age 60 Also Can Raise Benefits for Current and Former Family Members

But that's not all. There's another kicker, namely spousal benefits. Let's suppose Larry were married to someone his age who had never worked. In this case, her lifetime spousal benefits would rise from $345,586 to $413,570 were he to work till 80. So, in addition to picking up $168,466 for himself by working through age 80, he earns an extra $67,984 for his spouse.

There is a downside here or, at least, something that we know strikes many people as unfair. All covered wages are subject to payroll taxes (that FICA deduction) whether you retire at 62 or continue working until you're 92. So, even after you've begun receiving benefits, any subsequent wage earnings will be subject to payroll taxes. And while we've been emphasizing how additional earnings once you've retired can increase your benefits, this is not *always* the case. Many retirees pick up part-time jobs to augment their Social Security payments. These wages are not likely to be among their top 35 earnings years. Yet they will fork over payroll taxes anyway, even though doing so will not add a penny to their benefits. Many people believe they've already paid for their benefits when they've retired. So it's not surprising that they can't understand or accept the logic of continuing to pay taxes when they're not getting anything in return.

Now, this story changes for high earners. Few people know about the way post-60 work can raise their Social Security benefits. So, they may only look at how continued work could raise their tax bills, and for that reason they may be less inclined to continue working. It is true, in most cases, that these high-income earners will receive higher Social Security benefits. But they should be aware that the extra benefits may not be enough to offset their higher federal income taxes.

Imagine Beatrice, who never married, is now 63, started working at 22 earning $30,000 and received a 3.5 percent raise every year, so she is now earning $119,000. Beatrice is doing what we suggest and waiting till 70 to take her retirement benefit. If she works for one more year, her lifetime benefits would rise by roughly only $4,000, but her extra Social Security taxes would be more than $7,000. So this is not a net win for Beatrice. On the other hand, had Beatrice started working at age 40, earning the same amount between 40 and now, her lifetime benefits would rise by $14,000, which would cover her extra taxes by 7 grand!

THE EARNINGS TEST DOESN'T MEAN WHAT YOU THINK

But all this raises a serious empirical question: Why in the world do roughly two-thirds of claimants not only take Social Security before their FRA but, in many instances, consider it a justification, if not a mandate, to *stop working*? Or, at least, to stop working full-time?

We understand their desire to take Social Security benefits right away for fear that deferring them would cause retirees to lose benefits if they die early, presumably causing them to run short of money in heaven. But we're concerned that something else may be holding you back, as with many people we've interviewed. We're concerned, that is, that you may feel that if you take your benefits early, you'll have to give them back to the system via its *Earnings Test* unless you stop working. Or you may be tired of paying more Social Security taxes each year and getting nothing back on your contributions. For you, then, here are the facts.

For now let's assume that you are collecting Social Security benefits and continuing to earn wage income. You may have heard that if you earn more than a certain amount, your Social Security benefits will be reduced. This is true. But *it is only true in the short run.* In the longer run, those reductions will, except for some important exceptions, be *paid back to you.* Here's how.

SOCIAL SECURITY ADJUSTMENT OF THE REDUCTION FACTOR

Social Security applies what it calls a "retirement Earnings Test" to the benefits of recipients who are younger than their normal retirement ages (remember, this is 66 for most people now near retirement age). So, if you are taking benefits and younger than your FRA in 2014, Social Security will withhold $1 in benefits for every $2 in wages that you earn above a threshold amount of $15,480 in 2014. If you are celebrating your 66th birthday in 2014 — and thus reaching your FRA — the agency uses a much higher threshold of $41,400 of wage income, and then withholds only $1 in benefits for each $3 you earn above this higher threshold, and only for those months in 2014 before you turn 66.

This higher threshold is, in a sense, the

agency's way of being fair to people receiving benefits who are near their FRA. That's because there is no retirement Earnings Test once you have reached your 66th birthday. None of Warren Buffett's wage income will reduce his Social Security benefits. So, in this respect at least, when you hit your FRA, you and Warren will be in the same boat.

Up to this point, having your benefits reduced for wage income seems like a bad deal and certainly not an incentive to continue working. But wait. As is nearly always the case with Social Security, there is more. And the agency emphasizes this prominently in its explanatory consumer publications and on its website: "It is important to note, though, that these benefit reductions are not truly lost. Your benefit will be increased at your FRA to account for benefits withheld due to earlier earnings. (Spouses and survivors who receive benefits because they have minor or disabled children in their care do not receive increased benefits at FRA if benefits were withheld because of work.)"

Once you reach FRA, Social Security will repay you, in the form of permanently higher benefits from this age on, any dollars it earlier withheld from you. The way it reduces your benefits and, later, restores them, is important and can have a big impact on your cash flow. Let's take a year when a person aged 62 through 65 is receiving his or her retirement benefits. During this year, the person expects to earn $8,400 more than the threshold amount and have their benefits reduced by $4,200.

If the person was getting $1,000 in monthly benefits, the agency would eliminate all benefit payments for 5 months and then restore the $1,000 monthly payment in the 6th month and thereafter. It uses round numbers in calculating the number of forgone monthly benefits. In this case, it is cutting $5,000 even though the reduction is only $4,200. The $800 difference, Social Security says, will be paid back to you the following year.

SOCIAL SECURITY VERBATIM
ARE YOU UP THE
RIGHT KIND OF CREEK?

"Work you do in connection with the ordinary upkeep, repair, and replacement of an *existing water system* is agricultural labor [and] is covered by Social Security." But work "in connection with the construction of a *new system or the extension of an existing system* [is] not agricultural labor [and] not covered."

ALL QUOTES FROM OFFICIAL
SOCIAL SECURITY RULES

AGENCY EXPLAINS EARNINGS TEST RULES, OR DOES IT?

Does this sound confusing? You bet. What's worse is that Social Security expects you to estimate your annual earnings at the beginning of the earnings year, tell the agency what you expect them to be, and begin any benefit reductions right away. We're sorry, but the world doesn't work that way. Most people probably have no clue that the Earnings Test even exists or that they might have their benefits reduced. Almost certainly, they would be surprised to learn that the benefit reductions would mean they would get no benefits at all until all reductions had occurred. For a household counting on regular Social Security payments, losing them for an extended period is a hardship.

We posed all these questions to Social Security. To be fair, Social Security's official answers are necessarily broad and incredibly bureaucratic. When your decisions affect most of the people in America, often in a big way, you learn to be deliberate. And the agency has had 80 years to perfect its goobledygook. So, here's their answer on matters pertaining to the Earnings Test:

Beneficiaries who earn over the annual exempt amount and receive some benefits during the year are required by law to file an annual report with Social Security (SSA) after the close of the tax year. Beginning with reporting year 1996 and each year thereafter, SSA considers the W-2 filed by the employer and the SE tax return information by the beneficiary to be the report required by law. Social Security (SSA) will use that information along with other pertinent information in our records to reduce a beneficiary's monthly benefits by the amount of his or her earnings that exceed the annual exempt amount if the beneficiary is under or in the year of Full Retirement Age (FRA).

To administer the Earnings Test (ET), SSA will:

- identify working beneficiaries during the initial claims process, explain the Social Security ET and code our records with the work and earnings information;
- ask beneficiaries to report any change in their work activity that will result in significant changes in their earnings level;
- send a mid-year mailer letter to certain beneficiaries asking them to update their estimate for the current year and give us an estimate of their next year's earnings;
- ask certain beneficiaries to report their earnings to us at the end of the year;
- use the earnings posted to our records along with other pertinent information in our records to adjust benefits under the ET and ensure proper payment of benefits.

Got all that?

You Get the Money Back Except When You Don't

The Earnings Test repayments (with the exceptions we noted) begin when you reach your FRA. They take the form of a monthly benefit that is higher than what you otherwise would receive. The size of the bump-up in your benefit depends on the amount of your earlier benefit reductions.

Here is an illustration provided by the agency:

As an example, let us say you claim retirement benefits upon turning 62 in 2013 and your payment is $750 per month. Then, you return to work and have 12 months of benefits withheld. We would recalculate your benefit at your Full Retirement Age of 66 and pay you $800 a month (in today's dollars). Or, maybe you earn so much between the ages of 62 and 66 that all benefits in those years are withheld. In that case, we would pay you $1,000 a month starting at age 66.

But, and this is a very big but, someone who switches from one Social Security benefit to another will never be able to enjoy the restoration of benefits lost to the Earnings Test. Imagine if you take your retirement benefit starting now, lose some retirement benefits due to the Earnings Test, and then switch to, say, a higher widow's benefit at FRA. What you get is the greater of the two — the retirement benefit and the amount of the widow benefit that is greater than your retirement benefit. So, even though Social Security will say your retirement benefit is larger, and it is, the excess portion of your widow's benefit will be declining, so your overall benefit will not be increased, and you will not be getting any money back from the Earnings Test adjustment.

Our message here, to sum up, is that you shouldn't always stop working because you think you won't get back the money taken by the Earnings Test. You *will* get it back in many cases.

8
PLAYING SOCIAL SECURITY'S MARITAL STATUS GAME

Social Security provides strong incentives with respect to marriage. There are, depending on your circumstances, reasons to get married, reasons to *stay* married, incentives to divorce, to remarry, and *not* to remarry. These decisions hinge on many factors, of course. But play your Social Security marital status cards right and it can mean making or keeping a lot of money. Play them wrong and you can get seriously singed for the rest of your life.

We're going to catalog the incentives and try to make them memorable with the titillating tale of one William H. Gigolo (the *H* stands for Hypothetical), who spends his life playing Social Security's marital status game to great personal profit.

FIRST INCENTIVE: THE PAYOFF TO GETTING MARRIED

To help celebrate your marriage, Social Security provides you with two special wedding gifts. The first comes after you have been married for 9 months. The second arrives on your first wedding anniversary.

The first gift isn't a Cuisinart that got lost in the mail, of course, or a Ginsu knife set. It's a pair of life insurance policies for you and your beloved, based on your two earnings records, and the policies go into effect once you've been married 9 months, assuming that each spouse has enough covered earnings to qualify for Social Security benefits.

From 9 months on, either spouse can buy the farm and the other will be eligible for survivor benefits, as well as mother or father benefits if there are children, and the children themselves — whether premarital, newborn, adopted, or from previous relationships — will be eligible for child survivor benefits.

The second wedding present, which kicks in one year after the vow exchange, is the ability for one of you to collect a full spousal benefit at FRA, provided you jointly and properly time your benefit collection. In some circumstances, one of you can collect a full spousal benefit for a while, after which the other can collect an excess spousal benefit. And even if you *don't* correctly time your joint benefit collection, one of you may be able to collect a positive excess spousal benefit.

Moreover, if you have sufficiently young children or a child who became disabled before the age of 22, there are *unreduced* child-in-care full spousal benefits to be had even *before* you take your own retirement benefit. That is to say, taking these benefits before FRA does not trigger the dreaded deeming problem.

The spousal benefits are nice, or course, once you come of (more-than-middle) age. But the bigger Social Security payoff to being married for a year or more would come were your spouse to die. (That's why this gift is an *insurance* policy.) And the payoff is especially valuable if your spouse was a much higher earner than you. In this case, you could, when the time comes, take your reduced retirement benefit for a while and then flip onto your higher survivor benefit, thanking yourself for the rest of your days for having married so well. If *you* were the higher earner, taking your survivor benefit early and waiting until, say, 70, to collect your own retirement benefit will generate maximum lifetime benefits. But either way, you're protected, so long as one of you shall live.

SECOND INCENTIVE: THE PAYOFF TO *STAYING* MARRIED FOR AT LEAST TEN YEARS

Somewhere between 40 percent and half of all American first marriages end in divorce. Second marriages? 50–67 percent of *them* untie the knot. And a discouraging 75 percent of *third* marriages dissolve, despite having been entered into with the benefit of boots-on-the-ground experience, firm conviction, we assume, and eternal optimism.

It turns out that, for Americans who get divorced, the median length of first marriages in the United States — the length of time by which 50 percent of them end — is 8 years. That means more than half of the divorced are making a big financial mistake. It's a big *tactical* mistake with regard to future Social Security benefits, especially for our female readers. Women currently file roughly two-thirds of divorce cases in the United States, but women are the prime beneficiaries of sticking out a marriage for 10 years.

The simple fact is that you need to stay married 10 years and not a day less to be able to collect *spousal* and *survivor* benefits as an ex. The benefits can be significant. We caution you not to officially unhitch before a decade's up without at least considering these costs. Social Security has no requirement that you consort with, or for that matter even *live* with, your spouse. You two can move to the opposite ends of the earth and still qualify for spousal and survivor benefits based on the other's work record.

Yes, this would be an example of gaming the system, and we have no intention of corrupting those of you who feel that is inappropriate. But this book is written for people like those of you who have been married for 9 years and 11 months, are now about to get divorced, and only shortly after having done so, learn of the 10-year rule — to their everlasting regret. Are you less entitled to benefits than the Social Security–savvy people who knew to wait a decade before divorcing?

THIRD INCENTIVE: TO *GET* DIVORCED ONCE A DECADE OF MARRIAGE HAS PASSED

You now understand that, having been married for a decade, once you get divorced, you retain the right to collect spousal and survivor benefits.

But this creates an incentive best described as perverse. The incentive is to get divorced after 10 years because, if you do, both exes, upon reaching FRA of 66,[1] can file *just for a spousal benefit* and wait until age 70 to collect their largest possible retirement benefit. This advantage is of greatest benefit to couples in which both spouses are high earners.

Imagine Peter and Mary: meeting in college in 1973, falling in love, marrying — too young, as it turns out. Both work, both begin to appreciate the less-worse things in life. Peter decides to attend business school and heads to Wall Street. Mary winds up in advertising and prospers as well. The more they earn, the more devoted they become not only to the perks of wealth, but to its nuances. And this has led them to the intricacies of the Social Security system. So when this couple discovers, as so many do, that they have grown apart, they don't simply split. They stick it out for the requisite decade and a day because they know it will pay off.

Now, having reached their FRA of 66, they are primed to cash in. That's because, having waited long enough for an official divorce, they would *both* be eligible to take spousal benefits — on *each other's* considerable lifetime income — while waiting until 70 to collect their own maximum retirement payments. So Peter *and* Mary would be able to collect more than $60,000 in today's dollars in spousal benefits over the next four years. When they reach 70, their roughly $15,000 per year spousal benefits would be replaced with their $40,000-plus per year retirement benefit.

So, thanks to their being divorced, Peter and Mary each pull down $60,000 in spousal benefits, whereas had they remained married only one of them could have collected the $60,000.

A caveat: When you divorce, even after 10 years of marriage, you do lose the right to collect the spousal benefit associated with having young or disabled children of your former spouse in your care.

FOURTH INCENTIVE:
THE PAYOFF TO REMARRYING

Once you are divorced or widowed, you have the option to go shopping for a new high-earning spouse, marriage to whom, after only 9 and then 12 months, will occasion two new Social Security wedding gifts.

Will getting remarried wipe out your ability to collect spousal and survivor benefits on your prior spouse's work record? *Yes,* when it comes to spousal benefits, *no,* when it comes to widow(er) benefits, provided you remarry after 60.

Is there potentially a big payoff to getting remarried? Definitely.

First, you may wind up marrying someone with a higher earnings record than your former spouse and get *larger* spousal and survivor benefits as a result. Second, if you stick it out with the second (or third or fourth) spouse for 10 years, you can collect divorcee spousal benefits sequentially on your different exes, as the tale of William H. Gigolo is about to illustrate. Third, if any of your spouses dies, you can collect survivor benefits, sequentially, on each. Fourth, if you stick it out for a decade with one or more exes and also have one or more decedent former spouses to work with, you can sequentially collect on the exes *and* the decedents.

And one of the best parts of spouse-hopping is this: when you start collecting early on a different former spouse's work record, Early Retirement Reductions from taking benefits on another spouse at an earlier date don't carry over.

Fifth Incentive: The Payoff to *Not* Remarrying

Why would anyone want to not remarry?

Because remarrying wipes out your ticket

to spousal benefits on any ex's work record as long as you *stay* remarried.

Remarrying before age 60 also wipes out your eligibility for survivor benefits on any decedent *former* spouse's work record for as long as you stay remarried.

So be careful before you strategically remarry. Unless, that is, you are a real pro. Like William H.

PLAYING THE SOCIAL SECURITY MARITAL STATUS GAME TO THE HILT

It is time at last for the story of William H. Gigolo, our hypothetical master of Social Security's marital status game. He worked not a day in his life, but instead lived off the relatively high earnings of three lovely ex-wives — call them Sarah, Sally, and Suzie. In each case, William waited until their 10th anniversary, chose a romantic restaurant, and over dessert, announced he was filing for divorce.

Positing William as a sociopath, we picture him pleased to have lived off successive exes and helped himself to half their assets thereafter. Now 62 and single for two years, he remains attractive to women, a sad testament to the gender imbalance between eligible baby boomers because women still tend to marry older men, though it was never true, as *Newsweek* famously mis-reported in 1986, that "a woman over age 40 has a better chance of being killed by a terrorist than to get married." (That mythical single girl would be pushing or past 70 today.)

Since a wife has to be at least 62 for the husband to collect spousal benefits, William was careful to marry at least one ex older than himself. This wife, Sarah, is 64 and the lowest earner. The next-highest earner is Sally, 60. Suzie is only 56, but she's earned more than the others.

To maximize his lifetime Social Security benefits, William files for a divorced spousal benefit at 62 and starts to collect half of Sarah's full retirement benefit, although reduced by 30 percent because he takes it early. Then, after 2 years, when *Sally* turns 62, William files for a divorcé spousal benefit based on *her* earnings record.

And why not? Since he's now eligible to collect on two exes, he can file for benefits on both. He won't get two divorcée spousal benefits — just the larger of the two. But since Sally's full retirement benefit is larger than Sarah's, he flips to hers. And here's another advantage from William's perspective: he'll be able to collect half of Sally's full retirement benefit, but it will be reduced by only 13.3 percent, *not 30 percent*! Why? Because William is now 64 and his early claiming reduction is smaller.

So far, so good, as long as you've got no scruples. We have already stipulated that William doesn't. So his cash-out plan is working. And here's a yet more perverse part three. When Suzie reaches 62 and William hits 68, he can flip onto Suzie's heftier earnings record and start collecting a completely unreduced divorcé spousal benefit since he doesn't start collecting this particular benefit (which exceeds the other two) until after he reaches his FRA.

Is William done with his optimization? Not necessarily. Let's fast-forward to his 70th birthday and suppose that Sally, who waited until FRA to start collecting her benefit, dies. Sally's full retirement benefit, while lower than Suzie's, exceeds the half of it on which William has most recently been collecting. So William can now file for and begin collecting a completely *unreduced* spousal survivor benefit on Sally's record. That benefit would be equal to 100 percent of Sally's full retirement benefit.

Fast-forward again. William is now 76 and Suzie dies, having also waited until FRA to collect her retirement benefit. What might William do? He could file for an unreduced survivor benefit based on *Suzie's* earnings record.

Fast-forward one last time. William is now 88. He's met a very lovely 94-year-old named Sandra, who earned more than any of the exes and is on her last legs. William realizes that he can marry Sandra and, after 9 months, qualify for survivor benefits on Sandra's earnings record. He whisks Sandra off to Las Vegas for a quickie marriage and, 9 months to the day of their nuptials, Sandra falls and breaks her hip. Her last leg gives out. So does the rest of her.

William leaves the funeral early in order to get to the local Social Security office before it closes and file for a full (unreduced) survivor benefit on Sandra's account.

This appears to be William's last Social Security play, but who knows. He's still got his looks and, as you read this, he is on Match.com checking out his options. Considering that there were 3.2 million women aged 85 and older in 2012, and only 1.8 million men of those ages, William's pickings are far from slim.

IF YOU'RE SINGLE, IT MAY PAY TO GET HITCHED

If you receive very low Social Security benefits — or expect to — you might take a deep breath and consider the following secret strategy: Find an attractive, single 80-year-old who is receiving a higher Social Security benefit and propose marriage. What might once have been scorned "a marriage of convenience" could very well be a marriage of necessity if you are in danger of outliving your savings.

After one year of mutual nuptial accommodation, you'll be able to collect a full spousal benefit on your new mate's work record. Depending on your age and whether you've filed for your own retirement benefit, you'll collect either a full or excess spousal benefit.

Better yet — from a strictly pecuniary point of view — marry someone on their last legs who receives a much larger benefit than you currently do or can ever hope to. Once you've been married for just 9 months, you'll be eligible to receive a *survivor* benefit, which, depending on when you take it, can equal as much as your unbeloved was collecting before his or her expiration date.

9
MARRIED WITH BENEFITS

Tarzan and Jane were exhausted from the Big Apple's ticker-tape parade for them. It was 1940 and they had just returned from their latest adventure in the wild. The twentieth century's version of Adam and Eve had once again captured the world's attention. Now they were in their suite at the Plaza, trying with their son, Korak, to coax Cheeta down from the drapes. After resting up for a few days, it would be on to visit Jane's family in the urban jungle of Baltimore.

Life had been good to the tree-swinger and his resourceful partner (Jane, not Cheeta). For the better part of two decades they had been alternating African expeditions with increasingly lucrative visits to the States. Tarzan wasn't keen on being a loincloth-clad pitchman but it sure beat hunting for a living. And the money was good, so good that after they presented a beaming Cheeta with a large bunch of bananas and slipped Korak a sawbuck, they were on their way to a meeting with their financial adviser.

The topic for the day was Social Security, a still-new program begun in 1935 that was just beginning to pay out benefits five years later.

We hope you will have figured out by now that we've taken some liberties with the story of Tarzan and Jane, who of course never really existed and, even within their fabricated tales, never set foot in a Social Security office as far as we can tell. Also, many current provisions of Social Security did not exist in 1940. But we're assuming they did so that Tarzan's and Jane's decisions make sense to you and your very real Social Security needs.

As a top earner, Tarzan paid the maximum amount of payroll taxes. Jane did not earn an income, but based on the rules of the program she stood to collect a substantial spousal benefit in her later years based on Tarzan's work history. Of course, Tarzan had been born in Great Britain, Jane pointed out, and maintained dual citizenship. This, too, might affect his and her Social Security benefits. So many coconuts to juggle!

Furthermore, while longevity tables were

not common in 1940, their financial adviser had read, in *Tarzan's Quest,* about the Apeman having received an immortality drug and explained that he ought therefore to wait until 70 to start his benefits, for obvious reasons. Moreover, he diplomatically pointed out, if the life span of the jungle man turned out to be brief, due to accident, the longer that Tarzan waited to claim retirement benefits, the greater would be Jane's widow benefit should he wind up on the wrong end of a poison-tipped spear. And then there was Korak to think about. He might also qualify for Social Security benefits.

We'd like to say that wives and husbands — real as well as fictional — have been having similarly fruitful discussions with each other and/or their financial advisers about Social Security over the ensuing 75 years. But they haven't. Every year, couples make uninformed claiming decisions that deny them and their family members access to billions and billions of benefit dollars. With retirement prospects dimmer than expected for tens of millions of baby boomers, claiming every possible dollar in Social Security should be a national pastime. Instead, it's an American afterthought. The Home Shopping Network teaches people far more about cubic zirconia than they ever learn about the nation's most basic and important retirement benefit.

What is clear is that, for all but the über-rich, a core part of a couple's retirement strategy should be an informed and optimal approach to their Social Security spousal benefits. *An obvious fact that we nonetheless feel obliged to note:* it's essential that both spouses understand their estimated benefits, especially how they are affected by waiting to claim benefits.

So allow us to review the options for those of you who are married. And please forgive us for yet again repeating ourselves. The worst that can happen, we figure, is that you'll simply skim and skip ahead. Much worse would be your forgetting a key option and thus nullifying, at least for yourself, the whole point of this book. And for those of you who might be cursing yourselves for forgetting what we've already tried to hammer home, know that we ourselves still check our notes on these items when we hit the key age milestones, despite having swung on Social Security's convoluted vines for years.

SPOUSAL BENEFIT
STEPPING-STONES

Step One in this process is to create an account on the Social Security website that provides each spouse access to an individualized Your Social Security Statement. We explained how to do this in Chapter 3. To begin, go to "my Social Security" at http://socialsecurity.gov/my account/.

Step Two is to revisit the crucial role played in spousal benefits (and lots of other Social Security claiming situations) by Social Security's rules about what it calls full or normal retirement age. Remember: Full Retirement Age is 66 for anyone born between 1943 and 1954. It then rises in two-month steps for those born from 1955 to 1959, and hits 67 for anyone born in 1960 or later years. (Many current reform proposals would increase this age to 68 or even older but as of this writing, the official FRA is as we've described it.)

Again, the significance of Full Retirement Age is that Social Security benefits claimed before reaching it are treated differently, and much less favorably, than claims at FRA and later.

Step Three is to understand how spousal benefits actually work. If a couple is married for at least a year, both spouses qualify for spousal benefits. However, only one of them can get a full spousal benefit. And as we've stressed, for this to happen they need to follow our three general rules — waiting to file until their benefits have reached their higher possible levels and only filing for one benefit at a time (a spousal benefit in this case) while letting a second benefit (their own retirement benefit) rise in value. In most cases — *but not all!* — a spousal benefit is equal to half of the Primary Insurance Amount — the retirement benefit the other spouse would receive upon reaching their FRA. Because upwards of two-thirds of men and women file for their retirement benefits before reaching their FRAs, their actual spousal benefits are less than half of the other spouse's PIA. And even for people who don't take benefits until well past their FRAs, Social Security rules say that half the full retirement benefit is the most that a spousal benefit can total.

Step Four: Review the basic options, which will be some variant of what you and your partner do between the ages of 62 (earliest claiming age) and 70 (the latest).[1] We've laid out the case for how one spouse can claim spousal benefits at FRA while letting their own retirement benefits build up by 8 percent each year from Delayed Retirement Credits. But there are many, many other options. You should model them using either Larry's software (http://www .maximizemysocialsecurity.com/) or someone else's.

Step Five: Build your optimal plan and then stay the course and follow it.

Now for some real-life spousal claiming questions posed to Larry and answered on Paul's Making Sen$e site at PBS.org.

SOCIAL SECURITY VERBATIM AND SOCIAL SECURITY WOULD KNOW THIS HOW?

"Third parties may assist a claimant when completing the iClaim [online] application, but the claimant must be present to select the 'Submit Now' button."

ALL QUOTES FROM OFFICIAL SOCIAL SECURITY RULES

WHAT IF ONE SPOUSE HAS NEVER WORKED?

Q: I am 52 years old and a full-time homemaker. My husband and I have been married for 33 years and have

seven children. So far, he has been the sole source of income for our family; my work has all been in the home. Will I be entitled to any Social Security at all?

A: Once your husband files for his retirement benefit, you'll be able to collect a spouse with child-in-care benefit if you have a child under age 16 or a child of any age who was disabled before age 22. You can collect a spousal benefit as early as age 62, a widow's benefit if your husband predeceases you and you are at least 60, or a mother's benefit if your husband dies while at least one of your children is under age 16 or one of your children is disabled (having become disabled before age 22). When your husband files for his retirement benefit, your children under 18 (or 19 if they are still in elementary or secondary school) can collect child benefits.

If you take a spousal benefit before FRA, it will be permanently reduced. If you take your widow's benefit before FRA, it may be less than the benefit your husband was collecting if he files for his retirement benefit early. (But if your husband files for his retirement benefit early and then passes away, there will be a point before FRA when you will have no further incentive to wait to collect your widow's benefit.)

The spousal and child benefits are half of your husband's Primary Insurance Amount but they may be affected by the Family Maximum Benefit (see Chapter 3 or the Glossary for details). When your husband dies, the child survivor benefit is 75 percent of your husband's PIA. And your widow's benefit (depending on when you take it and when your husband took his retirement benefit or, if he didn't take his retirement benefit, his age when he died) can range from 71.5 percent to 132 percent of his PIA.

HOW TO GET THE BEST DEAL ON
SPOUSAL BENEFITS

Q: I am 67 years old; my husband is 63. We are both still working full-time. Neither of us plans to claim Social Security benefits until we are 70, and we both plan to continue working full-time until that time. How might either of us be able to claim a spousal benefit without jeopardizing our full retirement benefits at age 70?

A: Sounds like the optimal thing to do is for you both (as you plan to do) to take your retirement benefit at 70 and for your husband to file just for a spousal benefit based on your work record when he reaches his

FRA of 66.

LOSING YOUR SPOUSAL BENEFIT BY NOT REQUESTING IT

Q: I am 70 and have been drawing my Social Security benefits since I was 62. My husband is 65 and started drawing his Social Security at age 62. Am I entitled to file for spousal benefits?

A: You were able to file for spousal benefits when your husband filed for his retirement benefit, which was three years ago. But your excess spousal benefit could have been zero since it's the difference between half of your husband's full retirement benefit less 100 percent of your full retirement benefit.

Even if Social Security knows you are married, you won't get this excess spousal benefit unless you apply for it. I recommend you rush over to the local Social Security office and file for your spousal benefit. If your excess spousal benefit is zero, you lose nothing but some time applying. If it's positive, your monthly check will be that amount higher for the rest of your life.

If this doesn't seem right, you should get in touch with Social Security. Maybe they did not know you were married or failed to accurately compute your benefit. Also, if your husband continues to work, his PIA might increase. If it did, your spousal benefit might increase by enough to make your excess spousal benefit more than zero.

Easy question. Complicated answer.

CAN YOU CLAIM SPOUSAL BENEFITS AND THEN CANCEL THEM?

Q: Why can't a spouse cancel spousal benefits after his wife suspends her retirement benefit? I decided to wait until I retired and was told my husband could cancel his spousal benefits. When he tried, he was told he could not do this. Is that true?

A: You can withdraw a spousal benefit and tell Social Security not to send you the money, but you can't suspend it and start it up later at a higher value. In other words, once you take a spousal benefit, there is no advantage to stopping the checks. We are allowed to suspend our retirement benefit (between FRA and age 70) and restart it again before or at age 70. We aren't allowed to do the same with spousal or survivor benefits. We don't see the logic.

HE TOOK EARLY BUT SHE CAN STILL GET A GOOD DEAL

Q: My husband of 25 years started drawing his reduced Social Security

benefits 10 years ago at the age of 62. Is there a spousal benefit for which I am eligible? I am 65, and we are thinking about my filing for spousal benefits at 66 and deferring my own Social Security until 70. Since he is on reduced benefits for taking it early, would my spousal benefit be based on his current benefit amount or what he would have received if he had waited until 65?

A: If you wait until 66 to file, you'll be able, as you correctly understand, to apply just for your own spousal benefit while letting your own retirement benefit grow by 32 percent through age 70. In this case, your spousal benefit will equal your full spousal benefit, which is half of your husband's PIA — not half of what he's currently collecting. What he's currently collecting is a reduced retirement benefit since he started his own benefit at 62. So your spousal benefit will be more than half of the retirement benefit he's now getting.

How Beatrice and Max Avoided Deeming — An Example

Beatrice just turned 70 and started taking her retirement benefit. Max, her husband, is 65 and just retired. They both earned the taxable maximum throughout their careers, so they were solidly upper-middle-class. Max has heard he can collect spousal benefit starting right away and then go for his own retirement benefit at 70.

Max has heard right, but he's also heard wrong. This is what makes Social Security so bedeviling. You can be told you can get something and you can get that something, but that something can turn out to be nothing.

In Max's case, if he applies at 65 for his spousal benefit, *which he can do* (because Beatrice has filed for her own retirement benefit), he'll be deemed to be filing for his own retirement benefit. As a result he'll get just the larger of the two benefits. More precisely, he'll get his retirement benefit reduced, because he's taking it before FRA, plus his excess spousal benefit, which, in his case, is zero.

So Max can get his spousal benefit, but he can't. Were Max to wait a year, until he reached FRA, and then file *just* for his spousal benefit, he not only could, but would, get his spousal benefit. At 70 he would then go for his own retirement benefit.

What's the dollar value to Beatrice and Max in lifetime Social Security benefits from avoiding deeming? It's $410,936![2]

That's huge. It reflects three things. First, the couple is older and closer to collecting, so the present value of their future benefits is larger. Second, if Max files for his spousal benefit and is deemed, his spousal benefit will be zero and his retirement benefit will be $29,599. But if he maximizes, his spousal benefit starting at 66 (his FRA) will be $15,611 for four years, and then at 70 he'll flip onto a $41,862 retirement benefit.

CHECKLIST OF SPOUSAL SOCIAL SECURITY TACTICS

File and Suspend

For one spouse to claim spousal benefits, the other spouse has to have filed for their own retirement benefits. Once they reach Full Retirement Age, they can file for retirement benefits and then suspend them at the same time. This action enables their spouse to file for spousal benefits while allowing the one who files and suspends to defer taking their own retirement benefits for up to 4 years until they turn 70. During the suspension period, they will earn Delayed Retirement Credits, raising their eventual monthly benefit in real terms by 8 percent a year. (Further file-and-suspend details were provided in Chapter 5.)

206

Restricted Application

When a spouse claims spousal benefits at FRA, they can do so with a restricted application. This will permit them to receive spousal benefits *without* triggering a simultaneous claim for their own retirement benefits. This strategy will permit them to collect spousal benefits for up to 4 years and then switch to their own retirement benefit at age 70, including any DRCs they've accrued by deferring it. This, recall, is the strategy Larry gave Paul at the tennis court, which made him nearly 50 grand.

Start, Stop, Start

If you need to begin benefits before FRA, remember that doing so may trigger "deeming," which will reduce your benefits or eliminate them forever. But don't forget that you can suspend your own benefits with a phone call once you reach FRA and resume them at any time until turning 70. This "start, stop, start" strategy can be optimal in order to permit your spouse or children to collect benefits on your work record much sooner than would otherwise be the case.

START, STOP, START — THE CASE OF ONE FAMILY COLLECTING EIGHT DIFFERENT SOCIAL SECURITY BENEFITS

John, 62, and Jane, 44, are married. They have a disabled five-year-old child, Joe. John was earning $38,000 when he retired last year. Jane earned $44,000 last year. But she's decided to quit work to spend time with John and their son. John wants to wait until 66 — full retirement age — to collect his retirement benefit. Jane wants to collect her retirement benefit at 62.

These are the wrong collection decisions in terms of maximizing the couple's lifetime benefits. But let us tell you what their selected strategy entails and then we'll explain what they should do.

Although they aren't following the optimal plan, John and Jane's Social Security benefit collection plan does deliver. In fact, it delivers $1,174,858 in combined lifetime benefits!

John and Jane are Social Security millionaires?

Yes, indeed. The $1,174,858 is the present value (using a 2 percent real discount rate) of the couple's benefits right through their maximum ages of life, which are 85 for John and 100 for Jane. Table 1, generated by Larry's software, shows the couple's annual benefits based on their planned/ selected benefit collection dates. All amounts are in today's dollars.

Please look at the row for the year 2018. That's when John hits full retirement age and starts collecting his full retirement benefit of $20,504. That's big money compared to the $38,000 he was making before he retired. But total family benefits are even higher — $37,144. That's because son Joe can now collect an $8,320 child benefit based on John's work record. And Jane can also collect $8,320 in annual spousal benefits as a spouse with a child in care of a retired worker. The combined child and spousal with child-in-care benefits are, however, subject to Social Security's maximum family benefit provision. Otherwise Jane and Joe would each be receiving even larger checks.

When Jane reaches 62 she starts collecting her own retirement benefit, which is $15,804 on an annual basis. The amount at age 62 is smaller than at age 63 because it reflects only 11 months of retirement benefits. Why? Because Social Security requires you to be a full month above age 62 before you are entitled to collect an early retirement benefit.

Jane's retirement benefit is smaller than John's because she's taking her benefit at age 62, not at full retirement age. But still, $15,804 is a good-size check and certainly larger than the $8,320 she was collecting as a spousal-with-child-in-care benefit. On the other hand, it would be roughly 76 percent larger were she to wait until 70 to start collecting her retirement.

But there is a silver lining to Jane's collecting on her own work record. Joe's child benefit rises from $8,320 to $11,222 on an annual basis. Why? Because he now can collect a child benefit based on either John's or Jane's work records, depending on which of the two has the larger full retirement benefit (PIA).

Jane, despite having a shorter work span, has the higher PIA. Hence, Joe starts collecting on Jane's work record and receives the full child benefit, namely half of Jane's PIA (not half of the reduced PIA that Jane is receiving as a early retirement benefit). We say full child benefit because the maximum family benefit associated with Jane's work record doesn't come into play due to the fact that only one family member — Joe — is trying to collect on Jane's work record.

When John reaches age 85, he dies thanks to his assumed age-85 maximum age of life.

At this point Jane receives not just her own reduced retirement benefit, but also her excess widow's benefit or $4,700. And Joe stops collecting a $11,222 child benefit based on Jane's work record. Instead, he collects a child survivor benefit of roughly $15,375 based on John's work record. The child survivor benefit is 75 percent of the deceased parent's PIA and 75 percent of John's PIA exceeds 50 percent of Jane's PIA.

To recap, we have John, Jane, and Joe receiving seven different benefits: John's retirement benefit, Joe's child benefit based on John's work record, Jane's child-in-care spousal benefit based on John's work record, Jane's retirement benefit, Joe's child benefit based on Jane's work record, Jane's excess widow's benefit, and Joe's child survivor benefit.

That's a lot of different benefits. So it might seem that John and Jane are doing the right thing.

They aren't. Instead, they are leaving $111,400 on the table.

So where's the extra $111,400 coming from? First, it's from having John start, stop, start. Specifically, the maximized solution, which the software found by checking 45,327 collection date combinations, entails

John's filing for his early retirement benefit immediately, i.e., at his current age of 62. This permits Jane and Joe to collect child-in-care spousal benefits and child benefits four years sooner than the couple's own strategy allowed. Once John reaches full retirement age, the optimal plan says he should suspend his retirement benefit and start it up again at 70. As Table 2, which presents annual benefits based on the optimal strategy, shows, John gets zero benefits between 66 and 70. That's a big hit. But once he reaches 70, he restarts his retirement benefit at a 32 percent higher level, again all measured in today's dollars.

Second, it's from having Jane take widow's benefits at ages 68 and 69, after John dies. During this time, Joe collects a child survivor benefit. And then at 70, Jane collects her largest possible retirement benefit, while Joe continues to collect a child survivor benefit off John's work record. As you can see from comparing Tables 1 and 2 for, say, the year 2050, when Jane is 80, her total annual benefit under the maximized solution is $27,829 — much larger than the $20,504 she collects under the couple's own benefit collection strategy.

The maximized solution also entails the collection of seven benefits: John's early retirement benefit, John's restarted age-70 retirement benefit, Jane's child-in-care spousal benefit, Joe's child benefit from John's work record, Joe's survivor benefit from John's work record, Jane's widow's benefit, and Jane's retirement benefit. Actually, there is an eighth benefit. When Jane passes away at 100, Joe will collect a child survivor benefit based on Jane's work record.

And so, another story with the familiar moral: Getting what's yours isn't easy.

Getting a Do-Over by Withdrawing

You might make a retirement benefit claiming decision you later regret. Welcome to a very large club and one whose membership is growing as millions of baby boomers begin claiming Social Security every year. But you can wipe the slate clean by withdrawing your benefits (see Chapter 3) within one year of the date at which you become entitled to collect your first retirement benefit check. This permits you to be regarded by Social Security as never having taken benefits. But you must repay all benefits received on your work record, including spousal and child benefits. And your repayment must be gross of any deductions from your check for Medicare Part B

TABLE 1 ANNUAL F
JOHN, JANE, AND JOE—

YEAR	AGES		RETIREMENT BENEFITS	
	John	Jane	John	Ja▪
2014 through 2017	62-65	44-47	$0	$
2018 through 2031	66-79	48-61	$20,504	$
2032 through 2037	80-85	62-67	$20,504	$15,80
2038 through 2070	DECEASED	68-100	$0	$15,80

TABLE 2 ANNUAL I
JOHN, JANE, AND JOE—1

YEAR	AGES		RETIREMENT BENEFITS	
	John	Jane	John	Ja▪
2014	62	44	$14,175	$
2015 through 2017	63-65	45-47	$15,463	$
2018 through 2021	66-69	48-51	$0	$
2022 through 2037	70-85	52-67	$20,412	$
2038 and 2039	DECEASED	68-69	$0	$
2040 through 2070	DECEASED	70-100	$0	$27,8▪

EFITS FOR

EIR STRATEGY

POUSAL ENEFITS	SURVIVOR BENEFITS	CHILDREN'S BENEFITS	NET BENEFIT
Jane	Jane	Joe	
$0	$0	$0	$0
$8,320	$0	$8,320	$37,144
$0	$0	$11,222	$47,529
$0	$4,700	$15,378	$35,882

EFITS FOR

BEST STRATEGY

POUSAL ENEFITS	SURVIVOR BENEFITS	CHILDREN'S BENEFITS	NET BENEFIT
Jane	Jane	Joe	
$7,626	$0	$7,626	$29,427
$8,320	$0	$8,320	$32,103
$8,320	$0	$8,320	$16,640
$8,320	$0	$8,320	$37,051
$0	$20,412	$15,378	$35,790
$0	$0	$15,374	$43,204

premiums. And, if it's a claim for retirement benefits, you must withdraw within a year of first collecting.

Some Final Warnings

Social Security asks for your marital history when you file for benefits. But in some cases, your best strategy may not involve filing for benefits. And, as we've shown repeatedly, the system is hardly flawless. So, when your marital status is or becomes an integral part of your claiming strategy, contact the agency and make sure it has an accurate record of your entire marital history.

Your best benefit strategy can change even after you've mapped out a solid plan. For example, if you or your spouse continued to work after one of you applied for retirement benefits, it's possible that the working spouse's full retirement benefit will have increased. Now, say that you looked earlier and decided against spousal benefits because your own retirement benefit (or your spouse's) was greater than half your spouse's Primary Insurance Amount (or half of yours). But if one of your PIAs has increased appreciably due to continued employment, perhaps the case for spousal benefits has also become attractive. It's certainly worth checking out.

10
GAY COUPLES GET TO CLAIM WHAT'S THEIRS

As we write this, the legalization of same-sex marriages is sweeping the nation. Citizens and courts are pushing for equal treatment, keyed to the Supreme Court's historic June 2013 decision that the 1996 federal Defense of Marriage Act was unconstitutional. States containing nearly two-thirds of the nation's population allowed same-sex marriages as of late 2014. Legal challenges to state laws banning the same-sex marriages have been lodged in *every* other state. And public opinion polls show an ever-growing majority of Americans supports the rights of same-sex couples to marry and enjoy all the legal, tax, health-care, and other rights long reserved for heterosexual couples.

Among these rights, none is more important financially than the extension of Social Security benefits to gay couples, their children, and other qualifying present,

217

former, and deceased family members. We're talking about hundreds of thousands of dollars in lifetime benefits that would not otherwise be available to same-sex households. And therefore more secure retirements. And therefore long, long futures that now can be more reliably and predictably funded. And, in our view, we're talking about a country that is taking a huge step toward living up to its promise of equal rights for all.

To understand these newly extended Social Security benefits, the best way to begin is to read the chapters, secrets, gotchas, and basics in *Get What's Yours* that apply to married persons. Such a simple change, yet so profound in its ramifications.

To date, the biggest effect of the DOMA ruling has been educational, according to Stuart H. Armstrong II, a Massachusetts financial planner at Centinel Financial Group who advises many LGBT clients. "Because this is such a sea change in the way of thinking, it is important for people to be aware of these benefits," says Armstrong, also a national board member of the Financial Planning Association. "A lot of us are still pinching ourselves, realizing that this has happened so fast."

Some provisions of Social Security don't

apply as yet to same-sex couples because of how new the laws are. Massachusetts was the first state to approve same-sex marriages, and that was only in 2004. Because divorce benefits require a marriage to have lasted 10 years before permitting such benefits, it will be many years before substantial numbers of same-sex ex-spouses will qualify for them.

More immediately, however, Armstrong advises same-sex couples to review any recent Social Security claiming decisions made before they were married. Such decisions, made as individuals, might be less appealing than decisions available to a married spouse. Under Social Security rules, benefit decisions less than a year old can be withdrawn and claimants can get a "fresh slate" as regards their benefits. (They would have to repay any Social Security benefits already received, including Medicare Part B premiums for hospital insurance.) Even if the claiming decision is more than a year old, it may be worth your time to contest it. There are no penalties or costs for doing so, and the Obama administration's strongly pro-LGBT policies toward federal benefits may predispose the SSA toward generous responses.

We could have just tucked this advice in

Chapter 3 where withdrawing benefits was discussed. But to us, legalizing same-sex marriage is fundamental, not parenthetical. So we wanted to provide it with its own chapter.

We also want to stress that true equality for same-sex couples is not yet close to arriving when it comes to Social Security benefits. The agency's unfolding response to the DOMA decision has been as confusing as many of its other policies. And if you look for a clear statement on its website, good luck.

For example, the agency repeatedly and strongly encourages spouses in same-sex marriages to file for any benefit they feel is now open to them — benefits for spouses, for children, for survivors, and so on. This sounds great, right? And we agree that it's very important to submit a legally binding time stamp for benefits.

However, the agency is placing many if not most of these requests on hold and is not processing them for approval. How many? We don't know because the SSA declined to tell us.

For starters, however, let's talk about what the agency is approving. The largest category of benefit approvals involves people married in one of more than 30 states (plus the District of Columbia) where same-sex unions are legal and recognized (as of this writing, of course; by the time you read this, we hope the number is much larger). The SSA also has broadened its recognition of civil unions. If the couple has been married long enough (9 months for survivor and 12 months for spousal benefits), the agency will approve a request for spousal benefits if the couple not only is legally married but also lives in one of the states that has legalized same-sex unions. (It's more nuanced than this, as you'll see shortly in some examples.)

However, if the couple was married in one of those states or the District, but the applicant for benefits resides in one of the states that *does not* sanction same-sex marriages, the application for spousal benefits will be put on hold.[1]

According to the Human Rights Campaign, which has led efforts to broaden legal recognition for gays, the preferred position it thinks federal agencies should adopt regarding LGBT benefits is what is known as a "state of celebration" interpretation of the law. Under this approach, all applicable federal protections will be provided to people regardless of where they live so long as their marriage was legal in the state where it was performed or celebrated. The

IRS has adopted a state of celebration approach to applying its rules, which has been widely hailed by same-sex marriage supporters.

The Justice Department agreed in a June 2014 memo to President Obama outlining the response of federal agencies since the DOMA ruling: "Agencies have overwhelmingly chosen to recognize marriages as valid based on the law of the jurisdiction where the marriage took place (the 'place of celebration') regardless of where the couple currently resides (the 'place of domicile')."

The department noted, however, that the SSA and the Department of Veterans Affairs were prohibited by current law from adopting place of celebrations standards:

The Social Security Administration and the Department of Veterans Affairs are required by law to confer certain marriage-related benefits based on the law of the state in which the married couple resides or resided, preventing the extension of benefits to same-sex married couples living in states that do not allow or recognize same-sex marriages.

Current law[2] has largely limited the approval for benefits to those claims where the person *whose earnings record is the basis for the claim* (this is the nuance we referred to) actually lives in a state that permits same-sex unions. Legislation has been introduced to change the law but we are not encouraged at the prospects for passage by our divided and largely dysfunctional Congress.

**SOCIAL SECURITY VERBATIM
DEATH IS NO EXCUSE I**

"If the overpaid beneficiary or payee has died, the estate is liable for repayment. We may ask the legal representative to make a refund, or we may withhold benefits due the estate . . . and if an RSDI [retirement, survivors and disability insurance] overpayment cannot be recovered from the overpaid beneficiary, the payee, or the estate, benefits may be withheld from other persons entitled to benefits on the same earnings record."

*ALL QUOTES FROM OFFICIAL
SOCIAL SECURITY RULES*

In terms of spousal benefits, here are the agency's internal guidelines for treating benefit applications.[3] In these hypothetical examples, Massachusetts and California are the states where same-sex marriage is legal; Texas represents the states where it is not. The language and maniacal abbreviations are Social Security's, not ours, save for an occasional snarky comment in brackets — and in our translation after each of the administration's case studies. One simple rule of thumb: if neither member of a same-sex couple has yet to file for spousal benefits, beware of relocating to a state that hasn't legalized same-sex marriage.

Here are Social Security's cases in point, in the SSA's words.

CLAIMS THAT WOULD BE APPROVED:

Liz (the claimant) and Allison (the NH) ["number holder" in Social Security–speak] marry in Massachusetts (MA) after MA recognizes same-sex marriage. They are domiciled in MA. Liz files for spouse's benefits on Allison's record while they are domiciled in MA. They meet all other factors of entitlement. Approve the claim.

[In other words, if you married and still live in a state that approved same-sex nuptials before you tied the knot, you're good.]

Richard (the claimant) and Melvin (the NH) marry in MA after MA recognizes same-sex marriage. Richard moves and becomes domiciled in California (CA). Melvin remains domiciled in MA. Richard files for spouse's benefits on Melvin's record. They meet all other factors of entitlement. Approve the claim.

[Again, the marriage, rather obviously, has to have taken place *after* same-sex union has been legalized. This case is meant to show that even if the dependent spouse then moves out of state, if it is to a state that has also legalized same-sex marriage, Social Security benefits are the same as for any married couple.]

Jennifer (the claimant) and Ellie (the NH) marry in MA after MA recognizes same-sex marriage. Jennifer and Ellie move and become domiciled in California (CA). Jennifer files for spouse's benefits on Ellie's record. They meet all other factors of entitlement. Approve the claim.

[No problem even if *both* spouses move to another state that has legalized same-sex marriage.]

Colton (the claimant) and Carson (the NH) marry in MA after MA recognizes same-sex marriage. Colton moves and becomes domiciled in Texas (TX). Carson remains domiciled in MA. Colton files for spouse's benefits on Carson's record. They meet all other factors of entitlement. Approve the claim.

[Ah, this is encouraging. The spouse who claims benefits on the partner's earnings record can move to a state that does *not* recognize same-sex marriage, but so long as the partner — Carson — remains in a recognizing state, benefits are honored.]

Susan (the claimant) and Gail (the NH) are domiciled and marry in MA after MA recognizes same-sex marriage. Susan files for spouse's benefits on Gail's record while domiciled in MA. While the application is pending, Susan and Gail move to and become domiciled in Texas (TX). They meet all other factors of entitlement. Approve the claim because when the claim was filed, Susan and Gail were domiciled in a state that recognizes same-sex marriage. Use the date of filing in MA to determine month of entitlement.

[The relevant point here is actually quite clear: "when the claim was filed, Susan and Gail were domiciled in a state that recognizes same-sex marriage." End of story.]

James (the claimant) and Sheldon (the NH) are domiciled in TX and marry while on vacation in MA after MA recognizes same-sex marriage. James files for spouse's benefits on Sheldon's record while domiciled in TX. While the application is pending, James and Sheldon move to and become domiciled in MA. They meet all other factors of entitlement. Approve the claim because while the claim was pending a final determination James and Sheldon became domiciled in a state that recognizes same-sex marriage. Use the date of filing in TX to determine month of entitlement.

[Again, Social Security's reasoning is clear. The claim is approved "because while the claim was pending a final determination James and Sheldon became domiciled in a state that recognizes same-sex marriage."]

And now for the bad news. Or, as Social Security puts it:

CLAIMS THAT WOULD BE PLACED ON HOLD:

Brad (the claimant) and George (the NH) marry in MA after MA recognizes same-sex marriage. They were domiciled in MA. They move to and become domiciled in Texas (TX). Brad files for spouse's benefits on George's record while they are domiciled in TX. They meet all other factors of entitlement. Hold the claim.

["Hold the claim" means that Social Security will *turn it down,* unless the status changes. The moral of this case history is loud and clarion: If you marry in a same-sex state, *do not wait* until moving to a non-same-sex state to file for a dependent spousal claim.]

Sarah (the claimant) and Wanda (the NH) marry in MA after MA recognizes same-sex marriage. They were domiciled in MA. Wanda then moves and becomes domiciled in TX while Sarah remains domiciled in MA. Sarah files for spouse's benefits on Wanda's record. They meet all other factors of entitlement. Hold the claim.

[Again, *don't wait,* even if the partner claiming spousal benefits stays in the same-sex state. You both have to be in a same-sex state when you first claim.]

Shawn (the claimant) and Sam (the NH) marry in MA after MA recognizes same-sex marriage, but are domiciled in Texas (TX). Shawn files for spouse's benefits on Sam's record. They meet all other factors of entitlement. Hold the claim.

[The punch line of this paragraph — may our friends in Texas forgive us: if you're gay and married, don't move to the Lone Star State. Not yet, anyway.]

None of these distinctions would matter if Social Security adopted the so-called "celebration model" for awarding benefits: that is, once you're married in a same-sex state, nothing else matters. We hope it has done so by the time you read this. For now, we urge married couples whose claims have been placed on hold to take the time to fully understand Social Security's rules so they can plan for the future. We also urge them to continue pushing for change. Or, barring all else, to consider moving to a state that fully honors — and celebrates — their mutual commitment.

11
DIVORCED? DARK CLOUDS
AND SILVER LININGS

In Chapter 8, we provided a tongue-in-cheek, hypothetical illustration of how serial marriage and divorce (after 10 years) and some well-timed deaths can provide opportunities to maximize lifetime Social Security benefits that you might call special — or perverse.

In this chapter, we're going to look at some actual and hypothetical questions and case studies of the divorced. These questions, you'll recall, are culled from the "Ask Larry" columns on Paul's Making Sen$e website on PBS.org. They are meant to reassure any of the divorced who feel at sea about which benefits to collect and when. And you're not alone here. In fact, some 41 percent of you who were married at some point and are now in your fifties are currently divorced. This share is up from 36 percent back in the mid-1990s.

Let's start with the biggest question about

divorce benefits, namely whether your ex-spouse or your ex's current spouse can control what you can receive. The answer here is no and yes.

IF MY EX'S NEW WIFE COLLECTS ON HIS EARNINGS RECORD, CAN I COLLECT TOO?

Q: If my husband's ex-wife tries to collect spousal benefits when my husband starts collecting, how does that affect any spousal benefit I am eligible for when my husband is deceased or if we divorce? Does her claim reduce mine?

A: Whether she files for a divorcée spousal benefit and what she collects has no impact on what you can collect as a spouse or, for that matter, as a surviving widow, were your ex-husband to predecease you. The last thing Social Security wants is to be in the middle of family feuds over who should get what benefits.

HOW CAN I KEEP MY AWFUL EX FROM COLLECTING ON MY WORK RECORD?

Q: I don't want my horrible ex-husband collecting benefits on my work record. How can I prevent that?

A: Sorry, but your ability to restrict what

232

your ex-spouse receives based on your work record is limited. Your best move in this regard is simply to get divorced before 10 years are up. In this case, your ex can't receive any benefits of any kind based on your work record. But this cuts both ways. You'll no longer be able to collect any benefits based on her or his earning record.

If you were married for 10 years prior to getting divorced, the only way to reduce the divorced spousal benefits available to your ex is by limiting your future covered earnings. This may reduce your Average Indexed Monthly Earnings (AIME) compared to what would otherwise be the case. And having a smaller AIME means having a smaller Primary Insurance Amount (PIA), upon which your ex's divorced spousal benefit is based.

How about divorced widower's benefits? Here you can limit what your ex receives by taking your own retirement benefit early. This will reduce your own retirement benefit, which directly or indirectly affects the calculation of your ex's divorced widower's benefit.

But trying to spite your ex by earning less or taking your own retirement benefit early can limit your own retirement benefits as well as the spousal, child, and widower benefits that any new spouse and existing and new children can collect on your earnings record.

WHY IS SOCIAL SECURITY PUTTING MANY/MOST OF THE POOR INTO EXCESS BENEFIT HELL?

Q: I am 62 and divorced from my long-term (over 10 year) marriage to a much older man (and higher earner) who is still living. I have worked steadily all my life but always at low-wage jobs so I'm probably at the lowest rung of benefits. But I am desperate for any income. With my savings nearly gone, I am contemplating early Social Security claiming as no other income seems possible. If I do claim early Social Security, does this mean I can never benefit from claiming against my former husband's Social Security? I know effectively I would have zeroed out benefits if I claimed under his benefits as well as mine. But if I just claim only mine early am I forever precluded from benefiting under his? I am desperate and the people at Social Security won't give me a straight answer!

A: I'm terribly sorry to tell you this, but if you file for your retirement benefit early (which most low-income people are forced to do because they need the money), you'll be forced to file for your spousal benefit early as well, since your ex is over 62. The second you file for your retirement benefit, you plunge into what I call "excess benefit hell," in which you can never ever again collect one benefit by itself while letting the other one grow. Instead, your divorced spousal or divorced widow's benefit (when your ex dies) becomes your excess spousal or excess widow's benefit.

Note that because you are divorced, for you to be deemed to be filing for an early spousal benefit, your ex needs to be only 62 or older. He (she) does not need to be a) over 62 and also b) have filed for his or her retirement benefit in order for you to be deemed. So this is a disadvantage that the divorced face relative to married spouses.

Your excess spousal benefit is calculated as 50 percent of your ex's PIA, less 100 percent of your PIA, augmented by any Delayed Retirement Credits. Your excess widow's benefit is calculated as your widow's benefit less your own retirement benefit, reduced by any early retirement reduction factors and augmented by any Delayed Retirement Credits. If either excess benefit is negative, it's set to zero.

For those with their own Social Security earnings, their excess spousal benefit is likely to be negative, so it will be set to zero.[1] If your own PIA is, however, less than your spousal benefit, your excess spousal benefit will be positive. In this event, Social Security will force you to take it, at a reduced level, immediately. This is our old nemesis, deeming, at work.[2] Furthermore, if you file now or anytime before Full Retirement Age for your spousal benefit, you'll be deemed to also be filing for your retirement benefit, plunging you into excess spousal benefit hell.

Bottom line? Filing for a retirement benefit now likely will wipe out your spousal benefit forever. You will have the option at FRA to suspend your retirement benefit and start it up again at 70 at a 32 percent, inflation-adjusted higher value. But since you have landed in excess spousal benefit hell, you're stuck there forever. And even during the period when your retirement benefit is suspended, your spousal benefit will be calculated as your excess spousal benefit, which, again, will likely be zero.

If you could make it until FRA without filing for any benefits, you could file just for your spousal benefit and then let your own retirement benefit grow. But since you are strapped for cash, you don't have this option.

This is just one of the very many ways that Social Security disadvantages low-income people. On the surface, the system's benefits seem to be calculated in a highly progressive manner. They are. But then there are all these catch-22s and monstrously complex provisions that hurt the poor.

DO I NEED TO BE MARRIED FOR 10 CONSECUTIVE YEARS TO COLLECT DIVORCE BENEFITS?

Q: I married my ex in January 1972. We divorced in June 1981, remarried each other in November 1983 and divorced again in May 1993. We were married to each other a total of just under 20 years. He is 64 and still working. I am 62 and am on SSI and have never remarried. Am I eligible to collect on his Social Security earnings?

A: Unfortunately, the answer is no because you weren't married for 10 consecutive years in either case. Social Security restarts the 10-year marriage clock required for divorced spouses to collect when they remarry, including when they remarry their former spouse. But, as always, there is an exception. If you remarry your former

spouse in the same calendar year or in the
calendar year immediately following the
year of your divorce, the marriages are
considered continuous for purposes of
meeting the 10-year duration of marriage
requirement if you do subsequently call it
quits for good.

You're in Love. Great. But Think Twice About Getting Married!

**Q: I am getting laid off and would like
to collect my ex-husband's Social Security
when I am 66. I am 64 now, and am
not remarried. My ex is still alive. I am
also considering marriage to my civil
union partner; if I should marry her,
can I still collect his benefits at 66 and
delay mine until 70?**

A: No, I'm sorry, but you can't collect
spousal benefits from an ex while being
married. You can collect survivor benefits if
you remarry after 60, which would be your
case. So, short of doing in your ex (which I
don't advise) or his passing away, remar-
riage will mean you'll need to look to your
partner for a spousal benefit.

Getting Hit by Three Whammies

**Q: I was a police officer for 33 years.
Prior to that I worked at various jobs,**

but I am 10 quarters short to collect Social Security. I had always planned on working again after retiring from the police department in order to accrue the required Social Security quarters. However, as I was preparing to retire, I was diagnosed with oral cancer, which left me unable to work. Is there any way to collect from my current wife or my ex-wife? Things are really hard right now, and any help would be appreciated. I was married to a teacher for 27 years, divorcing in 2001. I remarried in February 2013, at the age of 60, to a 62-year-old woman, who has worked most of her life. Thank you very much.

A: Unfortunately, you can't collect spousal benefits on your ex-spouse's earning record because you are married. On the other hand, since you remarried after age 60, you can collect a survivor benefit based on your ex once your ex passes away.

The good news is you can collect on your second wife's earnings record. The bad news is that your spousal benefit will be hit by three whammies if you take it starting at age 62. First, it will be reduced by two-thirds of your policeman's pension due to the Government Pension Offset (GPO) provision. Second, it will be reduced due to the early spousal benefits reduction factor. And third, your current wife will need to apply for reduced retirement benefits in order for you to be eligible to collect a spousal benefit. The GPO may also prevent you from drawing a surviving divorced spousal benefit — if your first wife dies before you.

Divorced? Say Goodbye to Child-in-Care Spousal Benefits

(Here's a question Larry made up.) **Q: I'm divorced. My kids are under age 16. Can I collect a spousal benefit? I was married for more than 10 years. My ex was a true jerk. He ran off with my best friend's cousin Sheila and left me with the kids. I should never have married the old cougar. Glad to be rid of him. But Sheila? Get outta here! She doesn't hold a flamethrower to me.**

My sister Charlene also married a geezer and has young kids. She's hanging in there with him, although he's no day in the park. The kids are collecting child benefits since he's collecting his retirement benefit. And get this — she's collecting a spousal benefit even though she's only 35 because the kids are under age 16. And those benefits aren't re-

duced because she's so young. Nor are they being clawed back via the Earnings Test because she doesn't work. Well, she works as a waitress, but it's all under the table, so Social Security never learns about it.

Anyhow, Charlene told me to ask you if I can collect divorcée spousal benefits just like she's collecting. I could sure use the money. Sheila's squeezing my creep ex for every penny he's got and the bills keep piling up.

A: Unfortunately, I've got bad news. Divorcée spousal benefits are not available to mothers of children under age 16 (even though your ex has filed for his retirement benefit) — unless the mother is 62 or older. If that were the case, you could collect those benefits with no reduction for being under FRA. And provided you didn't file for your own retirement benefit, you'd get the full spousal benefit for an ex-spouse with a child in your care. Plus, if the kids all reached age 16 before you reached FRA, you could wait until then to apply just for your full divorcée spousal benefit.

But you aren't age 62 or older. You are too young and you're divorced, therefore Social Security treats you differently from someone who is young but married. If you find this outrageous and unfair, I'm with you. But someone — probably a male — decided a very long time ago that divorced spouses with young children weren't as worthy or needy as married spouses with young children. You might want to write your congresswoman and ask her if she thinks this stinks and when she is going to fix it.

CAN I CLAIM HALF OF MY EX'S BENEFIT?

Q: Is it true that I can only claim half of my ex's Social Security benefit? I live in Texas and we were married for 37 years. I have not remarried.

A: The truth may be worse than this. If you ever filed for your own retirement benefit, even if you suspended it after reaching FRA in order to start it up at a higher value later, you won't get the full spousal benefit, which is half of your ex's PIA (not what he actually collects as a retirement benefit, which can be larger or smaller than his PIA, which is the retirement benefit due him at his FRA). Instead, you'll get an excess spousal benefit equal to your full spousal benefit (i.e., half of *his* PIA) minus 100 percent of *your* PIA if you filed at or before FRA or your actual retirement benefit if you filed at or after FRA.

How Social Security Keeps the Divorced and Widows in the Dark About Their Benefits

Q: Why can't I get access to my ex-spouse's earnings record? I need this information to do my own Social Security planning. Will Social Security notify me if my ex starts collecting his Social Security retirement benefit? This decision can, in special cases, affect when I can start my divorced spousal benefit.

A: The Social Security Administration won't let the divorced have access to their ex-spouses' earnings records. Nor will it let widows and widowers have access to their late spouses' earnings records.

The Social Security Administration does spouses a disservice by not letting them see what their exes or late spouses were earning. Given Social Security's benefit formulas, the earnings histories of, say, Mary's ex-husband, Joe, and Linda's late husband, Sam, are just as much the private property of Mary and Linda as they are of Joe and Sam.

Mary and Linda have a legal claim to benefits based on their former husbands' earnings records. But if they can't get ac-

243

cess to these earnings records, they can't properly plan when to retire, how much to save for retirement, in which order to take their spousal, retirement, and survivor benefits, or when to take them at all.

**SOCIAL SECURITY VERBATIM
DEATH IS NO EXCUSE II**

If someone formally requests that Social Security reconsider an adverse benefit decision: "In the event of claimant death, process the death termination. If there are no other parties, dismiss the request for reconsideration unless there is an over-payment on the record with no waiver request. A reconsidered determination should be rendered since recovery from the estate is possible."

*ALL QUOTES FROM OFFICIAL
SOCIAL SECURITY RULES*

BOTH DIVORCED SPOUSES CAN COLLECT FULL SPOUSAL BENEFITS

Q: I am 63 and my wife is 62. We have roughly equal lifetime earnings, and neither of us has yet filed for benefits.

If we are divorced prior to my 64th birthday, at age 66 (my FRA) can I file for spousal benefits, which would be half of her benefits at her age of 65? Can she, one year later, at her FRA, file for spousal benefits, which would be half of my benefits at my age of 67?

Can we then each, upon reaching age 70, file for our own benefits, which presumably will have been increasing all along? In addition, will the death of either former spouse during the period we are each receiving spousal benefits affect those benefits, or the ability at age 70 to file for our own full retirement benefits? In short, will divorce under these circumstances allow us each to receive spousal benefits, and then allow each of us at age 70 to switch to our own, higher benefits?

A: Yes, assuming you were married for at least 10 years, once you are divorced for 2 years, you can both, at FRA, file just for a full spousal benefit and then both take your own retirement benefits at 70 and, thereby, have those benefits start at their highest possible value. The ability for you both to receive full spousal benefits is an advantage provided to divorced spouses. In the case of married couples, only one can collect a full spousal benefit.

Finally, if you're getting divorced and taking your full spousal benefits, this will have no impact on your ability to collect survivor benefits based on your ex's work history.

DOES IT PAY TO LIVE IN SIN?

Q: If two people were married for 12 years, then got divorced and married other people, can the exes each collect Social Security benefits on their first spouses, even though they are married to other people now?

A: No. You can't collect a spousal benefit on an ex if you are remarried. But the answer changes to "yes" if you get divorced from your new spouses. Then you can both potentially collect spousal benefits on your first spouses' earnings records.

This raises the possibility that it might actually pay to get divorced, even if you don't want to, and then live together "in sin." Social Security doesn't care about such things. I'm not suggesting this, just pointing out the sometimes perverse incentives in the Social Security rules and regulations.

How Fast Can I Cash in on My Divorced Spousal Benefits?

Q: I turn 66 in August, reaching FRA. I want to take the spouse's benefits for which I qualify. One problem: my divorce becomes final next week (34-year marriage) and I noted on SSA's spousal benefits requirements that I don't qualify until 2 years after the divorce. Is this the case or do I qualify under other circumstances? I feel I am in limbo and will lose this important income. Thank you.

A: Divorced people who were married for 10 years or more can collect a spousal benefit based on the ex's earnings record, provided they are 62 or older and their ex is 62 or older and either: a) their ex has filed for his or her retirement benefit or b) they have been divorced for at least two years. So if your soon-to-be ex is over 62 and has already filed for his own retirement benefit, you don't need to wait 2 years. If he hasn't, you do.

Collecting Twice, Over Time, Off the Same Ex

Q: If, at 66, I file for my divorced spousal benefits and wait until 70 to collect my Social Security, then my ex-spouse dies with a larger Social Security, would I be able to file for it if it is larger than mine and I have already collected four years of divorced benefits between my age of 66 and 70?

A: Yes. And your divorced survivor benefit will exceed your divorced spousal benefit — possibly by a factor of 2!

BE VERY CAREFUL
WHAT YOU ASK FOR

Q: I just read your Social Security story, but am still not understanding one thing. I am divorced, just turned 66, and started getting half of my ex-husband's Social Security benefit because it was bigger than what I could get from my own earnings. When I turn 70, can I file again to receive more Social Security benefits from my own earnings in addition to half of my ex-husband's, or is it an either/or choice?

A: If, case A, you filed just for your spousal benefit — that is, you filed a restricted application — you can get your own retirement benefit starting at 70, inclusive of 4 years of Delayed Retirement Credits. Between now and then, you'll collect your full spousal benefit, namely half of your ex's full retirement benefit.

If, case B, you applied for *both* your divorced spousal benefit and your full retirement benefit, you are receiving your full retirement benefit plus your excess spousal benefit (the amount by which your full spousal benefit exceeds your retirement benefit). This monthly check would be the same amount *through age 70.*

Under case A, your retirement benefit will be 32 percent larger starting at age 70 thanks to the Delayed Retirement Credit. As of age 70, you may start receiving a larger total monthly check. This would be the case if your DRCs boost your retirement so it is greater than your spousal benefit.

In contrast, under case B, you won't be credited with Delayed Retirement Credits because you already filed for your retirement benefit.

So case A beats case B. If you are trying to collect a full divorce spousal benefit, apply just for it at FRA. And wait until age 70 to file for your own retirement benefit. There is no guarantee your total monthly check will rise at age 70. But it may if the Delayed Retirement Credits make a big enough difference.[3]

The Family Maximum Benefit Doesn't Apply to Ex-Spouses

Q: I'm 69 years old, and I read on the Social Security Administration (SSA) website that when my former husband, who's 80, dies, my benefit will be increased to 50 percent of his full retirement benefit. I currently receive a small supplement based on his account.

However, he remarried and his wife is much younger. The SSA says that there is a monthly collection limit of between 150 and 180 percent of the deceased's benefit amount. How would that affect me?

A: Provided your ex didn't collect his retirement before FRA, you can collect 100 percent of the benefit he was receiving when he dies. Otherwise, the crazy RIB-LIM formula kicks in.

My Ex Is Younger. Do I Need to Wait to Collect a Divorcé Spousal Benefit?

Q: I am 62, and I was married for 12 years. My ex-spouse is 54. I lost my job making $120,000 per year, however, I think I can get by on savings plus Social Security. Is it possible to claim a Social Security benefit on my ex-wife's work history? She is still working and makes about $90,000 per year. If yes, do I have to wait until she retires?

A: Yes, you can collect a spousal benefit on your ex, but you have to wait not until she retires, but until she reaches age 62. If she passes away, you can collect a survivor benefit starting immediately.

WHICH OF MY EX'S THREE WIVES CAN COLLECT?

Q: I am a second wife with a third after me. As far as Social Security goes from my ex, who among us has a claim? Of the three wives, I was married the longest at 14 years. Just wondering.

A: All three ex-wives can collect spousal and survivor benefits provided they were married at least 10 years and 1 second prior to getting divorced. So, yes, you can collect benefits — spousal, while your ex is still kicking — and survivor benefits after he dies.

IT MAY PAY TO GET DIVORCED AND LIVE IN SIN

Not that we're recommending this, of course, but we can imagine people living so close to the bone that they may want to take advantage of Social Security's incentive to get divorced. There is, in fact, an incentive for *everyone* who has been married for 10 or more (*long?*) years to do so.

The secret involves "spousal benefits" that all married spouses are entitled to collect on their mate's earnings, as long they meet certain conditions. If they play their cards right, one of the two spouses can collect a *full spousal benefit* equal to half of their partner's full retirement benefit while leaving their own retirement benefit to keep growing.

But if you get *divorced,* so long as you were married for at least 10 years, *both* you and your now-ex can, potentially, get full spousal benefits while putting off your *own* retirement benefit.

In other words, if you've been married or will be married long enough, it can pay to get divorced. It's true for low-income folks. It's true for those with average incomes. And it's even true for *high*-income people. Indeed, for fat (or merely plump) cats, getting divorced could bring in an extra $60,000 over four years: four very nice vacations abroad, perhaps, or a brand-new 328i BMW coupe convertible!

Three catches. 1) You need to reach FRA having *not filed for your own retirement benefit.* 2) You need to be divorced for 2 years before you can apply for a spousal benefit on your ex's earnings record, or your ex needs to have filed for their retirement benefit. 3) Your ex needs to be 62 or over or receiving disability benefits.

But what if I love my spouse?

Love has nothing to do with this. We're talking a 328i BMW coupe convertible, for gosh sakes! Furthermore, we're not saying you need to physically separate. You can continue to live together and behave in every way as spouses. (Of course, you also need to look at how divorce would affect your taxes.)

Okay, now to get serious. We're not really recommending you get divorced. That could be very expensive in terms of legal fees and time-consuming, requiring formally allocating assets between you and your would-be ex. The real point of this example is to make clear that divorced people can get something married people can't, namely two free full spousal benefits rather than just one.

SALLY SMARTY PANTS GETS DIVORCED

Sally Smarty Pants was very smart, except when it came to Social Security. She got divorced one day shy of 10 years after making a New Year's resolution not to spend a whole decade married to John Know It All. Now she's 63 and kicking herself not just for marrying that know-it-all, who turned out to know enough to make a lot of money. She also took her retirement benefits 366 days ago and wished she hadn't. It's now a day too late for her to repay every dollar she received and start up her benefit from scratch in the future at a much higher level.

What's Sally to do? She was a modest earner, having worked all her life at the neighborhood bookstore (telling people what books to read — hence her nickname). But the store closed six years ago, costing her $40,000 per year in salary. Now Sally's living off her $1,500 monthly retirement benefit check, whose lifetime value is $489,956. But Sally also has some retirement account assets thanks to her messy divorce. She's got enough to forgo receiving Social Security till 70, but she's given up that option by taking benefits early.

Not entirely! There is another strategy Sally can follow, namely to suspend her retirement benefit at Full Retirement Age (66 for her) and start it up again at 70. Her annual benefit will be $23,760, and her lifetime benefits, as of today, will be $542,608.[4] That 11 percent increase in benefits is not going to pay for a life in the fast lane, but it's extra money that Sally can definitely use and it's hers for free, with no risk, just by becoming a Social Security smarty!

SPEAKING OF LISA, WHO USED TO LOVE JOEY

Unlike Sally Smarty Pants, Lisa and Joey stuck it out for 10 long years and, luckily, 1 day, and, as a result, both of them can receive spousal benefits based on the other's work record.

Let's first consider Lisa, who is now 65 and is five years older than Joey. And let's assume that Lisa's and Joey's full retirement benefits are both $2,500.

Lisa and Joey got divorced a long time ago — when Lisa was 40. She hasn't talked to Joey for 25 years. She also has no idea she can collect benefits off Joey's work record.

If Lisa does what she's thinking of doing — taking retirement benefits immediately — she'll give up $92,664.[5] How come? Because if she waits until 70, she can collect a retirement benefit of $23,755, not $16,769 — the amount she'll get starting benefits at age 65. Plus, when Lisa is 67 — the year Joey reaches age 62 — she'll be eligible to collect a full spousal benefit based on Joey's earnings record. This will mean an extra $8,894 a year (in today's dollars) for three years. At 70, Lisa's spousal benefit will flip to an excess spousal benefit since at 70 she'll start collecting her own retirement benefit. (Recall that the act of filing for a retirement benefit means you can only collect roughly the larger of two benefits to which you are entitled.)

SPEAKING OF JOEY, WHO USED TO LOVE LISA

Joey, who is now 60, is thinking of taking his retirement benefit at 62. Big mistake. Doing so will leave $132,634 on the table. First, Joey will give up a full annual spousal benefit of $8,783 for 4 years starting at 66. Second, he'll be stuck with a retirement benefit of $13,681 — far below his potential age-70 starting value of $23,946.[6]

Why, you might ask, does Joey get to receive full (not excess) spousal benefits for 4 years, but Lisa gets to receive such benefits for only 3 years? And why, if Lisa weren't 5 years, but 8 years older than Joey, would she get to receive full (not excess) spousal benefits for zero years?

Beats us, but those indeed are the age-based quirks of the system. It seems like Social Security is, effectively, trying to have each spouse insure the other against divorce because two can live more cheaply than one. The spousal benefit can also be viewed as providing some earnings and child-bearing insurance. If you had low lifetime covered earnings because you were, say, unemployed for many years or because you spent years out of the workforce raising children, the spousal benefit would loom relatively large. But if Lisa were 8 years older than Joey, she'd receive zero spousal benefits until age 70 and only the excess spousal benefit thereafter even if she had stayed home raising their children for most of her potential working life.

12
WIDOWED? WHY SOCIAL SECURITY IS A MAJOR WOMEN'S ISSUE

About 10 million widows and widowers aged 65 and older were receiving monthly survivor's benefits in 2013. Of these, 80 percent were awarded to women. So, while we have been taking great pains throughout to discuss Social Security in gender-neutral terms, we won't do so here, even though we realize that with the increase in house husbands and the legalization of gay marriage, the gender ratio will probably shift in the future.

In short, this chapter's specifics apply mainly to women. But husbands ought to read the chapter, too, and read it closely, because their decisions about how long to work and when to begin claiming their own Social Security retirement benefits could have a substantial impact on the quality of their wives' later years. And, to be honest here, the odds favor that many of those years will be spent as widows. Adult children should read it as well and think about their mother's unmet financial needs in later life — needs that may fall on them to fund. Then they should talk to both their parents and make sure the claiming decisions of their moms and dads are made with the likely longevity of their moms in mind.

One more point before moving forward. A book of strategies for dealing with a bureaucracy and its rules invites little in the way of empathic emotions, save for frustration. But as all three of us have answered many benefit questions from "survivors," we first want to express our sincere condolences to every reader who has lost a spouse, an overwhelmingly significant other, or an irreplaceable parent. Losing a partner or parent is one of life's heaviest burdens, and we have often felt inadequate to the task of providing advice in such circumstances. But we're of sadly little use with regard to your loss, so from here on, we'll stick to pointers for dealing with what is cruelly inevitable.

Back to the hard realities:

1. Widowhood is a woman's issue.
2. The benefits paid to widows, particularly older ones, are crucial to avoiding years of poverty or something close to it.

3. Changing patterns of marriage and divorce mean that fewer women will be collecting survivor or divorce benefits in the future.

4. Rising labor-force participation rates for women, however, and, generally, rising wages as well, mean that women increasingly will be better able to fend for themselves in retirement, including receiving growing benefits as compared with those received by men.

5. And yet, ironically, despite their rising earnings profiles, women who marry increasingly face raw deals when their husbands die.

Here's a specific example that came in the form of a question to Larry on Paul's PBS Money Sen$e Web page from "Helen" of Eureka, California:

I am twice divorced and began taking my own Social Security benefit at age 66. My first husband died last year. We were married over 10 years. Am I eligible to collect his Social Security benefit?

Our answer: Yes, Helen — and everyone in her position — would be *eligible* to collect on a deceased former husband's earnings record, even if long divorced from him, even if she remarried (so long as she did so on or after her 60th birthday), all assuming that she was married to the deceased ex-husband for at least a decade, as she says she was.

To be clear as well as comprehensive, Helen, like everyone in such a position, would be in line to receive a survivor's benefit based on her husband's earnings record *or* she could continue to get her own retirement benefit, the one she already started taking at age 66. She would be eligible to receive the larger of the two benefits.

We weren't able to reach Helen to quiz her on the specifics, but since the average American man earns something like 25 percent more than the average woman does, let's assume that's the case here.

Now, if Helen were just taking a spousal benefit, the most she could collect would be half of his PIA. The math is simple. His PIA is only 25 percent higher than hers, so half of his would be only 62.5 percent of her PIA.

However, she's not taking a spousal benefit but a survivor's benefit. The math here may be much, much trickier. Helen is eligible to collect the greater of her retirement benefit or, depending on when he began taking benefits and the age at which he died, *all* of her late former husband's benefit. We don't know these facts in Helen's case. But if her late former husband didn't begin taking retirement benefits until he was 70, for example, they would be 132 percent of a PIA that already was 25 percent larger than Helen's. So her widow's benefit would be much larger than her own retirement benefit. Remember, she started taking that at her Full Retirement Age, so it would be only equal to her PIA (plus subsequent Cost of Living Adjustments). Again, an easy decision for her.

But if, like most men, he claimed retirement benefits early (before FRA), they would be reduced and so would her survivor's benefit. The only way to know for sure is to review the numbers carefully. A visit to her Social Security office *should* do the trick here. But we hope Helen brushes up on the portions of *Get What's Yours* that explain the benefit cuts caused by these RIB-LIM rules. (See Chapter 3 or Glossary for the RIB-LIM definition.)

But wait. Helen's situation suggests another possibility. Suppose Helen were to *suspend* her own retirement benefit until age 70 (assuming she can afford to) and instead take, between now and then, what's called her excess survivor's benefit. Remember from earlier discussions that the excess survivor benefit will be the difference between her survivor benefit and her own suspended retirement benefit. We're assuming here it will be positive.

If Helen did this, her own retirement benefit will be growing at 8 percent a year until age 70, inflation adjusted, due to those Delayed Retirement Credits we keep touting. In other words, as long as her survivor benefit is *greater* than her own current benefit, she will be getting *something* while waiting for her maximum possible benefit, which she can get by restarting her own *retirement benefit at 70.* Of course, this might not represent a lot of dollars, so problems in affording to delay her own retirement benefits might be an issue.

A SHORT (AND ADMITTEDLY DRY) PRIMER ON THE BASICS FOR WIDOWS AND WIDOWERS

Anyone married for more than 9 months is eligible to receive survivor's benefits keyed to the Social Security earnings record of their late spouse. Survivor's benefits based on the work record of a deceased and divorced spouse are also possible if you have not remarried before the age of 60.

Survivor's benefits begin as early as age 60, unlike retirement benefits, where 62 is the earliest age for filing. If you are disabled, you may elect to begin receiving survivor's benefits at the age of 50.

Survivor's benefits can be as much as the deceased spouse's actual retirement benefit, including up to 4 years' of Delayed Retirement Credits if he waited to claim benefits until turning 70. They also can be a lot less. It depends on the ages and Social Security claiming decisions of both spouses. Working through these possibilities is the key to making the optimal claiming decision.

There is a penalty for early filing, beginning at age 60 and ending when you reach FRA, which is 66 for anyone born between 1943 and 1954. During this 72-month period, survivor's benefits are reduced by just under four-tenths of a percent for each month prior to turning 66 (.396, to be precise). This works out to 4.75 percent a year, or a 28.5 percent early filing penalty for the full 6-year period between ages 60 and 66.

A final "basic," in the form of a mild warning: If you file for survivor's benefits early — before 66 — you could also be affected by the *Earnings Test,* the same one that temporarily reduces retirement benefits for early filers. But, as with those benefits, any survivor's benefits reduced by this test will be restored once you've reached FRA.

TIME FOR ANOTHER EXAMPLE

To return from the abstract to the concrete, here's a seemingly straightforward email from a Texas woman, who wrote:

> My husband died yesterday. I live in Houston, Texas. Am I entitled to his Social Security paycheck?

Well, the easy answer is "no, you're entitled to *your own* Social Security paycheck, in the form of your *survivor's* benefit." But if the emailer means "Am I entitled to the *amount* of my late husband's paycheck?" the answer, unfortunately, is that as with Helen's situation, there's no way to say without knowing exactly how much the husband was receiving, based on his earnings record, *when* he starting taking his benefits, and when the surviving widow decides to take her survivor's benefit.

The point of this case study is that Social Security does not make the process of finding such information easy. Here is what a widow like this woman in Houston would have to go through when trying to determine when to take her survivor's benefit.

First thing first. If she is 60 or over (or 50 or older and disabled), she can collect widow's benefits starting immediately, subject to early claiming reductions if she is younger than her FRA. That's the easy part of the answer. But how much will her widow's benefit be? It hinges on who takes (or in this case, *took*) their benefits *when*. There are four different situations to consider, and each one demands a different answer: 1) both wait (waited) until full eligibility age; 2) husband waited (until FRA) but *wife* now takes early; 3) husband took early, wife now waits; 4) both take (or took) early. Because there are bound to be readers facing the situation sketched in the email, we'll consider the answers one painstaking permutation at a time.

1. If husband took his retirement benefit after FRA and widow takes the survivor's benefit at or after her own FRA, she will, indeed, receive his actual retirement benefit — his full retirement benefit inclusive of his Delayed Retirement Credits. As it happens, this may be even *more* than the check he was receiving each month. Why? Because his

monthly Medicare Part B premium may have been withheld from his monthly Social Security check and of course those premiums no longer need to be paid. His check may also have been less than his retirement benefit for another reason: Social Security may have been withholding some of his retirement benefit for income taxes and the amount of this withholding could decline if his widow is in a lower federal income tax bracket after he dies.

2. Even if the husband took his retirement benefit at FRA, if the widow took her survivor's benefit *before* FRA, her survivor's benefit will be reduced. For example, it will be reduced by 28.5 percent if she took it at 60, assuming she was born between 1943 and 1954.

3. Now suppose the opposite: the husband took his retirement benefit early and the widow waits to take her survivor's benefit until her full eligibility age. In that case, the survivor's benefit would equal the larger of two payments: a) the early retirement benefit he was receiving or b) 82.5 percent of his full retire-

ment benefit. So, by way of example, let's say he took his retirement benefit at age 62. It would then have been smaller than 82.5 percent of his full retirement benefit. So, by waiting until her FRA, her survivor's benefit would exceed what her husband had been receiving.

4. If the husband took his retirement benefit early and the widow also takes her survivor's benefit early, the reduced survivor's benefit can be less than what he was receiving, depending on how early she starts taking. In this case, her survivor's benefit will equal her late spouse's full retirement benefit reduced by her survivor's benefit reduction factor.

THE WIDOW'S LIMIT (RIB-LIM)

When Social Security's foundational laws were enacted in the 1930s, the rules regarding women were shaped by men, thinking about what would happen to their predominantly nonworking wives when the men died. Here's what one of the program's primary oversight groups said back then, as cited in a 2010 SSA research paper on widows:

A haunting fear in the minds of many older men is the possibility, and frequently, the probability, that their widow will be in need after their death. The day of large families and of the farm economy, when aged parents were thereby assured comfort in their declining years, has passed for a large proportion of our population. This change has had particularly devastating effect on the sense of security of the aged women of our country.

Survivor's benefits weren't even included in the law as originally enacted. In later years, debates on the level of widow benefits included discussions that concluded that widows could live more cheaply than widowers because they knew how to take care of their domestic needs. Men, by contrast, were assumed to need more money. Among other reasons, it was assumed they could not cook and would thus have to buy their meals at a restaurant. We kid you not.

Even today, more than 75 years later, Social Security planners say that poverty rates of older widows are one of their greatest concerns. And one of the major causes of low widow benefits, besides having earned less and therefore saved less than men, is that their husbands overwhelmingly took their retirement benefits early, thus locking in lower survivor's benefits for their widows for the rest of their lives.

This is reflected in what's called the Retirement Income Benefit Limit, or, like some abbreviation out of the old Soviet Union, RIB-LIM. It is also called the widow's limit in some Social Security discussions. We discussed RIB-LIM at some length in Chapter 3 and will spare you an encore here. But it affects lots of women: roughly 3 million, or about 3 out of every 8 widows, according to a 2010 research paper. In cases involving the retirement benefits of nondisabled husbands who died, nearly 60 percent of their widows saw their survivor's benefits reduced by RIB-LIM.[1]

Okay, here's another survivor's question that came in over the electronic transom:

My 70-year-old husband passed away and he was collecting Social Security at 62. I am 64 and still working. Will I receive a portion of my husband's Social Security?

Our answer: Yes, but your timing here is crucial. Remember that if someone tries to take her own retirement benefit and her survivor's benefit at the same time, she'll get only the larger of the two benefits. (You might remember from an earlier discussion that deeming does not affect survivor benefits.)

Normally, we'd recommend that a widow in this position take the smaller of the two benefits earlier, allowing the second benefit to rise in value, and then switch to it after it no longer rises with age.

But in this case, because the husband took his retirement benefit early, the survivor's benefit is calculated based on the RIB-LIM referred to above, which means the survivor's benefit will be 82.5 percent of the husband's full retirement benefit, regardless of whether or not it is taken immediately or not until FRA.

In other words, for the widow in this situation, there is no advantage to waiting to collect her survivor's benefit. There is, however, a possible advantage — and a large one — from waiting to collect her own retirement benefit. If she waits, for example, until age 70, when it's as large as possible, it may exceed her survivor's benefit, in which case she'll collect *it* rather than her survivor's benefit.

But it's also possible that her retirement benefit may exceed her survivor's benefit even *before* age 70. So we think she and people in her situation should apply right now for their survivor's benefit and then apply for their own retirement benefit at or after the point that their retirement benefit exceeds the survivor's benefit, which, again, may never happen. There's some homework to do here, but by this point in *Get What's Yours,* we are confident you'll be up to it!

A last caveat: the annual Earnings Test may prevent this widow from receiving all or part of her potential survivor's benefit before FRA. But, as we've often pointed out, she'll get the money back eventually.

SOCIAL SECURITY VERBATIM
DEATH IS NO EXCUSE III (NEITHER IS BAD GRAMMAR)

"If a numberholder dies during a period of voluntary suspension and *a survivor requests that benefits for months prior to death is reinstated and paid* as an underpayment to the estate, do not reinstate benefits. There is no basis to change the numberholder's decision merely because an underpayment is created."

ALL QUOTES FROM OFFICIAL SOCIAL SECURITY RULES

MIXED SOCIAL SECURITY BLESSING FOR WIDOWS: MORE WOMEN IN THE WORKFORCE

In the "olden days," of course, many wives *never* worked outside the home. Without survivor benefits, they would have been destitute. Thus it is that a woman whose husband died at age 70, after deferring his retirement benefit and enjoying 4 years of Delayed Retirement Credits, may be eligible to receive his entire benefit for the rest of her life, including annual increases to adjust for the effect of inflation. And she may receive this without ever having worked for Social Security–covered wages a day in her life.

More likely in this era, however, wives will have worked but will still have earned less than their husbands. This means that their benefits as surviving spouses may be higher than their own retirement benefits, for which they have paid taxes their entire working lives. As an agency 2010 research paper observed, "The auxiliary benefit provisions, including spousal and widow's benefits, mean that many women do not receive higher benefits in return for their contributions than they would have received had they never worked or contributed to the program."

On the other hand, as more women have entered the workforce and as more of them have begun to earn higher salaries, a growing percentage of women has begun to earn Social Security retirement benefits on a par with men in general and their husbands in particular.

The problem is, it will take decades for this trend to take full effect. (Recall, if you will, that benefits are tied to a person's top *35* years of covered earnings.) Moreover, fewer women are getting married. And to compound the problem, a rising percentage is getting divorced, more and more of them after fewer than 10 years of marriage, the minimum needed to qualify for survivor divorced spousal benefits.

The net effect of these trends is that despite women's slow and steady entry into the workforce, there's been a slow and steady countereffect on what surviving female spouses can expect from Social Security. Just look at the so-called income replacement rate: the percentage of a person's pre-retirement income represented by their Social Security benefits. This rate is a key measure of the impact and adequacy of Social Security benefits, and it has been declining in a big way. Without getting into the minutiae of demographic shifts, women's changing role in the workforce, and other statistical details, the bottom line here is that everyone — but particularly women — will be depending on Social Security for an ever-shrinking share of their retirement income needs, and therefore had better get as much as they possibly can.

Everyone — aging wives and their husbands, as well as their grown children — needs to think carefully about women's relatively greater needs for retirement security. And the sooner such recognition is incorporated into a family's financial plans, the more likely widows are to live the kinds of lives their husbands and children want for them.

A Last (and Touching) Case Study

I am 67 and married and have been diagnosed with terminal cancer. I have another five years at most to live. The people at my local Social Security office said I should file to begin taking my retirement benefits right away so I'd at least get something back before I die for all my years of contributions. What do you think?

This question was posed to Larry in person and so we let him narrate the rest of the story, and his answer:

You could not meet a nicer or better man, and he's facing his situation with joy for all the good he's done and experienced and with determination to live out his remaining days helping others, all while living life to the fullest.

In between telling me about his recent and pending fly-fishing expeditions, which he can partake in thanks to oral chemotherapy, he asked if he should follow the

Social Security office's strong advice.

I told him this probably was bad advice for the following reason: Each year between FRA and 70 that he waits to collect will increase by 8 percent (not compounded) the real (inflation-adjusted) amount of Social Security survivor's benefits his wife, who hadn't worked much, will receive for the rest of her life after he passes away. For example, if he survives to 70, his wife will receive a 24 percent higher survivor's benefit check every month.

The reason the wife's work history matters, I told him, is that she'll get a check equal to the larger of her own retirement benefit or her survivor's benefit. If she had earned more than her husband and waited, say, to age 70 to collect her retirement benefit, the survivor's benefit wouldn't matter because she'd never collect it.

One moral to this story is to be very careful taking Social Security's advice. Another is to bear in mind that your decision about when to take your own retirement benefit will impact what your spouse and, indeed, any ex-spouses to whom you were married for 10 or more years, will receive in survivor's benefits.

Social Security Administration employees are specifically trained not to advise people what to do but instead to explain their options and let them decide what is best for them. Some employees hesitate to mention what will happen in the event of a person's death simply because it's an uncomfortable subject. But we sometimes have the worst of both worlds: they give advice when they shouldn't and then don't do a very good job of it.

13
NEVER MARRIED OR
DIVORCED TOO SOON

Social Security provides a host of incentives to strategically tie the knot, as we explained in Chapter 8. But what about those of you who never marry? What strategies and tactics are unique to *you*?

This is not an idle question because there are more than a few of you out there. Indeed, the ranks of the unmarried have swelled in recent years and decades, perhaps because the stigma against what used to be scornfully called *cohabitation* — or even *out-of-wedlock* child rearing — has faded. It's true that less than 10 percent of people in the U.S. aged 55 to 64 have never been married. But the Census Bureau reports that this figure is higher for younger age brackets and has steadily been increasing in recent decades. Currently, the percentages of never-married persons is 12.5 percent for those 50 to 54; 14 percent for people aged 45 to 49; 17.5 percent for the 40–44 age group, and more than 23 percent for persons aged 35 to 39.

Let's say you're between 50 and 64 and you never married. There were *6.5 million* of you as of 2013,[1] 6.5 million people who should both be stressing about — and *doing* something about — your Social Security and retirement needs, even if the "doing" has involved nothing more to date than getting this book as a gift.

Another 10.3 million Americans between 50 and 64 were divorced. And these days, more than 50 percent of people who married don't stay hitched for the 10 years needed to qualify for Social Security divorce benefits. In short, lots of people may have benefit pressures and choices similar, if not identical, to the never-hitched.

So let's get down to cases. Say you're single with neither kids nor ex, or you were married for fewer than 10 years and thus have no basis for receiving spousal benefits. In this case, your Social Security choices hinge on the following three questions:

1. When do you want to begin receiving benefits?
2. If you're already getting benefits, might it be worth your while to change your mind?

3. If you do change your mind, what do you do?

MEET PATRICIA D., SINGLE AND 66

Patricia D. of Connecticut turned 66 at the end of 2013. We interviewed her in the spring of 2014. She, like thousands of others, had sent an email to "Ask Larry," the Web feature that began appearing on Paul's PBS Making Sen$e site in the summer of 2012.

Should you ever have thought — before reading "Ask Larry" or this book — that the benefit elections of a single person were simple, or that the advice of Social Security was always clear or accurate, Patricia would have begged to differ. She learned firsthand that her decisions and those of millions of other single persons include challenging issues about not only Social Security but their broader finances, their health, and the type of lives they hope to live.

Here is part of her email to Larry as it appeared on Making Sen$e:

I will be 66 at the end of this month. I will receive my first Social Security check in January. I'm single, never married. When I went to Social Security to sign up, I asked if I could suspend my payment in the next year. I was told that I could but that I would have to pay back all payments that I have received. This is never mentioned in your articles.

Patricia, the folks at Social Security, or both were mixing up *suspending* and *withdrawing* retirement benefits. This is not a hypothetical distinction. If Patricia had not done her homework and, as you will read shortly, stuck to her guns, following the agency's information could have led her to make lifelong decisions that would have cost her dearly.

When you *suspend* benefits, you put them on hold and let them accumulate Delayed Retirement Credits. You have no obligation to repay anything. (You will, however, have an obligation to pay Medicare premiums yourself, because they can no longer be deducted from your now-suspended Social Security payment.)

If Patricia had wanted, instead, to *withdraw* her benefit, then Social Security would have been correct, though she would have had to make this request within one year of beginning to receive payments from Social Security. (Waiting even one day beyond this deadline would have canceled her ability to withdraw her benefit.) So, if she did "withdraw," she would, indeed, need to repay the Social Security benefits she had so far received. Withdrawing and repaying her past received retirement benefits would effectively reset her Social Security status to that of someone who had never filed for retirement benefits at all. Also, this would ensure that she received Delayed Retirement Credits when she finally did begin to collect her retirement benefit. As we suggested in Chapter 3, *withdrawing* is a do-over option after having made a decision, at Full Retirement Age, that you wish to change within a year. *Suspending,* by contrast, is a strategy to be adopted at Full Retirement Age that can be reversed at any time.

Very few people, single or otherwise, withdraw their benefits. First, it can cost a lot of money to repay up to a year's benefits. Second, few people know this right even exists. Third, the reasons that more than 98 percent of people begin claiming Social Security retirement benefits before age 70 are not likely to go away, so most people simply will never consider withdrawing them.

**SOCIAL SECURITY VERBATIM
TOUGHER THAN THE IRS**

"Your personal records showing wages paid to you are not of high investigative probative value."

*ALL QUOTES FROM OFFICIAL
SOCIAL SECURITY RULES*

DOCUMENT YOUR INTERACTIONS WITH SOCIAL SECURITY

It's always possible that Patricia and the Social Security representative with whom she spoke misunderstood one another. This is one reason we urge you to take notes and keep solid records of your communications with Social Security. Sadly, the art of letter writing may be dead. But the benefits of having a written record of your dealings with Social Security could be enormous. If the agency did make a mistake or misunderstood your claiming preferences, putting a time stamp on when you logged your request can lock in a claiming date. To be sure communications are properly logged, go to any Social Security office and formally document your intentions. Or, send a certified letter to the agency, requiring a signed acknowledgment of its receipt.

We spoke with Patricia to make sure we understood her situation. It was clear she had no intention to withdraw benefits, which, after all, hadn't even begun yet. She had been living for decades on a very tight budget. She had continued to work well into her 60s and, in fact, would have continued to work past age 66 had she been able to find a job that paid her enough to allow her to defer collecting her Social Security and watch her Delayed Retirement Credits add 8 percent a year — in today's dollars — to her monthly benefit.

Last decade's Great Recession cost Patricia her last full-time job in 2009, and she spent the next four years working part-time whenever she could. A close reader of Larry's blog, Patricia knew that once she reached Full Retirement Age at 66 she would enjoy two aspects of that milestone: 1) none of her outside earnings would reduce her Social Security benefits, even temporarily, and 2) if she got a job that paid well enough, she could suspend her benefits once she reached FRA and restart them at any time until she turned 70 (when Social Security would automatically restart them for her).

PLAYING THE BENEFITS
WAITING GAME

"What I was doing was waiting to claim until 66," Patricia said. "So, I would begin claiming at 66 and then keep looking for a job. And if I found one, I would then suspend" — her benefit, that is. That was the question that she posed to Social Security.

Despite the bum information, Patricia stuck to her plans and decided not to claim benefits early. Had she begun claiming at age 62, Patricia said, her Social Security benefit would have been $740. When she finally began claiming after she turned 66, her benefit was $1,052 a month.

"And I'm still looking for work but I'm not necessarily focused on getting a full-time position," she explained. "I am looking for something that I would like to do. I am not trying to make the round ball fit into the square box."

Realistically, the idea of suspending is not feasible for her unless she were to get a high wage, she added. In fact, Patricia's income is so low that she qualifies for reduced Medicare premiums and also gets food stamps. Fortunately, she is in good health and her only prescription drug costs $10 for a three-month supply. "From what I get from Social Security I can pay my bills, but I can't buy food."

Because a new job could end her eligibility for food stamps and other forms of government assistance, Patricia figures any new job would have to pay her at least 25 percent more than her Social Security benefit for her to consider suspending and reapplying later.

HOW TO SUSPEND BENEFITS

If Patricia *had* decided to suspend her benefit, however, she would only have had to call, visit, or write her local Social Security office. Here's what the agency has to say, officially:

You do not have to sign your request to suspend benefit payments. You may ask us orally or in writing. [Remember, we prefer writing because it establishes the time of your request. And while the agency doesn't specify sending a certified letter, we think this is prudent.] If your benefit payments are suspended, they will start automatically the month you reach age 70. If you change your mind and want the payments to start before age 70, just tell us when you want your benefits reinstated (orally or in writing). Your request may include benefits for any months when your payments were suspended.

UNDERSTANDING LUMP-SUM PAYMENTS

If Patricia or any other person facing a similar decision suspends her benefits (and, please recall, she can only do this if she has reached FRA, in her case, 66), she should be aware that she could decide later to collect the cumulative value of these suspended benefits as a lump-sum payment should an emergency or the siren song of that bucket-list trip to Bali beckon.

This is nice to know because it means that suspending payments doesn't deny you funds if, for example, you became ill and had an emergency need for cash. By contrast, withdrawing benefits eliminates your option to collect benefits you could have received in a single lump sum. Two points to keep in mind here: 1) it takes time to process this request, so don't expect the funds right away; and 2) if you request a lump-sum payment of suspended benefits, Social Security will treat this as if you had filed for retirement at the retroactive date of your payment request.

What does "retroactive" mean? Well, say Patricia decided before she turned 70 that she wanted a lump-sum payment. Social Security would pay her a lump sum for the number of months from the time she turned 66 to her age when she requested the lump-sum payment. This payment would include any Cost of Living Adjustments that affected benefits during the period.

If she asked for the lump-sum payment because she needed the money, she also would likely ask the agency to begin her monthly benefit payments *in addition to* the retroactive lump-sum income she would receive. The agency would do so but — and here's the rub — her lump-sum payment would be based on the benefits that would have been due her at age 66, not the age when she requested the payment. And her regular monthly payments thereafter also would be based on a claiming age of 66. In other words, she would *lose* any and all Delayed Retirement Credits she had accumulated.

But what if she didn't need *all* that money but, instead, say, just one year's worth? At age 69, she could tell the agency she wanted to resume her benefits as of the age of 68 (remember, they have been suspended since age 66). She would get a lump sum equal to just one year's worth of those payments. But when she started her regular monthly benefits at age 69, she would enjoy two years of Delayed Retirement Credits. That is, her monthly benefit would be 16 percent higher than at age 66. And it's this higher payment that she would receive each month for the rest of her life.

WHY SINGLES SHOULD SUSPEND AT FRA

Now here comes one of those sentences worthy of boldface: **For most people, we advise great caution before filing and suspending benefits.** For married people or those with former or deceased spouses, or with qualifying children (or even parents), suspending Social Security benefits eliminates the ability to claim a stand-alone auxiliary benefit. This is because the act of filing for a retirement benefit, even though you suspend it, can trigger a simultaneous claim for an auxiliary benefit. And, as we've said throughout the book, you can collect only one benefit at a time.

But for singles with no prospects of collecting an auxiliary benefit, such caution can be thrown to the winds, or wherever they're throwing caution these days. Anyone who plans to delay their retirement benefits past FRA to as late as age 70 should look at file and suspend as a free insurance policy.

Otherwise, the most you could get back in retroactive benefits is six months' worth, as we explain in Secret 16, in Chapter 16, "Some Filers Can Get Retroactive Benefits."

Let us summarize with this general advice. If you were never married and are quite sure you won't be getting married before age 70, you should *always* file for your retirement benefit as soon as you reach FRA. If you can wait and want to wait to take advantage of the Delayed Retirement Credit, then suspend your retirement benefit. This will put you in the same boat as not filing-and-suspending when it comes to collecting these credits. But it will also give you the option of collecting all suspended benefits in a lump sum should an emergency arise.

HOW TO WITHDRAW BENEFITS

If Patricia instead got a terrific job and could afford to withdraw the benefits she began at age 66, she has until the day before her 67th birthday to do so. A *withdrawal* does require a form — SSA-521. Call Social Security to have one mailed to you or enter SSA-521 in an Internet search engine and you can print out your own. Compared to other SSA forms, this one is a snap.

The only open-ended information required on the form is its request that you provide a reason for your decision. There are only two boxes — the first says you are withdrawing because you intend to keep working. It also has what we'll call a "heads-up" notice: "I have been advised of the alternatives to withdrawal for applicants under FRA and still wish to withdraw my application." This is bewildering, as the only alternative we know of is simply to continue receiving benefits. Remember that the only other choice — *suspending* benefits — is not available to a claimant until FRA.

If Patricia *does* withdraw, she needs to repay all her benefits, including any Medicare premiums. If she was or had been married, or had qualifying children, any benefits any of these folks received on her record would also need to be repaid.

And finally, if she does withdraw, she must reapply for benefits when she wants them to resume. Social Security will *not* automatically restart them, even when she turns 70.

14
HIDDEN BENEFITS
FOR THE DISABLED

Just as Social Security has become the dominant source of income for most older Americans, so has it become the nation's default welfare program. Neither role was part of the agency's founding mission, which envisioned Social Security as a modest source of supplement income to augment people's savings and pensions. Yet here the program finds itself, some 80 years later, paying out benefits under two programs to more than 20 million disabled Americans. That's a huge number in its own right and even more so considering how many additional lives and livelihoods are affected by the $200 billion in annual benefits the disabled receive.

It used to be otherwise. More than 14 million Americans were dependent on federal welfare as recently as 1993, when President Bill Clinton took office. But with his vow "to end welfare as we know it" and the advent of welfare-to-work reform, welfare now provides benefits to barely *4 million* Americans, though the US population has increased by 60 million since 1993. The tax code has helped a lot here. Refundable tax credits totaled about $150 billion in 2013, nearly all to low-income households. And then there is "disability."

Supplemental Security Income (SSI) and Social Security Disability Insurance (SSDI) compensate for the disappearance of traditional welfare. SSI is for disabled adults, older Americans, and disabled children with limited incomes and resources. SSDI is hardly welfare in the classic sense but nonetheless a huge support program, available to workers who are certified as disabled and who have logged the requisite "covered" work under Social Security rules, which we'll relegate to an endnote, quoting the official language.[1] (Even if it's not relevant to you or yours, you might take a look to reassure yourself that you'd rather be reading our prose than that of the Social Security Administration.)

There were nearly 8.3 million SSI recipients as of August 2014, including 1.3 million under the age of 18, 4.9 million aged 18 to 64, and 2.1 million who were 65 or older.[2]

Total SSI payments are now projected to be well north of $60 billion a year, and the average monthly payment is approaching $550. The number of SSI recipients has doubled since 1985 and began a sustained rise in the 1990s. Even the end of the Great Recession has not ended the annual increases.

SSDI is different: a distinct program is available to all disabled persons who qualify. Its ranks have swelled as well. The agency projects it will pay out between $150 billion and $160 billion in annual SSDI benefits, more than 90 percent to disabled workers and the rest to their children and spouses.

There were nearly 11 million SSDI recipients as of August 2014. As with SSI, the numbers of SSDI beneficiaries has been steadily climbing, mostly due to the general aging of the population. The recession also drove more people to seek disability payments because of job losses and family economic pressures.

It should be noted that when it comes to qualifying for the programs, neither SSI nor SSDI is a slam dunk. Barely a third of disability claimants are accepted into the programs when they initially apply. Many of those turned down hire lawyers to appeal their denials. But though the success rate for "reconsideration" varies drastically by state, the national average was barely 13 percent as of a few years ago. Fraud remains a serious problem, although some claim it is not as acute as in the past.

Are recipients scamming the system? It depends what you mean by *scamming*. More than a few seem to exaggerate or even feign symptoms in order to qualify, as the sharply differing rates in percentage of "disabled" by state suggests. Theoretically, it could be the case that inhabitants of the so-called "disability belt" (Appalachia, the Mid-South, and the Mississippi Delta) become physically or mentally unable to work at double the rate of a state like Utah, for example, or that back problems have become far more disabling than in the past, as the data now indicate. A simpler explanation is that in poor states and a difficult job market, more people are functionally unable to find work, for *whatever* reason. And remember, fewer than half of applicants actually wind up getting benefits.

But regardless of whether or not you think *you* might be less generous were you doling out disability money for the Social Security system itself, as things stand, disability programs are a big and growing expense. And while a dedicated part of Social Security payroll taxes go to SSDI programs, it is scheduled to run short of money in 2016. Even our divided Congress cannot continue to ignore this funding shortfall.

On the assumption that this chapter will be read primarily by those who might qualify for SSDI, because of their work record, and are not among the indigent disabled who have rarely or ever been able to work (SSI recipients), the rest of this chapter concerns SSDI strategies. SSI deserves a book of its own. Understanding Social Security's treatment of the disabled matters to more than 20 percent of households. Indeed, it may eventually matter to many of today's 140 million nondisabled workers, given the considerable odds that they or their spouses someday will become disabled.

Those receiving Social Security disability benefits enjoy 9 advantages relative to other covered workers, but they are also subject to some bad-news provisions. First the good news.

ADVANTAGE 1 — EFFECTIVELY TAKING RETIREMENT BENEFITS EARLY WITH NO REDUCTION

Workers who qualify for disability benefits are able to receive them through Full

Retirement Age. At that point they formally convert to the worker's full retirement benefit. The conversion doesn't change the amount of the benefit, just its name.

If the same-size benefit is being called a full retirement benefit after FRA and a disability benefit before FRA, we can just as well say that disabled workers are able to receive their full retirement benefit throughout all the years of their retirement benefit eligibility that is, from age 62 onward.

This fact, that disabled workers can receive retirement benefits (even if they are called disability benefits) early (between 62 and FRA), *but subject to no reduction,* is an advantage — a big one. Indeed, for disabled workers now reaching 62, their benefits from age 62 through the ends of their lives are one-third larger than would be the case for a nondisabled worker with the same full retirement benefit who takes retirement benefits starting at age 62.[3]

ADVANTAGE 2 — THE DISABLED AREN'T SUBJECT TO DEEMING

Disabled workers collecting their benefits before their FRA aren't deemed to be filing for their spousal benefit even if their spouse has already filed for retirement benefits. This exemption carries over to divorced disabled workers. Disabled workers thus aren't forced to take the larger of their disability and spousal (or divorced spousal) benefits prior to reaching full retirement.

ADVANTAGE 3 — WITHDRAWING BENEFITS ENABLES THE DISABLED TO MAX OUT AUXILIARY BENEFITS

Even though they can collect just their auxiliary benefit from FRA through age 70 (while letting their own retirement benefits grow), disabled workers need to do something special — *they need to file form 521 and withdraw their retirement benefit.*

If they don't withdraw their retirement benefit (see Chapter 3 for details), their disability benefit will automatically convert to their retirement benefit, at which point they can no longer take an auxiliary benefit (a spousal or a widow[er] benefit) by itself while letting their own retirement benefit grow. (Note that *suspending* your retirement benefit won't do the trick here; it is not the same as *withdrawing* it.)

You can only withdraw your retirement benefit beginning 4 months before your FRA, and up to 1 year after. But waiting more than 6 months beyond FRA to withdraw can cost you in terms of your ability to collect all of your auxiliary benefits in the first year after reaching FRA. Social Security will pay benefits taken after FRA retroactively, but only up to a maximum of 6 months.

(The relevant auxiliary benefits here are spousal, divorced spousal, widow[er] and divorced widow[er] benefits.)

ADVANTAGE 4 — OLDER SPOUSES (AND EXES) CAN COLLECT SPOUSAL BENEFITS EARLIER

The conditions under which spouses, ex-spouses, and children of disabled workers can collect auxiliary benefits based on the work record of the disabled worker are the same as in the case of retired workers, with one exception: the spouse or ex-spouse who is at least 62 can collect a spousal or divorced spousal benefit regardless of the age of the disabled worker.

ADVANTAGE 5 — THE DISABLED CAN TAKE EXCESS SPOUSAL BENEFITS EARLY AND STILL GET A FULL BUT REDUCED SPOUSAL BENEFIT AFTER FULL RETIREMENT WHILE LETTING THEIR OWN RETIREMENT BENEFIT GROW THROUGH AGE 70

As we pointed out in Advantage 2, the disabled aren't subject to deeming. This

300

means that if their spouse has filed for a retirement benefit, they aren't forced to take their spousal benefit early at a reduced rate. But here's a nice twist.

Those on disability can take their excess spousal benefit early and then, when they reach their own Full Retirement Age, withdraw their retirement benefit. But here's the advantage: they don't have to pay back the excess spousal benefit because it's a "disability" benefit, not a "retirement" benefit.

So why "withdraw" instead of "suspend"? Because withdrawing clears the slate, preventing the disability benefit from automatically converting into a retirement benefit. It's as if they're starting from scratch. So they can file for a full spousal benefit at their FRA while letting their own retirement benefit grow through age 70.

This advantage is subject to one arcane gotcha, however: the full spousal benefit will be hit with the early spousal benefit reduction factor because they took their *excess spousal benefit* early. And that's as simple as we can make it.

ADVANTAGE 6 — THE DISABLED CAN TAKE REDUCED WIDOW(ER) BENEFITS STARTING AT AGE 50

If you're receiving a disability benefit and your spouse (or ex-spouse of 10 or more years) has passed away, you can collect reduced widow(er) or divorced widow(er) benefits 10 years earlier — at age 50, not 60 — than if you aren't disabled. Furthermore, there is no additional reduction for taking the widow(er) survivor benefit starting at age 50 or at any other age before age 60.

There is a condition attached to this advantage, however. You have to become disabled within 7 years of your spouse's death to take your disabled widow(er)'s benefit between ages 50 and 60. But — surprise! — there's a condition: if you were entitled to collect a mother's benefit after your spouse died (because you had a child under 16 or a disabled child of your deceased spouse in your care), the 7-year clock won't start ticking until you stop collecting that benefit.

ADVANTAGE 7 — ONCE DISABLED WIDOW(ER)S REACH FULL RETIREMENT, THE EARLY WIDOW-BENEFIT REDUCTION GOES AWAY

Let's assume you become disabled before your spouse died and take your disabled widow(er) benefit starting early, indeed as early as age 50. If so, when you reach FRA, this benefit no longer will be reduced even though you began taking it early. However, if your deceased spouse began taking *their* retirement benefit early, the amount you receive will be affected by the RIB-LIM provision we explained in Chapter 3.

ADVANTAGE 8 — SPECIAL RIB-LIM FORMULA FOR DISABLED WIDOW(ER)S

Survivor benefits for a disabled widow(er) whose spouse took benefits early are calculated using a special formula that can be more generous than if the widow(er) was not disabled. The formula includes complex RIB-LIM calculations that should be discussed with a Social Security Technical Expert.

ADVANTAGE 9 — YOU DON'T HAVE TO WORK SUPERLONG OR EARN LOTS OF MONEY TO QUALITY FOR DISABILITY BENEFITS

The rules for disability benefit eligibility are quite demanding. They are less strict if you are younger, however. For example, someone who is disabled prior to age 25 can collect disability benefits with only 6 quarters of covered earnings. For middle-aged workers, the requirement is 20 quarters of covered work out of the prior 40 quarters (ending with the quarter in which you become disabled) and having accumulated sufficient overall quarters of coverage to obtain fully insured status. Obtaining fully insured status doesn't require the 40 quarters that would apply to nondisabled workers. Another key point: you can obtain more than 1 quarter (indeed, as many as 4 quarters) of coverage in a given quarter simply by earning enough money in that quarter.

SOCIAL SECURITY VERBATIM
THE DEFINITION OF A
CIRCULAR DEFINITION

"What does actually paid mean? Actual payment occurs when you are actually paid. . . ."

ALL QUOTES FROM OFFICIAL SOCIAL SECURITY RULES

BUT, AS ALWAYS WITH SOCIAL SECURITY, DANGER LURKS

So much for the advantages. But they assume you're doing everything right. And keep in mind that SSDI benefits are often reduced because of worker's compensation payments and public disability benefits. So, if you've received them, be aware that they might reduce your SSDI payments. Here's one other very big thing to watch out for:

A TRULY NASTY FAMILY MAXIMUM BENEFIT FOR DISABLED WORKERS

Disabled workers face a different and potentially far more restrictive formula for the Family Maximum Benefits (FMB) available to themselves and their qualifying children and spouses. For nondisabled workers, as we told you in Chapter 3, the FMB ranges from 1.5 to 1.87 times the worker's Primary Insurance Amount.

But for disabled workers it's the smaller of 1.5 times the disabled worker's PIA and a second amount. This second amount is, itself, the larger of two numbers, namely 85 percent of the disabled worker's Average Indexed Monthly Earnings (AIME) and the disabled worker's PIA.

The real problem, however, is that for many disabled workers who were low earners, the FMB will end up equaling just the worker's PIA and not a penny more. This means that the child and child-in-care spousal benefits available to children and spouses will be *zero*! This seems unfair and heartless to our disabled citizens and their families.

Now disabled workers between ages 62 and FRA who are in this situation could opt to take their reduced retirement rather than disability benefits. This would raise their family benefit max during those years. But doing so would entail forfeiting the right to withdraw their retirement benefit and receive just a spousal benefit while letting their own retirement benefit grow.

To try to make some of this concrete, here

are a few examples.

DISABILITY HITS THE JONESES

Ted and Martha Jones know, unfortunately, all too much about disability. Ted became disabled at 45 due to a traffic accident. Although he can't work, his life expectancy hasn't changed. Ted's now 65 and Martha's 62. Ted's collecting $2,000 per month in disability insurance benefits. Martha is thinking of applying for her retirement benefit right away and waiting until FRA to collect her spousal benefit. Her full retirement benefit is $1,250 per month.

What Martha wants to do and can do are two different things. If she files for her retirement benefit, she'll be deemed to be filing for her spousal benefit as well. The reason is that for purposes of deeming, Social Security treats a spouse (Ted in this case) who is over 62 and is collecting disability benefits as having filed for a retirement benefit.

If Martha follows her plan, she'll receive only her retirement benefit. That's because her excess spousal benefit will be zero, since her spousal benefit is *less* than her own retirement benefit. For spouses of disabled workers, the excess spousal benefit is the difference between half of the disabled

307

worker's disability benefit and 100 percent of the spouse's own full retirement benefit. For Martha, this amount is negative, wiping out her excess spousal benefit entirely.

If Martha follows her game plan and Ted continues to receive his disability benefit after reaching FRA — at which point it will be called a retirement benefit — the couple would have lifetime benefits of $915,551, using a current longevity table like the one on p. 300.

But they can do better. At FRA (66 in this case), Ted can withdraw his retirement benefit and start it up again at 70 at a 32 percent larger value, after inflation. And Martha can wait until FRA and collect a full (as opposed to an excess) spousal benefit through age 70 and then switch to her retirement benefit. This strategy would produce $244,979 more in lifetime benefits!

DISABILITY HITS THE SMITHS

Lisa Smith is disabled, age 62, and is receiving $500 per month. Her husband, Bill, is 66, meaning he has just reached FRA. He has a $3,000-per-month full retirement benefit. Lisa's projected lifespan is relatively short: age 75. Their plan is to have Bill wait till 70 to collect his highest possible retirement benefit of $3,960.

But they can do better. Bill can file and suspend, thus permitting Lisa to get an excess spousal benefit of $700 a month through FRA. This will raise her total check to $1,200 per month.[4]

15
GOVERNMENT PENSIONS AND WINDFALL PENALTIES

Millions of people work or have worked at jobs that are not covered by Social Security laws; many state and local government employees, for example. They don't have to worry every year about those relentlessly rising FICA payments listed on their W-2s or, for the self-employed, the substantial FICA contributions on their tax returns. Lots of these folks, however — at least a million and a half — also work or have worked at different jobs that *are* covered by Social Security. More will do so in the future. And even if they haven't, perhaps their spouses have, or will.

From this fact flows a question: where a person's work history involves both non-covered *and* covered employment, how are their Social Security benefits affected? Those of their spouses? Their children?

Not to worry. As we've seen in about every other realm of working life, Social Security has programs and rules for these situations. They are covered in the Windfall Elimination Provision and the Government Pension Offset, which we'll be calling WEP and GPO. These rules are meant to produce a rough degree of fairness in the treatment of people who have earned retirement pensions from work not subject to Social Security payment taxes, as compared with those whose pensions do stem from such covered employment. Like much else, this is another situation where Ricky Ricardo might say, as he is credited with telling his wife on the *I Love Lucy* show, "Social Security, you have some 'splaining to do!"

As we've emphasized, the formula used to determine the Primary Insurance Amount is very progressive. This means that lower-paid workers get a Social Security retirement benefit that represents a much higher percentage of their pre-retirement earnings than do more highly paid persons. The PIA (see Chapter 3 for more details) is calculated by dividing a worker's lifetime average covered earnings into three pieces separated by two bend points. It then credits lower earnings amounts by much higher percentages than higher earnings. In 2015, the PIA included 90 percent of the first bend point (up to $826 of average monthly earnings),

32 percent of the next $4,980, and 15 percent of any amount higher than this. Thus, the less you earned, the greater the percentage of your total earnings that are replaced by Social Security benefits.

Fine and dandy, perhaps, but this created the problems that spawned the WEP. People who earned plenty of *non-covered* income might have *covered* income as well — but not that much of it. Yet they would benefit from the progressivity adjustment as if they hadn't earned much at all. Social Security would, and did, treat them as lowly compensated earners and rewarded them accordingly with very progressive PIAs, even if they had a boatload of non-covered income.

An *unfair* windfall, you might say.

GETTING WEP'D OUT

And so, the major Social Security reforms of 1983 included the Windfall Elimination Provision — the WEP — to cancel out the progressivity adjustment for people it was never aimed to help. It did so by modifying the formula for calculating the PIAs of such people. For people subject to the WEP, the 90 percent adjustment that had been applied to the first bend point became *40* percent instead.

WEP applies only to the first bend point,

since that's where almost all the benefit is in the progressivity adjustment. Remember, the first bend in 2015 comes at $826 of Average Indexed Monthly Wages. Before the WEP, beneficiaries would get 90 percent of that: $743. Reducing that to only 40 percent gives you only $330 — $413 a month less. So, this is the most that *you* can lose due to the WEP. But auxiliary benefits based on your earnings record — for spousal, divorced, child-in-care spousal, and child benefits — are also affected.

Fortunately for those affected, there are other factors limiting the WEP.

First, you can lose only up to half of your Social Security pension from non-covered earnings. An example will make this clear. Say your non-covered pension is $600 a month. Under the WEP, your Social Security benefits can't be reduced by more than half this amount, which is $300. So even though the WEP could potentially reduce your benefits by up to $413, they actually will be reduced by only $300 — half of your non-covered pension.

Next, in its continuing quest for fairness, the agency figured that the more years someone spent in covered employment, the smaller the impact of the WEP should be. So, regardless of how large your pension from non-covered employment might be, you wouldn't be penalized if you made Social Security tax payments for a long enough period of time. At a maximum, there's no WEP effect at all if your work record includes a full 30 years of substantial covered employment, and there's a sliding scale for the WEP reduction, in percentage terms, depending on how many years of *substantial* covered earnings you've logged.

Years of Substantial Earnings[1]	Percentage Adjustment
30 or more	90 (no WEP impact)
29	85 percent of WEP applies
28	80
27	75
26	70
25	65
24	60
23	55
22	50
21	45
20 or less	40 (maximum WEP impact)

Source: Social Security Administration.

Using this chart is anything but simple. If the WEP applies to you, you'll need to access your official Social Security earnings record, see whether each year of covered earnings officially qualifies as "substantial," figure out how many years of substantial earnings you have, and then determine what percentage the agency will use in determining your benefits under the WEP. Larry might say this is bedevilingly difficult and a good example of Social Security's extravagant and unnecessary complexity. Paul would chalk it up to the inevitable tangle of a rules-based system trying to be as fair as it can. Phil sees both of their points.

BACK TO THE WEP RULES THEMSELVES

But you're presumably more interested in the particulars than our value judgments about them, and so there's another set of WEP rules that may apply to you and yours. Since the WEP reduces your PIA and thus your retirement benefits, it will, while you are alive, *also* reduce benefits to anyone else who stands to collect benefits based on your record. The good news, if you want to call it that, is that the WEP does not reduce the benefits of your survivors when you die. That first bend point of your earnings base is automatically reset to 90 percent.

We've already explained how much Social Security likes calculators, offering four different ones for figuring out retirement benefits (which don't always agree with one another). You may be excited to learn that the agency also has not one but two calculators to estimate WEP benefits — simple and detailed. The simple one is located online at http://www.socialsecurity.gov/retire2/anyPiaWepjs04.htm. It resembles the Online Calculator for regular Social Security benefits (http://www.ssa.gov/retire2/AnypiaApplet.html) but has added a place to enter the amount of any non-covered pension payments. It then calculates the WEP reduction in determining your Social Security benefits. The detailed WEP calculator actually is the identical calculator used to determine regular benefits (http://www.ssa.gov/OACT/anypia/anypia.html). It includes a non-covered pension choice that is simply left blank for those without a non-covered pension.

All of the things that can affect your retirement benefit — the annual Cost of Living Adjustment, the early retirement reduction, and the Delayed Retirement Credit — are applied to your lower WEP PIA. But be aware that these adjustments are applied to your benefit only after your basic WEP benefit has been determined.

ANOTHER COUNTRY

Here's a situation that may apply to more than a few readers. What if your non-covered pension is from work done in another country — as ambassador to Dristanistan, say? In rare cases like these, WEP reductions to your *Social Security* earnings will still apply. Unless — you'll especially like this wrinkle, we think — you worked in one of the 25 countries with which the United States currently has what is called a totalization agreement. Of course, this being Social Security, these agreements have different rules. In some cases, a non-covered pension based on work outside the United States will WEP you; in other cases, it will not. For example, in Canada, some of your U.S. covered earnings may be credited toward your Canadian pension, and so you may not be WEP'd by that pension. (You can find details and a list of the countries at http://www.ssa.gov/international/agreements_overview.html.)

How big is the impact of the WEP? Consider a 60-year-old minimum wage worker who works only 10 years in covered employment — just enough to qualify for a retirement benefit. Her full Social Security retirement benefit will be about $7,700 if she doesn't collect a non-covered pension and

$3,400 if she collects such a pension equal to $10,000 — close to half her final salary. So being WEP'd would reduce her Social Security benefit by 56 percent.

Now suppose she earns four times as much, but, again, doesn't work in non-covered employment. In this case, her full retirement benefit would be close to $13,400. If she does work in non-covered employment, receiving a $40,000 annual non-covered pension, her full retirement benefit would be cut to $8,500, by 37 percent.

These two cases illustrate two things. First, the WEP can lower benefits a lot. Second, the WEP hits low earners disproportionately hard because it reduces covered earnings only in the first bend-point bracket.

The irony here is not lost on us. The WEP was designed so that people with non-covered pensions and relatively low covered earnings would not benefit from the program's progressivity. Yet the effects of the WEP are felt more heavily by lower than higher earners. We would just remind you that we don't make the rules (and, because we can't avoid piling on, that we hope never to make up rules with such unintended, il-logical, and unfair impacts as some of the doozies brought to us by the SSA).

GETTING GPO'D

Like the WEP, the GPO — the Government Pension Offset — is tied to receiving retirement income from non-covered employment. But it applies to *dependent* benefits, in this case, spousal and child benefits that you and your kids can receive based on the work records of your current or former spouses.

The GPO — enacted in 1977 and amended in 1983 — eliminated a perceived windfall benefit that occurred when a person who worked in non-covered employment was receiving a Social Security spousal benefit based on the covered earnings of a current or former spouse. Before the GPO,

319

the non-covered spouse could receive their own pension *and* all of their Social Security spousal benefit. That would be more, by comparison, than had this person been in covered employment, where they could receive only the greater of their own retirement benefit *or* their spousal benefit.

Like the WEP, the GPO is designed to eliminate what the agency perceived as windfalls to non-covered employees. If you get a pension from a government or other non-covered employer, the GPO says that two-thirds of this amount will be deducted from any spousal or widow/widower Social Security benefit linked to your spouse's Social Security earnings record. If your non-covered pension is based on work in foreign countries, it will not trigger the GPO.

Here's an example provided by Social Security: a person is receiving a $600 monthly government pension and is also eligible for a $500 Social Security benefit as a living or surviving spouse. After deducting two-thirds of their government pension from this amount, or $400, Social Security will pay them only $100. Their total monthly retirement benefit from these two sources thus will be $700, not $1,100. The provision works the same way even if the person takes their government pension in a lump sum. In that case, Social Security will determine what the monthly government pension benefits would have been and make the appropriate deduction from any monthly Social Security payments due to the person based on their spouse's covered earnings record.

There are several exemptions from the GPO related to the timing of non-covered employment and pension entitlement, and the conversion of some government jobs from non-covered to covered status. Further, non-covered employment in foreign countries doesn't trigger the GPO. The relevant details can be found at http://www.ssa.gov/retire2/gpo.htm. When mastering them, may the Force be with you.

THE WEP AND GPO: A RECAP

To recap. If you get a noncovered pension:

The WEP reduces your own Social Security retirement benefits and those of your family members collecting on your work record while you are alive. Once you die, the WEP doesn't affect your family members' survivor benefits.

The GPO reduces your Social Security spousal, child-in-care spousal, widow(er) divorced spousal, mother (father), divorced widow(er), and divorced mother (father) benefits based on the work records of your spouse (current or ex, alive or deceased). The reduction is two-thirds of your non-covered pension. If you take your pension benefits in a lump sum, Social Security will calculate an equivalent non-covered pension and reduce your spousal and survivor benefits by two-thirds of this amount. If two-thirds of your non-covered pension exceeds your benefit, you'll get zero benefit unless and until this is no longer the case.

In short, the WEP and the GPO can add disheartening details to your job of getting Social Security right. So we are ending this chapter with a sextet of approaches to cope with these two challenging acronyms.

MAXIMIZING LIFETIME BENEFITS UNDER WEP/GPO

1. If Possible, Wait to Collect a Larger Non-Covered Pension and Take SS Benefits Early

The WEP and GPO don't kick in until you begin collecting your non-covered pension. So consider delaying your pension's start date, *but only if it will rise in value during this deferral period by enough to compensate for the later start date.* In the meantime, you can collect your Social Security benefits without being WEP'd or GPO'd. Adopting this strategy involves taking your retirement benefit early, which will permanently reduce the benefits available to those whose benefits depend on yours. As we note below in item 4, this caveat is *very* important when it comes to your current or former spouses. Their widow(er) benefits won't be WEP'd after you die, but they will be lower if you take your retirement benefit early.

If your spouse, rather than you, takes their retirement benefit early while deferring their non-covered pension (to delay being WEP'd), you may want to take your spousal benefit before your spouse starts taking their non-covered pension. Recall that your spousal benefit is based on your spouse's PIA. If your spouse delays their non-covered pension, the WEP will not kick in and their PIA will not be reduced by the WEP adjustment. If their PIA is not reduced, of course, this means that your spousal benefit will be higher. If this makes your head spin, as it did ours, we recommend assuming a lotus position and lots of deep breathing. But it is, as they say, a true fact.

2. Once Your Spouse Is WEP'd and GPO'd, Joint Optimizing May Be Less Important

Suppose your husband has a non-covered pension and you don't, and that he's already started taking it. This limits the spousal benefit you can receive from his work record, since his PIA will be WEP'd. It also means that the spousal and widow's benefit he can receive from your work record will be reduced, if not eliminated, since these benefits will be GPO'd. Furthermore, if he dies after you start taking your retirement benefit and your own benefit exceeds your widow's benefit, which is based on his work record, you'll never collect a widow's benefit.

In this case, where there is little he can collect off you and little or nothing you can collect from him, there may be scant reason to coordinate your Social Security decisions.

3. Accumulate More Years of Covered Earnings to Limit or Avoid the WEP

Take a 60-year-old with 10 years of covered earnings who makes four times the minimum wage. If she works 20 years, not 10, her annual full retirement benefit rises from $8,500 to $17,000! In terms of lifetime benefits (measured as a present value as of age 60), this represents almost a $200,000 increase. And if she squeezes in a full 30 years in covered employment, she'll have enough substantial earnings to avoid the WEP entirely and end up collecting $27,000 per year or more than $420,000 in extra lifetime benefits as of age 60.

4. If You Have a Young Spouse and Are Being WEP'd, Waiting Till 70 to Collect Your Retirement Benefit May Beat Approach #1

Roughly 1 in 5 married men are married to women 6 or more years younger. There is also a significant life expectancy difference in favor of women. If, for example, you are a 60-year-old male and your wife is 52, you can expect to die 14 years before she does.

If she's had a low earnings history and you've had a decent amount of covered earnings, waiting till 70 to collect may be the best way to maximize your joint benefits. This is particularly the case if you have a medical condition that makes your early demise relatively certain. By waiting to collect, you'll be able to bequeath the highest possible widow's benefit to your wife.

But, again, this is tricky. If her own retirement benefit exceeds her widow's benefit and you die after she's age 70 and is taking her own retirement benefit, she'll never collect a penny of her widow's benefit. Why not? Because she'll receive the larger of her own retirement benefit and the widow's benefit.

If you can count on dying before your eight-years-younger wife was, say, at FRA, she could collect the widow's benefit through age 70 and let her own, larger, retirement benefit keep growing. But while death and taxes are the only sure things in life, you generally can't count on dying young.

This discussion assumes that approach #1 — taking Social Security before your non-covered pension begins — is feasible. If your non-covered pension starts, say, at 62 and there is no option to let it grow and take it later, you are going to be WEP'd no matter when you start collecting. In this case, waiting until 70 to maximize your retirement benefit will likely be best.

5. Even If You Are Currently Fully GPO'd, Consider Filing for Your Spousal and Widow(er) Benefit

Be aware of whether your non-covered pension has cost-of-living adjustments each year, as does Social Security. If it doesn't, then the impact of the GPO may decrease over time. This is because the inflation-adjusted value of your pension will decline compared with your Social Security benefit. The GPO, recall, subtracts two-thirds of your non-covered pension from your auxiliary Social Security benefit. But if your non-covered pension is fixed in dollar terms, what's being subtracted will also be fixed in dollar terms. Meanwhile, your auxiliary benefit will, in dollar terms, rise through time thanks to Social Security's annual COLA. Hence, even though you may receive no auxiliary benefit initially, over time it may become positive. Yes, we know it may be time to assume the lotus position again.

6. Taking Your Non-Covered Pension Early May Be Best

Say you are 55 and have the option of taking your non-covered pension now or waiting to take a larger benefit later. Also say you have a decent amount of covered earnings under your belt. In this case, taking your non-covered pension early has some advantages in terms of getting more from Social Security.

Remember that the WEP can't lower your PIA by more than half your non-covered pension. And if your non-covered pension is smaller, this can limit the amount of damage inflicted by the WEP. Also remember that your auxiliary benefits from current and former spouse (alive and dead) will be reduced by two-thirds of your non-covered pension. But if your non-covered pension is smaller because you've decided to take a smaller sum for more years, the impact of the GPO will be smaller and less damaging.

16
50 Good-News Secrets to Higher Lifetime Benefits

You could say that the first edition of this book was a post Larry submitted several years ago for Paul's *PBS NewsHour* daily blog: Making Sen$e. In it, Larry simply listed 34 Social Security "secrets" he'd come across in his years of researching the system while designing maximizing-benefits software. The post drew several hundred thousand readers. This response prompted Paul to propose that Making Sen$e solicit questions from the public for Larry to answer. The "Ask Larry" Q&A column has been featured each Monday ever since.

In the meantime, the list of "secrets" has swelled to an even 50. We print it for the first time here, knowing that many people may not have the energy or inclination to read a whole book, but that lots of people will use a good, quick list to get their bearings. Also, we figure that pretty much everyone enjoys a treasure hunt. So consider this the optimist's approach to Social Security: an engaging search for the path to optimal lifetime benefits.

It is also a *unique* path, because what's best for any given household critically depends on a host of variables: that household's specific marital status, age(s), covered earnings histories, projected course of future covered earnings, presence and ages of children, disability status of children, maximum age(s) of life, pensions from non-covered employment, and other factors.

In fact, there are so many combinations of these factors that it's impossible to consider them separately, even in a book like this one. That's why Larry's column continues to draw a flood of questions, nearly three years after it began in mid-2012.

The best we can do is provide more or less general rules, the most important specific strategies, key clues for finding your unique Social Security Easter (nest) egg, and case studies illustrating specifically how to get what's yours. But part of aiding your treasure hunt is to take you into the weeds and point out some very nitty-gritty but extremely important secrets, many of which you'll never likely learn on your own. So here's our latest and greatest list. For those who have paid close attention up till now, consider it a review or better, read the titles of each secret and see if you now know the answer.

THE SECRETS

1. Don't Assume You Know About All Your Benefits

Social Security has so many different benefits and provisions about these benefits that you may be entitled to benefits you don't even know exist. Or you may be ineligible for benefits you thought would soon be yours.

2. Unless You Ask, You Won't Receive

Social Security doesn't know to whom you are married, whom you've divorced, whom you will divorce, whether your spouse or ex-spouse(s) died, whether you have young or disabled children, whether you are taking care of dependent parents. It knows nothing about your family — absolutely nothing. So if you can collect benefits for yourself based on the work histories of current or former relatives or if current relatives can collect benefits based on your work record, *you must tell the agency.* Furthermore, if your marital situation changes, or a former or current spouse dies and this can affect your current benefits, *you must tell the agency.* Don't expect your benefits to change unless you *tell the agency.*

3. Patience in Benefit Collection Can Pay Off Big-Time

Social Security provides very strong incentives for you to wait to collect benefits. For example, your age-70 retirement benefit is 76 percent higher, after inflation, than your age-62 retirement benefit. Taking much higher benefits for somewhat fewer years can maximize lifetime benefits. And don't focus on the break-even date — it is only one of many dates at which you can die. Worry about the broke date — the date you can't pay all your bills because you took benefits that were too low, too early.

4. So Can the Timing of Benefit Collection

If you are able to collect two benefits, you'll want to take one early and the other later. Why? Because you can't collect two benefits at once, just the larger of the two or something very close to that. By timing your benefit collection, you can take one benefit early while letting the other benefit's starting value grow.

5. There Is No Advantage to Waiting Past 70 to Take Your Retirement Benefit or Past Full Retirement Age to Take Spousal or Widow(er) Benefits

If you wait to collect your retirement benefit beyond FRA (66 these days), it will be increased due to the Delayed Retirement Credit. This credit applies only to retirement benefits and ends at 70. There is no incentive beyond FRA to wait to collect either spousal or widow(er) benefits.

6. There May Be No Advantage to Waiting Until FRA to Collect Widow(er) Benefits

If you are widowed (or were widowed but remarried after age 60) and your deceased spouse took retirement benefits early, there may be no incentive in waiting to collect survivor benefits even *before* you reach FRA.

7. Already Collecting? Consider Suspending and Restarting Your Benefits Later

If you are already collecting your retirement benefit and want to raise it, there may be a way. Between FRA and age 70, you have the option to suspend your retirement benefit and restart it at any time up to age 70. Social Security will add its Delayed Retirement Credit — 8 percent a year or 32 percent for 4 years — to your existing benefit.

8. You Can File and Suspend to Get Benefits for Your Spouse

To enable your spouse to receive spousal benefits, you need to file for your retirement benefit. But you don't need to take your retirement benefit if you file after reaching FRA. You can, instead, *file and suspend* — that is, file for your benefit, but suspend its collection. This way you can wait until 70 to begin taking your own retirement benefit, when it will be at its largest value thanks to the Delayed Retirement Credit.

9. Even If You Suspend, Family Benefits Can Continue

If you have filed for your retirement benefit, but suspended its collection, your unmarried children under 18 (under 20 if still in elementary or high school) as well as your unmarried disabled children (if they are older than 18 and became disabled before age 22), regardless of age, can collect child benefits equal to 50 percent of your full retirement benefit, but subject to the Family Maximum Benefit.

334

10. Start, Stop, Start Can Be a Winning Strategy for Some

If you have an older spouse, starting your retirement benefit early and then stopping it (by suspending it after reaching FRA) and then restarting it at 70 can permit your spouse or a minor or disabled child or both to collect benefits without reducing your age-70 retirement benefit by too much.

11. Married? You Can Get Maximum Spousal and Retirement Benefits

If your husband (wife) files for their retirement benefit (regardless of whether they suspend it), you can, after reaching FRA, file just for a full spousal benefit (half of your spouse's full retirement benefit) and then wait until 70 to collect your largest possible retirement benefit.

12. Survivor Benefits Are More Generous than Spousal Benefits

Apart from any reduction for taking a widow(er) benefits early, your widow(er) benefit will equal at least what your spouse was collecting as a retirement benefit. Child survivor benefits are also larger than child benefits paid to young or disabled children of retired workers.

13. Take Your Widow(er) or Retirement Benefit First?

You can take one benefit early and let the other one grow. Which should you take first? Typically, the smaller of the two.

14. You Can "Repay and Replay," but Only Within One Year

Once you file for your retirement benefit, you have exactly one year — and not a day more — to *repay and replay,* that is, withdraw your benefit and be treated as if you had never yet filed at all. To repay and replay, you must repay all benefits (gross of any withholding for Medicare Part B premiums and federal income taxes) paid to you, your spouse, and your children on your earnings record.

15. You Can Collect Suspended Benefits in a Lump Sum, but at a Cost

After suspending, until age 70, you can request a lump-sum payment of all your suspended benefits: the benefits you *would have received* had you never suspended. But doing so will reset your monthly retirement benefit to the level it was at the time you suspended. And you will not be credited with any Delayed Retirement Credits — the bonus that prompted you to suspend in the first place.

16. Some Filers Can Get Retroactive Benefits

If you are above FRA and you realize that you should have filed in the past for a benefit, you can collect up to 6 months (for most people; see below for exceptions) of that benefit retroactively in a lump sum. Take Sally, a 67-year-old widow who never worked and whose husband died several years ago. Sally just learned she could have started taking widow's benefits at age 66, and that they will not increase if she waits to take them. Sally rushes over to the Social Security office and files. To her partial relief, she learns she lost only half a year's benefits, not a full year's benefits, because she can collect 6 months of benefits retroactively. Taking retroactive widow's or spousal benefits comes at no cost. That's not the case for retirement benefits. If Sally were a never-married worker applying for her retirement benefit retroactively, she'd also get a lump sum payment for 6 months of forgone retirement benefits, but she'd also lose 6 months of her Delayed Retirement Credit. The retroactivity period is up to a year for some but not all claims of disabled persons and their auxiliaries (spouse, ex-spouse, children, etc.). If you think you may qualify for this longer period, make sure you ask Social Security about it.

17. In Most Cases, There's No "Earnings Penalty" for Taking Benefits Early

If you take retirement, spousal, or widow/widower benefits early and lose some or all of them because of Social Security's Earnings Test, Social Security will make up (via its Adjustment of the Reduction Factor) for the loss in benefits starting at your FRA, based on the number of months of benefits you forfeited. This is true whether the benefits lost are based on your earnings record or on your spouse's or whether the loss of benefits reflects you or your spouse being hit by the Earnings Test.

18. But in Some Instances, the Earnings Penalty Is Never Recouped

Benefits that aren't reduced, specifically spousal and mother (father) benefits when there is a young or disabled child in care, and that are lost via the Earnings Test, aren't recouped via the Adjustment of the Reduction Factor because there was no reduction factor applied to begin with. Also, if, after reaching FRA, you start taking a different benefit (switching, for example, from a spousal benefit to your own retirement benefit), the level of that different benefit will *not* be increased to reflect the prior loss — due to the Earnings Test — in the benefit you were receiving.

19. Earnings Penalty Impacts Are Shared by All Beneficiaries off a Worker's Record

If a worker earns enough to trigger the Earnings Test, the reduction in benefits will be apportioned on a prorata basis to the benefits of the worker and the benefits of any family members who are collecting derived from his earnings record.

20. Working Longer May Mean Higher Benefits for You and Your Family

For many of you — and certainly *all* of you who will earn above Social Security's maximum taxable earnings level — the longer you work, the higher will be your Primary Insurance Amount, which determines your own retirement benefit and the auxiliary benefits available to your spouse, ex-spouses, and young and disabled children. This reflects Social Security's Recomputation of Benefits provision that replaces one of your previous 35 highest-earnings years with your latest year's earnings if it's higher. Any new top-35 earnings year, even one occurring when you're 90, will raise your earnings record and thus your PIA and all related benefit entitlements.

SOCIAL SECURITY VERBATIM
THE FAT LADY NEVER SINGS I

"We may always make a new initial determination whenever a change occurs in the factual situation despite how much time elapses from the date of that change."

ALL QUOTES FROM OFFICIAL
SOCIAL SECURITY RULES

21. Only One Spouse Can Get a Spousal Benefit by Itself

Suppose you are 62 and your spouse is at FRA, having not yet filed for his or her retirement benefit. In this case, you can file for your retirement benefit permitting your spouse to file just for a spousal benefit, while waiting until 70 to file for a retirement benefit. When your spouse hits 70 and does file for a retirement benefit, you get the green light to file for a spousal benefit based on their earnings history. But, because you've already filed for a retirement benefit, you can no longer collect just a spousal benefit by itself, while letting your retirement benefit grow. This is true even if you suspend your retirement benefit. If you were the much lower earner and your spousal benefit exceeds your retirement benefit,[1] you too may be able to collect a spousal benefit. And since you'll be trying to collect two benefits at once — your own retirement benefit and your spousal benefit — Social Security will only give you the larger of the two.

22. There's a Family Maximum Benefit Available on Each Worker's Record

There is a Family Maximum Benefit (FMB) that applies to the total benefits to you, your spouse, and your children that can be received on your earnings record. It ranges from 150 percent to 187 percent of your PIA. The exact multiple depends on the level of your PIA. This maximum includes your own full retirement benefit. This leaves only 50–87 percent of your PIA available to be split between your spouse and children regardless of whether you suspend your retirement benefit. But you can raise your Family Maximum Benefit if you keep working and thereby raise your PIA, which determines your FMB.

23. For Disabled Workers the FMB Is Potentially Much Smaller

One of Social Security's nastiest hidden provisions involves the maximum amount of benefits available to a disabled worker and their family while the worker is receiving disability benefits. Social Security uses a different formula for calculating this maximum than it does in the case of workers who have filed for their retirement benefits. The disabled FMB formula is less generous in general and far less generous in the case of low-earning workers. Indeed, the formula for low-earning disabled workers may keep their children and spouse from collecting any benefits whatsoever.

24. Die Early? Kids and Spouses (Including Exes) May Still Get Survivor Benefits

You could die as early as age 28 and still provide Social Security survivor benefits to family members and ex-spouses to whom you were married for 10 or more years based on your earnings record. You need to have worked at least one quarter a year in "covered" employment (periods when you paid payroll taxes to Social Security) for at least six years beginning from the time you turned 21 until your death. More limited death benefits are available if your 6 covered quarters of earnings occurred during a 13-quarter period including the quarter in which you die.

25. Unreduced Child-in-Care Benefits May Be Available at Any Age

If your spouse has filed for a retirement benefit and you have unmarried children of that spouse who are in your care (either under age 16 or disabled, having become disabled before age 22), you can receive a child-in-care spousal benefit at any age. It will not be reduced even if you collect it before FRA. The benefit is half of your spouse's PIA, but may be less due to the FMB. Father and mother benefits, available to surviving spouses with a child in care, are available at any age and are not reduced based on age.

26. Worker's Death Presents New Benefit Choices for Surviving Spouse

If the worker dies, the child-in-care spousal benefit would become a mother benefit if she still has a child in care, and rises to 75 percent of the deceased worker's PIA. If the spouse is aged 60 or older, she has the choice of continuing the mother benefit or filing to receive her widow's benefit. If she does file for her widow's benefit, Social

Security will pay her the greater of the two. If she is below FRA, her widow's benefit may be reduced. In that case, it might increase if she defers taking it, so she will need to evaluate the difference between the two to decide on her best course of action. She may, for example, decide to continue the mother benefit and let her widow benefit increase before filing for it.

27. Child Survivor Benefits Are Larger Than Child Dependent Benefits

The child benefit for a deceased worker is larger than for a retired worker. This is because the benefit for a qualified child of a retired worker is 50 percent of the worker's PIA. But the child survivor benefit is 75 percent of the deceased worker's PIA. A qualified child — a child eligible to collect a child benefit — is defined as any child who is unmarried, under 18, or under 19 and still in elementary or high school, or, if disabled, at any age if disabled before the age of 22.

28. A Different PIA Formula May Apply to Survivors

Surviving spouses and ex-spouses of workers who die at a relatively young age may benefit from a second PIA formula. This formula was designed to help survivors of workers with short earnings histories. It does so by raising the deceased worker's PIA.

29. Worker's Death Frees Up More of Family Maximum Benefit for Survivors

When a working spouse dies, any benefits received by his or her spouse and qualifying children are likely to increase. This is because the worker's benefits are no longer included in the FMB calculation, leaving more room under the maximum for other family members. Moreover, in the case of the death of a disabled worker, the FMB formula itself changes from the one pertaining to disabled workers to the more generous one pertaining to retired and deceased workers.

30. Your Delayed Retirement Credit Doesn't Increase Spousal and Child Benefits

Spousal (including divorced spousal benefits and child-in-care spousal benefits) and child benefits will not rise if you suspend and restart your retirement benefit at a higher level. This is because spousal and child benefits are based on your PIA, not the actual retirement benefit you collect.

31. Your Parents May Be Entitled to Survivor Benefits

Your parents, if age 62 or older and dependent on you for at least half of their financial support, can collect parent benefits on your earnings record after you die. One surviving parent would receive 82.5 percent of your PIA. If both parents qualify and are alive, each would receive 75 percent of your PIA. Both cases would be subject to the FMB.

32. Ex-Spouses May Need to Wait to Collect Divorce Spousal Benefits

If you are divorced, but were married for 10 or more years and are not married, you may be able to collect divorce spousal benefits starting at age 62. However, to do so, your ex-spouse must be at least 62 or receiving disability benefits. Further, you have to have been divorced for 2 years unless she/he has already filed for their own retirement or disability benefit.

33. Divorce Benefits Are Not Subject to the Family Maximum Benefit

Benefits to divorced ex-spouses are not restricted by the FMB and don't affect what your current spouse and children can receive. This secret means that the spousal benefit for your divorced ex-spouse may be higher than for your current spouse.

34. Divorced? Forget about Child-in-Care Benefits Until Your Ex Dies

You cannot get child-in-care benefits as a divorced spouse even if you have your ex-spouse's children in your care. However, once your ex dies, you can receive mother or father divorced surviving spouse benefits based on having a child in care.

35. Divorced? You Can Be Deemed Even If Your Ex Has Not Filed for a Retirement Benefit

Your ex over 62 is treated as having filed for a retirement benefit when Social Security considers whether to deem you when you file for a benefit. So, if you are under FRA, even if your ex has not actually filed for retirement, when you file for either your retirement or your ex-spousal benefit, you will be deemed to be filing for both and will collect only the greater of the two. This also means that both exes can be deemed.

36. Deeming Only Affects One Married Spouse

This one is easier to understand than to explain! For married spouses, as we've explained, deeming occurs when a spouse files for either retirement or spousal benefits before reaching FRA, and automatically triggers the simultaneous filing of the other benefit.[2] But, as we've also noted, you can't file for a spousal benefit unless your spouse already has filed for their retirement benefit. The *aha* recognition here is that, by definition, only one spouse can be the first to file for their retirement. The first spouse to do so thus cannot also be deemed to be filing for their spousal benefit, for the simple reason that their spouse has not yet filed for their retirement benefit.

37. Divorced? Think Before Remarrying

If you get divorced and then remarry, you will *not* be able to receive a spousal benefit based on your ex's work history as long as you remain remarried.

38. Remarrying Can Cost You, Big-Time

If your spouse or ex-spouse (of 10 or more years) dies, you won't be able to receive widow/widower benefits if you remarry, unless you remarry after age 60.

39. Marrying for a Nanosecond Can Pay Off

To get benefits based on your ex's work record, you need to have been married for 10 years. To get spousal benefits from your retired spouse's work record, you need to be married for a year. To get survivor benefits from your deceased spouse's work record, you need to be married for 9 months. But to get mother-father benefits (survivor benefits for spouses with a child in care), you need to be married only for a nanosecond or less. There's also no time requirement for receiving mother-father benefits as a divorced spouse.

40. Multiple Marriages? Multiple Benefit Choices

If you were married to more than one spouse, you can apply for spousal benefits or survivor benefits on the earnings record of whichever ex-spouse provides you the largest benefit. And you can switch at any time and apply for benefits from another ex-spouse. This might easily be the case, for example, if one ex-spouse died and your survivor benefit from that ex was higher than your spousal benefit from a different ex. The size of your new benefit will depend on when you claim it, but a reduction factor applied to one former spouse's benefit *does not apply* to a benefit you collect based on a different former spouse's work record.

41. If Your Spouse Dies Before Collecting Retirement Benefits

If your spouse dies before age 62, a specially calculated PIA will determine your widow/widower benefit. If your spouse dies between 62 and FRA, the benefit will be based on their full retirement benefit. If they die later, the benefit will be based on whatever retirement benefit they were entitled to, including any Delayed Retirement Credits.

42. Delaying Retirement Benefits Can Help Your Survivors

If you make it to FRA, delaying taking your retirement benefit — either by not filing for it or by filing and suspending it — will mean higher survivor benefits for your spouse, as well as ex-spouse(s), whenever you pass away.

43. Taking Retirement Benefits Early Can Hurt Your Survivors

Widow or widower benefits are normally equal to the deceased worker's (assume here he's the husband) benefit at his FRA or, if he dies later than this age, what he was entitled to receive at his death, including any Delayed Retirement Credits. However, if he filed for retirement benefits early, his widow will not receive his full PIA but something smaller based on a complicated formula involving his reduced benefit.[3]

44. Work in Non-Covered Jobs Can Reduce Your Social Security

The Windfall Elimination Provision (WEP) may reduce your Social Security benefit if you receive a pension from work where Social Security taxes were not taken out of your pay, such as a government agency or an employer in another country. The reduction arises through the application of a less generous PIA formula. If, however, you work 30 or more years in covered employment and earn above the substantial earnings amount, currently $22,050, there is no reduction. Furthermore, the reduction is less severe the more years you have substantial earnings in covered employment going from 20 up to 30 such years. There is, however, a limit to the amount of retirement benefits you can lose via the WEP, namely no more than half of the amount of the non-covered pension you receive.

45. Spousal and Survivor Benefits You Might Receive May Also Be Affected by Your Non-Covered Work

Thanks to the Government Pension Offset (GPO) provision, if you receive a pension from work where you did not pay Social Security taxes, your Social Security spousal, divorced spousal, widow, and divorced widow benefits based on any spouse's — current and former, living or dead — covered earnings record are reduced by two-thirds of your pension from non-covered employment. There are exceptions for some non-covered pensions, including pensions based on work abroad (foreign pensions).

46. It May Make Sense to Defer Non-Covered Pensions

Neither the Windfall Elimination Provision nor the Government Offset Provision kicks in until you start collecting your non-covered pensions. Hence it may behoove you to wait as long as possible to collect non-covered pensions, while starting as early as possible to collect your Social Security benefits. This would be the case if your non-covered pension compensates you for waiting to collect by providing a higher payment once you do so.

47. WEP Doesn't Affect Survivor Benefits

The Windfall Elimination Provision does not affect the survivor benefits your former spouse, your ex-spouse (if you were married more than 10 years before getting divorced), and your children can receive based on your covered earnings record.

48. Disability Benefits Automatically Convert to Retirement Benefits at FRA

When a disabled worker reaches FRA, she can withdraw her retirement benefit, and earn Delayed Retirement Credits until she files. If she doesn't do so, her disability benefit will automatically be converted to a retirement benefit and this conversion will be treated as her having filed for a retirement benefit.

49. Disabled Workers Can Collect Just Their Auxiliary Benefits Between FRA and 70

Disabled workers who withdraw their retirement benefits upon reaching FRA can apply just for their spousal, divorced spousal, or widow benefit and receive the full retirement benefit. At 70, they can then collect their full retirement benefit adjusted to reflect Delayed Retirement Credits.

50. Disabled Workers Aren't Subject to Deeming and Receive Special Widow(er) Benefits

Regardless of when they file for disability, workers aren't subject to deeming. They also can collect widow(er) benefits as early as age 50, and receive as much as if they had waited to age 60. There is a reduction if benefits are claimed before FRA, but upon reaching that age, the reduction factor is eliminated for widow(er)s or surviving divorced spouses who were also entitled to disability on their own work records when they began receiving survivor benefits.

17
25 Bad-News Gotchas That Can Reduce Your Benefits Forever

Hidden deep within Social Security's Handbook and Program Operations Manual System are lots of what Larry calls "gotchas." We've collected the 25 worst. Some will be familiar. Others won't. But we present the whole list here, in one spot, for easy reference. Take a look if you want reassurance that you aren't falling into any of the system's traps.

If your blood pressure rises, bear in mind that the folks at Social Security aren't to blame. They didn't design this maddening system, which despite its many deep flaws has done enormous good over the decades for hundreds of millions of Americans. No one at Social Security is trying to get us to make the wrong decisions and end up with lower benefits than possible. But very few people at Social Security know the rules well enough to guide us to the right choices. So, as the old saying goes, forewarned is forearmed.

1. If You Take Two Benefits at Once, You Lose One of the Two

Social Security won't pay you two different benefits at the same time. Instead it will pay you the larger of the two benefits (or something pretty close to this amount).[1] For example, if you are married and take or are forced to take your retirement benefit when you take your spousal benefit, you'll lose your retirement benefit if your spousal benefit is larger. Social Security won't say it has eliminated your retirement benefit. Instead, it will claim it's giving you your retirement benefit plus the difference or *excess* between the two. But, in reality, it has used the spousal benefit to wipe out your retirement benefit. You can receive two different benefits, but not at the same time.

2. Once You File for Your Retirement Benefit, You Can Never Take an Auxiliary Benefit by Itself

The instant you file for your retirement benefit you forfeit *forever* your ability to file for any other benefit just by itself. This is true even if you suspend your retirement benefit.

3. Your Retirement Benefit Will Generally Wipe Out Your Spousal or Divorced Spousal Benefit if Taken at the Same Time

As we discussed in Chapter 3, the formula that takes your Average Indexed Monthly Earnings and turns it into your Primary Insurance Amount — your full retirement benefit — is highly progressive. Benefits paid to lower-paid workers are a much higher percentage of their pre-retirement incomes than is the case for highly paid workers. Consequently, even if you've earned relatively low covered wages during your working life, taking your retirement benefit will likely mean never receiving a spousal benefit because a) taking your retirement benefit keeps you from ever taking another benefit by itself (Gotcha #2) and b) spousal benefits are at best only half of your spouse's PIA, so your retirement benefit will likely exceed your spousal or divorced spousal benefit and, therefore, wipe it out.

4. If You Take Your Retirement Benefit Early (Before FRA), You Can Be Deemed[2] to Be Taking Your Spousal or Divorced Spousal Benefit Early

If you are married, the deeming of spousal benefits happens if your spouse has filed for a retirement benefit at the time you file for your retirement benefit. And if you are divorced, the deeming of divorced spousal benefits happens if your ex is over 62 and a) you have been divorced for two or more years or b) your ex has filed for his or her retirement or disability benefit. If you are deemed, you'll trigger Gotcha #1, meaning one benefit — most likely your retirement benefit — will wipe out the other.

5. If You Take Your Spousal or Divorced Spousal Benefit Early (Before FRA), You'll Be Deemed to Be Taking Your Retirement Benefit Early

Many people think they can collect a spousal or a divorced spousal benefit by itself before FRA. Not the case. If you act on this misconception, four bad things will definitely or likely happen.

First, you will be deemed to be filing for your retirement benefit. Second, you will get only the larger of the two benefits (Gotcha #1). Third, you will likely never receive a spousal benefit (Gotchas #2 and #3). And fourth, you will have your retirement benefit permanently reduced.

Yes, you can undo some of the damage by suspending your retirement benefit at FRA and start it up again at 70 at a 32 percent higher real (after inflation) level. But this 32 percent kicker coming from the Delayed Retirement Credit will be applied to your reduced retirement benefit, not to your full retirement benefit. So once this gotcha gets you, you are gotten for life.

6. Deeming Dangers for the Disabled

If you are collecting a disability benefit and your spouse tries to collect just her Social Security benefit early, she will be deemed to be filing for her spousal benefits as well. If your spouse takes her retirement benefit early, she won't be able to delay taking a spousal benefit early, which means both her retirement and spousal benefits will be permanently reduced thanks to the early retirement benefit and early spousal benefit reduction factors. Furthermore, she will only receive, roughly speaking, the larger of the two reduced benefits.

7. While You Suspend Your Retirement Benefit, You Can Collect Only an Excess Auxiliary Benefit

You might think you can collect just your spousal, divorced spousal, widow(er), or divorced widow(er) benefit during any months between FRA and age 70 during which you suspend your retirement benefit.

Not true. During the suspension period, you'll receive, depending on your circumstances, just your *excess* benefit. The excess benefit is the difference, if positive, between your auxiliary (spousal, divorced spousal, widow, or divorced widow) benefit and your own retirement benefit. As Gotcha #3 makes clear, the excess spousal and excess divorced spousal benefits are often zero.

8. Only One Spouse in a Married Couple Can Receive a Spousal Benefit by Itself

In order to receive a spousal benefit, your partner needs to file for his retirement benefit. But when your partner files for a retirement benefit, he gets hit by Gotcha #2, meaning whenever he tries to take a spousal benefit, the amount paid out will be approximately the larger of the spousal benefit and the retirement benefit. And, given Gotcha #3, this will likely be simply the retirement benefit. (Note: *both* divorced ex-spouses can collect a spousal benefit by itself.)

9. If You Take Your Retirement Benefit Before Age 70, You May Permanently Reduce Your Surviving Spouse's Widow(er) Benefits

Your surviving spouse's widow(er) benefits may be based on the actual retirement benefit you were receiving when you passed away, so the earlier you take your benefit, the smaller this surviving benefit will be.

10. You Can Contribute to Social Security Your Entire Working Life and Receive Nothing Whatsoever in Extra Benefits

Suppose you start working at age 16 and continue working through FRA. Every week, week in and week out, you and your employer pay 12.4 percent of every dollar you earn in Social Security payroll (FICA) taxes. Also, suppose you earn relatively little in absolute terms and also relative to your spouse. Then you may do best to wait to collect your spousal benefit starting at FRA (spousal benefits don't increase after FRA), assuming your partner has filed for his or her retirement benefit.

At age 70, you file for your own retirement benefit, but now you get hit by Gotcha #1. And if your spousal benefit exceeds your age-70 retirement benefit (i.e., inclusive of the Delayed Retirement Credits), your total payment will continue to equal just your spousal benefit. Yes, Social Security will describe your total check as consisting of your own age-70 retirement benefit plus your excess spousal benefit. But the sum of these two components will just equal your spousal benefit. So you'll get nothing in extra benefits for all the years you contributed. Furthermore, when your spouse dies, you'll collect a survivor benefit based on their earnings record, which will be even larger than your spousal benefit, which is larger than your own retirement benefit.

11. If You Suspend Your Retirement Benefits and Don't Pay Your Medicare Part B Premiums, You May Lose Your Delayed Retirement Credits

Say you're a 62-year old husband and your wife is 66 — at her FRA. You'd like her to be able to collect "free" spousal benefits for four years and wait until 70 to take the highest retirement benefit possible. So you apply for your retirement benefit. When you hit 66, your wife is 70 and is collecting her retirement benefit. So now you say, "Gee, I can apply to get an excess spousal benefit on my partner's earnings record and suspend my own retirement benefit and start it up again at 70." So you apply for your spousal benefit and suspend your retirement benefit

But you're in Medicare Part B and you don't think about paying the Part B premium via a separate payment, since you're used to Social Security deducting the premium from your Social Security payment. Our understanding is that if you don't pay this out of your own pocket, your retirement benefit at age 70 will be no larger than when you suspended it, and you would have given up a positive retirement benefit for four years. As we've said, you are entitled to a lump-sum payment for those four years. But you must file this request before your 70th birthday or you'll be out of luck, and out of money.

12. Get Divorced a Day Too Early and Potentially Lose Tens of Thousands of Dollars in Divorced Spousal and Divorced Widow(er) Benefits

If you get divorced just one day shy of 10 years, neither you nor your spouse will collect a dime in spousal or survivor benefits. But if you wait one more day — just stick it out with the hate of your life for 24 more hours — you and your spouse can qualify for these benefits. For those who don't stay married for the full 10 years, but get close, and divorce not realizing the value of waiting it out, this is a real gotcha.

13. Remarry and Potentially Lose Divorced Spousal Benefits Potentially Worth Tens of Thousands of Dollars

Suppose you stick it out for 10 or more years with the hate of your life, who happened to be a high earner (thanks to your raising the kids). You then divorce the SOB, spend years looking for love in all the wrong places, and finally meet your own true love — an impoverished artist. If you marry your own true love, you will lose your spousal benefits from your ex. Depending on your ex's earnings record and your own, getting remarried can cost you big Social Security bucks over your remaining lifetime.

"The fact that we determine that a claimant meets the requirements for entitlement does not preclude us from making another determination that the claimant no longer meets those requirements at some subsequent date."

*ALL QUOTES FROM OFFICIAL
SOCIAL SECURITY RULES*

14. Remarry a Day Too Soon and Lose Divorcé(e) Widow(er) Benefits Potentially Worth Tens of Thousands of Dollars

You are a 59-year, 364-day-old divorcée who was miserably married to Mr. Big Bucks for 10-plus years until he dumped you for a starlet from *Real Stepford Housewives.* You are standing on the altar having just said, "I do" to Mr. Perfect. Your mother, who wasn't invited, swings open the church door and screams, "Stop, you idiots! You need to wait till tomorrow to get married." But it's too late. By remarrying before age 60, you just gave up your claim to divorcée survivor benefits on Mr. Big Bucks, who has recently been diagnosed with terminal cancer.

15. Working in Uncovered Employment Can Reduce Your Retirement Benefits from Working in Covered Employment

Jobs on which you fork over payroll taxes to Social Security are known as covered employment. Jobs for which you don't — mostly federal and some state and local jobs — are called non-covered employment. If you don't work 30 or more years in covered employment, the formula determining your full employment benefit (PIA) from covered employment becomes less and less generous (up to a limit) the longer you work in non-covered employment. This is called the Windfall Elimination Provision (WEP). It was implemented to keep non-covered workers from double dipping, which seems fair. But many non-covered workers may not realize how the WEP works and that you need to work 30 years in covered employment to fully escape its impact. If you are due retirement income from both covered and non-covered jobs, Chapter 15 explains the details you need to know to make smart claiming decisions.

16. Working in Non-Covered Employment Can Mean Reduced Spousal and Child Benefits for Your Spouse and Child, Even If Your Spouse Never Works in Non-Covered Employment

The WEP, if it reduces your PIA, will mean lower spousal and child benefits because those benefits are pegged to your PIA. The WEP does not, however, affect survivor benefits since the PIA for that calculation does not incorporate the WEP reduction.

17. Working in Jobs Not Covered by Social Security That Provide Pensions Can Cost You All or Most of Your Spousal and Divorced Spousal Widow(er) Benefits

If you receive a pension from uncovered work, the spousal, divorced spousal, survivor, and divorced survivor benefits for which you may be eligible based on your current spouse, ex-spouse, deceased spouse, or deceased ex-spouse's earnings record will be reduced by two-thirds of the pension you receive from the non-covered employment. This reduction is called the Government Pension Offset, or GPO.

From a fairness perspective, the GPO can lead to some troubling questions. Take Joe, who is married to Sally, who works in covered employment. Suppose Joe is a good-for-nothing lazy bum who doesn't work a day in his life. Doesn't matter. Joe can collect spousal benefits and survivor benefits on Sally's work record. Now suppose Joe is a good-for-something guy. Indeed, suppose Joe teaches school in a tough district his entire career, but the job isn't covered by Social Security. If Joe gets a decent-size pension from the uncovered job, his spousal and survivor benefits from Sally's work record will be wiped out by the GPO.

18. If You Make a Mistake in Your Retirement Benefit Filing Decision and Wait a Day Too Long to Fix It, Too Bad. You're Stuck

If you file for your retirement benefit, you have one year to withdraw your benefit, that is, to "repay and replay" — pay back every penny of benefits received on your work record (gross of any deductions for Medicare Part B premiums and withholdings for income tax) and start from scratch in making your Social Security collection decisions. If you decided on the 366th day to start over, you're out of luck. Unless it's a leap year, of course, in which case we will have to consult our Social Security rulebook again and get back to you.

19. Suspending Your Retirement Benefits Can Cost You Big Bucks

This gotcha pertains to those whose auxiliary benefit is larger than their retirement benefit even inclusive of the maximum amount of Delayed Retirement Credits that can be accumulated. For these people, the amount by which their auxiliary benefit exceeds their retirement benefit is treated by Social Security as their excess auxiliary benefit.

Now suppose you are in this boat and you suspend your retirement benefit. To do so you have to have filed for it. This immediately puts you into Gotcha #2, where you can't take an auxiliary benefit by itself. But suspending also puts you into Gotcha #6, where during the suspension period you receive just the excess auxiliary benefit. So, during the suspension period, you give up your retirement benefit; that is, you go from receiving your retirement benefit plus your excess auxiliary benefit to receiving just your excess auxiliary benefit.

Is this worth it? Well, when you restart your retirement benefit, say at 70, it will be larger because of the Delayed Retirement Credits you accumulate. But your excess auxiliary benefit will, at that point, be reset to a smaller amount such that your total retirement plus auxiliary benefit is either exactly the same amount as when you suspended or very close to it.

In other words, you would have suspended for nothing, losing potentially thousands of dollars in lifetime benefits. If you realize you made a mistake in suspending your retirement benefit (and seeing no change in your monthly payment is the clincher), you can undo the mistake and recover all your suspended payments. (See Secret #15 in Chapter 16.)

20. The Family Maximum Benefit (FMB) Means That Applying for Additional Benefits on a Worker's Record May Mean No Extra Benefits

The FMB — the most benefits available on your earnings record — is an awful piece of work. It can range from 150 to 187 percent of your PIA. But in order for family members to collect spousal or child benefits, you need to file for your retirement benefit. But since you are tagged for receiving 100 percent of your PIA in retirement benefits, *even if you have suspended your retirement benefit,* this leaves only 50 percent to 87 percent of your PIA available to other household members.

Since the child and spousal benefits available on your work record equal half of your PIA, it can take benefits to only one family member and at most two to hit the FMB. When this happens, the same 50–87 percent of your PIA will be proportionally divided up among your family members. So you may think you are getting an extra benefit for a spouse or a child in having them apply for a spousal or child benefit, but it's coming out of the pockets of your other family members.

21. Depending on Their Level and Your Other Income, 50 to 85 Percent of Your Social Security Benefits May Be Subject to Federal Income Taxation

Earning less than $25,000 ($32,000 for joint filers) in combined income means that none of your Social Security benefits are subject to federal income taxes. Combined income is defined as your non–Social Security income *plus* tax-exempt interest (on government securities, for example) *plus* half your Social Security benefit. Between $25,000 and $34,000 ($32,000 to $44,000 for joint filers), up to half of your benefits may be taxable. Above these amounts, 85 percent of your Social Security benefits may be taxable but never more than this percentage.

22. Social Security Benefit Taxation Rises with Inflation

The thresholds beyond which the first 50 percent and then 85 percent of your Social Security benefits are subject to federal income taxation are explicitly *not* indexed for inflation. Hence, eventually all Social Security recipients will be taxed on 85 percent of their Social Security benefits, assuming the rules don't change.

23. Disabled Workers Who File for a Spousal Benefit Early Can Get Hurt

If a disabled worker files for his spousal or divorced spousal benefit *before* FRA and then withdraws his retirement benefit *at* FRA, he can collect his spousal benefit by itself (i.e., he'll get his full, not his excess, spousal benefit), but the spousal benefit will be hit by the early spousal benefit reduction factor based on when he first started taking spousal benefits.

24. A Special Family Maximum Benefit Formula Can Hurt the Disabled

If you're disabled, Social Security has a special formula for calculating your FMB. It's less generous than the standard formula for many if not most disabled workers. And for those with very low earnings, it's draconian, permitting no benefits whatsoever to spouses over 62, spouses with children in care, or young or disabled children. If you are disabled or have a disabled family member, please read Chapter 14 to find out how to navigate Social Security's rules affecting benefits for disabled persons.

25. *Social Security Can Change Its Rules*

This is the gotcha of all gotchas! Social Security's existing rules give it broad leeway to change its mind. Even if it doesn't, Congress might. There was a proposal from the White House in the 2014 budget to eliminate the file-and-suspend strategy for higher-income households. It was not acted upon, but when broader reforms are put on the table — which we all feel will happen sooner rather than later — many benefit provisions could be changed.

18
WHITHER SOCIAL SECURITY?

We said at the outset that this book would be about how to get what's yours from Social Security, not about its finances or ways we think the program should be changed. We do, however, have strong thoughts about these matters. Here they are, starting with Paul.

Paul

It's as obvious as it is enervating: coauthorship demands compromise. Therefore the book you have just about finished, unless of course you first opened it to this chapter, represents a negotiated settlement. In a first draft, dear friend Larry would rail against the Social Security system, suggesting malign intent, a hopeless future, and general fecklessness. I would recoil at what I considered irresponsible hyperbole, animus, and undue pessimism and would then rewrite. Phil would — well, Phil can and will speak

374

for himself when he gets this chapter's last word.

In the dogged struggle between Larry and myself, there have been two fundamental bones of contention. One: the *reason* Social Security is so damnably complex. Two: woebegone predictions of Social Security's future.

SOCIAL SECURITY WAS DESIGNED TO PROTECT US, NOT TO DRIVE US MAD

Let's start with complexity. Larry likes to say that Social Security was designed to drive us mad. To the contrary, I think it's mad to say such a thing, even in jest.

I can hardly deny that Social Security, like every other piece of complex policy in a large and thus complicated and also thus highly politicized economy, has evolved in ways that are often confusing — bedeviling, even. But so has the tax code. The criminal justice code. Dodd-Frank. Ever scrutinize the Americans with Disabilities Act? Ever wonder what the Talmud was for? Scholasticism? Patriarchal Interpretations of the Quran?

Look, like any thoughtful polity, we're a nation of laws and rights. They're constantly changing with changing times, with changing mores, changing technology. In the process, they become more fine-tuned, more complicated, more gamed, more byzantine, and, as a result, they're frequently infuriating. Simplification would be great and often, perhaps, a stunning improvement. Even with the help of TurboTax, however, filing my taxes remains a humiliating hassle. It's simply a fantasy that laws and policy can simply be made simple.

Tell your neighbor that the right of way through your property is too damned complex to figure out so she can forget about it. Tell someone whose baby has been poisoned by lead paint from an unregulated toy made in China that federal regulations are just too complicated. Offer the same excuse to an investor accused of insider trading. Tell the stockholders of a corporation that's gone bankrupt through dastardly activity that it hid from the public that federal regulations are . . . you get the idea.

American society is often accused of being overly litigious. But is there so much litigation because our rules are deliberately complicated? Might it not be that they are complicated because of our insistence on "the rule of law," our widely heralded international competitive advantage? Our insistence on the ever more finely tuned checks and balances that have made the United States, for all its infamous flaws, the most stable long-standing democracy on earth?

Social Security has evolved in the same way. We write rules. People complain about their fairness, their clarity. So we make exceptions to those rules. That's because we're a large, pluralistic democracy. Those with a stake in the rules put up a fight. That's what they're *expected* to do. The administrators respond, just as *they* are expected to.

To the extent that Social Security is a hard-to-navigate system, it's due at least in part to our constantly balancing what we feel is fair against what we think we can afford — and because writing laws and regulations is really hard, never-ending work.

Personally, I have great sympathy for Social Security's plight, as I do for any government official or agency charged with writing and/or following the laws of the land.

BUT ISN'T SOCIAL SECURITY BANKRUPT?

Larry's second lament has been that both Social Security and America are bankrupt. Why? Because both have failed to account honestly for the promises they have made to current and future generations. These promises are essentially off the books, says Larry. To which I say: no kidding. You mean Americans want benefits, but don't much like paying for them? You mean human beings borrow against the future and then try to maintain a state of denial about their future obligations?

What do we suppose will actually happen with Social Security's promises and Uncle Sam's debt to pay off those promises? Like every other set of unrealistic promises, they will be renegotiated.

The Social Security system is much like other pension programs. When taxpayers on the hook for pension obligations find the burden too costly, they rebel. When they rebel, the rules change. Just look at what's been happening to local public pensions around the country.

In 1981, President Ronald Reagan and Congress appointed a commission to "reform" Social Security, chaired by the man who later became the chairman of the Federal Reserve Bank, Alan Greenspan. The so-called Greenspan Commission was asked "to study and make recommendations regarding the short-term financing crisis that Social Security faced at that time." The words are those of the Social Security Administration today, but the sense of crisis was acute even then.

The commission's recommendations inspired the Social Security Reform Act of 1983, featuring a host of changes, including a delay in cost-of-living benefits; a modest Social Security tax increase; increased tax rates on self-employment income to match what employees of firms have to pay; making up to 50 percent of Social Security income taxable for the first time (a ceiling later raised to 85 percent for higher earners); and eliminating "windfall benefits" for those with a pension from non-covered employment, as we explained in Chapter 15.

Amazingly, Congress then went the commission one better by lengthening the eligibility age for Social Security from 65 to 66, eventually to become 67 by 2027.

The crisis of the moment was averted — by changes that reflected the pressure of unyielding financial reality. That's what's likely to happen again.

Many of us will give a little. Some will give more than others. There will be a huge outcry, as there always is when people are asked to pay more or get less. Maybe members of the House will be besieged by seniors, as Congressman Dan Rostenkowski of Chicago famously was in 1988. (The footage on YouTube is unforgettable.) Seniors will vote to protect their benefits, and yes, there will be more seniors than ever.

But though we'll stub innumerable toes in the process, some way, somehow, we will probably once again kick the can down the road.

How *exactly*? Following the 2005 lead of Nobel Laureate economist Peter Diamond and former Clinton budget director Peter Orszag in *A Summary of Saving Social Security: A Balanced Approach* and the more recent book by Martin N. Baily and Jacob Funk Kirkegaard, *U.S. Pension Reform: Lessons from Other Countries,* I'd bet on some combination of the following:

- raising the Social Security (FICA) tax slightly from its current 12.4 percent total for employer and employee. As the eminent economist Alicia Munnell of the Center for Retirement Research at Boston College has said, a tax hike of another 1.2 percentage points on employers and the same hike on employees would completely eliminate the projected Social Security shortfall for the next 75 years. "We've just had a payroll tax cut of two percentage points," Munnell said when I interviewed her for *PBS NewsHour* in 2013. "I couldn't even tell and then they raised it again by two percentage points and I couldn't tell. There wasn't jubilation when it happened and it wasn't cataclysmic when it went back."

- hiking the ceiling on FICA taxes from today's $117,000, which rises annually, but only at the rate of inflation;
- making 100 percent of Social Security benefits income taxable;
- lengthening the retirement age gradually, in line with increased longevity and career spans;
- tinkering with the cost-of-living adjustment to lower it a bit;
- lowering benefits for better-off Americans by what financial expert Robert Pozen has proposed: "progressive indexation";
- increasing immigration because immigrants tend to be younger and thus pay Social Security taxes for decades while not collecting benefits;
- encouraging more Americans to continue to work later in life, and thus

continue to pay more and more FICA taxes;

- finally, if the tech futurologists are right, there will be a surge in economic growth that would bring in enough taxes to make the system whole.

As it happens, President Obama has already mentioned the cost-of-living adjustment and has hinted at preventing the well-off from taking certain benefits, including perhaps some of the ones we've highlighted in this book.

In fact, after we had finished the manuscript for this book, the Social Security agency's chief actuary issued a report (fall of 2014) on the impact of various program changes proposed at one time or another (or perhaps concocted by the actuary for purposes of discussion or illustration). So, for example, if we changed, starting in 2021, the way in which benefits are indexed — from average wage growth to inflation — the actuary reports that we would not only wipe out the entire Social Security deficit over the next 75 years but build a substantial *surplus*. Indeed, even over the infinite time horizon Larry favors 89 percent of the deficit would be eliminated by this one change alone.

Or we could "maintain current-law benefits for earners at the 30th percentile and below" and change the index from wage growth to inflation for everyone else. That would erase 82 percent of the 75-year shortfall — more than half of the deficit over an infinite time horizon.

Alternatively, according to the actuary, we could increase the normal retirement age three months per year starting for those aged 62 in 2017 until it reaches 70 in 2032 and increase it one month every two years thereafter. Deficit reduction? Sixty percent over 75 years; 48 percent, infinite horizon.

Also on the list: "Apply the 12.4 percent payroll tax rate on earnings above $250,000 starting in 2015," says the actuary's report, "and tax all earnings once the current-law taxable maximum exceeds $250,000." That change would eliminate 75 percent of the infinite horizon deficit. Just phasing in, over the next decade, an increase in the taxable maximum such that 90 percent of earnings would be subject to the payroll tax would eliminate a third of the infinite deficit.

Combine a few of these changes, and Social Security insecurity would become a bugaboo of the past.

Is the Future 75 Years Away — or Forever?

Larry and I differ in another fundamental way about Social Security's solvency. He insists that we use not 75 years, as most do, but an infinite time horizon when talking about the system's "unfunded liabilities" — its promises of future benefits for which money has not been set aside. By that measure, the system is a depth-defying $23 trillion or so underwater.

But I end by again quoting Alicia Munnell, when confronted with Larry's number and infinite time horizon. Her reply?

"When I'm talking about Larry Kotlikoff, whom I love, I need to separate some things that I agree with him on and some things that I don't agree with him on. I think using this trillion-dollar number is not very helpful at all because big numbers happen over a long period of time and other stuff also happens over a long period of time." In other words, things will change — a lot sooner than before we reach the end of the universe.

Larry

Our Social Security system is a disgrace, not in its objectives or in the tremendous help it has provided older people over the years, but in the way it's been designed and the way it's been financed.

Its complexity is beyond belief. The formula for the Social Security benefits of a married spouse involves 10 complex mathematical functions, one of which is in four dimensions! It leads all kinds of people to make all kinds of mistakes in deciding when to take benefits and what benefits to take. That's why we wrote this book — to help people get what's theirs.

Paul, I love you dearly, but you almost fell victim to the system's caprice to the tune of $40,000. I wonder how you would feel today had we never discussed your Social Security strategy and had you then discovered that you'd lost upwards of $40,000 of benefits you'd paid for but didn't know about.

Would you be saying, "No problem. This is the price of democracy"?

I think you'd be outraged, and properly so. But there are people who are losing out every day on their benefits because they can't figure out what they are actually owed and the best way to get what's theirs.

I love our country as much as you do, but I'm not going to wave the flag and say it's perfect. Nor am I going to let pass your suggestion that ours is the longest stable democracy.

Frankly, I don't know when to date the start of our democracy. Is it 1783, when we defeated the British, but kept millions of our countrymen in chains? Or is it the Civil War, when we freed the slaves, but kept half the population from voting? Or was it just a century ago, when women were given the right to vote? Or was it only a half century ago, when the Civil Rights Act was passed and blacks were actually able to vote?

The truth is, our democracy was and is very deeply flawed. Social Security's complexity and fiscal condition confirm this. Democracy is collective choice by the people. But having indecipherable institutions, be they our Social Security system, our tax system, our health-care system, or our financial system, deprives the people of the knowledge they need to make choices. Instead it leaves social choice not to the people but to the bureaucrats, who get to decide what's best.

I say bureaucrats rather than elected officials because our representatives are also at the mercy of the bureaucrats. Indeed, there is, I'd wager, not a single member of Congress with detailed knowledge of Social Security's 1,728 rules or its tens of thousands of rules about those rules. And when it comes to Social Security, the big picture is the sum of all the small pictures.

Bureaucracy is not a sine qua non of democracy. New Zealand is a pretty good democracy from everything I can discern. Its social security system has one rule: You reach retirement age and you get a monthly check — the same check as everyone else.

I'm not advocating New Zealand's system for the United States. Instead, I'm proposing we freeze the current Social Security system and replace it with the Purple Social Security Plan presented at www.thepurple socialsecurityplan.org, which is a remarkably simple, progressive, compulsory saving system. Phil views me as politically naïve for proposing radical reforms like this. But if you look across countries and over time, you see huge changes by governments in their old-age pension systems.

Indeed, radical change in our Social Security system is inevitable for the simple reason that the system is broke — indeed, in worse fiscal shape than Detroit's pensions when that city declared bankruptcy.

My evidence for this?

It's the $23 trillion infinite horizon fiscal gap shown in table 6 of the 2014 Social Security Trustees Report. Paul, you and Alicia Munnell, whom I love dearly, may not approve of looking out to the "end of the universe" in measuring today's Social Security unfunded liability. But that characterization is off base for the simple reason that the fiscal gap is a *present value* measure that more heavily *discounts* the system's future cash flows the further out they are in the future. The reason we need to look out to the infinite horizon fiscal gap is due to an economics labeling problem. This problem exists because government can label its receipts and expenditures in a myriad of ways, each of which changes the 75-year fiscal gap, on which you, Paul, and Alicia, are focused, but leaves the infinite horizon fiscal gap unchanged. The economics labeling problem is the reason that the Inform Act has been endorsed by more than 1,200 economists, including seventeen Nobel laureates (see www.theinformact.org).

The Inform Act mandates infinite horizon fiscal gap accounting by government agencies for the entire fiscal enterprise. My own estimate based on the Congressional Budget Office's Alternative Fiscal Scenario Projections puts the country's overall fiscal gap at $210 trillion for 2014. This is 57 percent of the present value of all future federal taxes, so our federal government, taken as a whole, is 57 percent underfunded. This table shows that Social Security is 23 percent under-funded. Stated differently, we need a 58 percent hike in *all* federal taxes to permit our federal government to meet all its expenditure commitments. And if one focuses just on Social Security, the requisite immediate and permanent tax hike to ensure that Social Security pays all sched-uled benefits is 33 percent!

Paul, I know you love your children and grandchildren more than life itself. But what you seem to be ignoring is that paying for what the government spends is, generation-ally speaking, a zero-sum game. The less our generation pays, the more your own kids and grandkids will have to pay; mine too. And we are moving full speed ahead to leave our kids and grandkids with fiscal bills that are far, far beyond their capacity to pay. This transformation of the American dream into the American nightmare is a terrible act of immortality. Yes, Paul, I know you and Phil feel this will never happen and that small adjustments will be made and that all will be fine. This is Panglossian in the extreme, as a quick glance at Argentina's century-long economic decline confirms. Yes, things that can't go on will stop. But they will stop too late.

Phil

Larry has interesting ideas for replacing Social Security with a fairer and better program. They're never going to happen. We're not going to replace an 80-year-old program that has become an enormous bureaucracy, with rules to match, and that touches the lives of virtually every American.

Can you imagine, for example, that tax reform — if it ever happens — would include replacing or reinventing the Internal Revenue Service? The IRS is a 100-plus year-old creature that has become the giant squid of bureaucracies. Our tax system is so complicated that an army of lawyers, accountants, tax experts, and other financial advisers has become necessary to comply with provisions that are impenetrable to untrained eyes.

And, unfortunately, you can add health care to the list of essential components of an advanced society that are increasingly too complicated to be understood by the public they are supposed to serve.

Such is the nature of national government. It is a major failing of the United States. It is a source of rising public anger and disaffection toward government that weakens our democracy and provides oxygen to the fires that are stoked by antigovernment extremists. It debases political discourse and puts needed political compromises out of reach. This situation is not about the welfare state, nor is it an indictment of the aims of these programs. It is an inescapable truth of complexities — of the systems we've built to govern ourselves, of the technology that has evolved to do so, and of the underlying challenges our social, economic, and political problems present.

LET'S KEEP SOCIAL SECURITY MOSTLY THE WAY IT IS

Still, short of a societal collapse of dystopian proportions, it is impossible for me to see a Social Security program in 50 years that looks a whole lot different from the one we have today. And while Larry and other brilliant and civic-minded reformers might lament this observation, I do not.

We've spent an entire book telling you about the complexities and shortcomings of Social Security. But it's appropriate here to take a big step back from these details, see the larger picture, and, just perhaps, gain some perspective.

Social Security pays out roughly three-quarters of a trillion dollars each year in benefits to Americans. It does so very efficiently and with a cost structure that would be impossible for any private company to match.

It is an economic lifeline for most older Americans. Today, people who are 65 and older have the *lowest* poverty rate of any age group in the nation. Before Social Security was adopted, older citizens had the nation's *highest* poverty rate. It's not the tooth fairy that caused this hugely important shift. It's been Social Security and, for the past 50 years, Medicare.

Social Security retirement and disability benefits (not including the SSI program) have been self-funded and have not added a penny to the US budget deficit. I'm going to spend some time on this topic. It's important and, further, I encounter many well-meaning critics of Social Security who rail about the way it's added to unsustainable budget deficits.

SOCIAL SECURITY
AND BUDGET DEFICITS

Major changes were made to Social Security in 1983 as part of the nonpartisan commission led by former Federal Reserve Board chair Alan Greenspan. The baby boomers were a big deal even 30-plus years ago. We knew then what today's Age Wave would look like. And so the 1983 changes created (among other things and not always on purpose) a funding system for Social Security that has built big surpluses to prepare for the years when millions of boomers would be taking Social Security benefits.

These program surpluses are invested in a special series of US Treasury securities, which have generated interest income to the program. Many books have been written about whether Social Security would have been better off placing its surpluses in non-government stocks and bonds. That's an interesting discussion, to be sure, but the point here is that Social Security did not fritter away its surpluses. That work was done by a succession of shortsighted Congresses and Presidents, who spent the dollars they received from Social Security on other government programs. This is hardly the fault of Social Security, and blaming it for Washington's fiscal besottedness is way off base.

Social Security's self-sufficiency has been essential to its success. Whatever we do, it would be an enormous mistake to commingle its funding with the rest of the federal budget, and thereby expose it to annual political popularity contests. This has been, in fact, what has happened to the Social Security Administration's annual operating budget in recent years. The result has been huge cuts in staffing, a reduction in the numbers of Social Security offices around the country, and a reduction in hours that the remaining offices are open to the public. It is just madness to have done these things to the agency just as its workload was poised to soar, courtesy of the front end of the boomer generation turning 65, at a rate of 10,000 a day during the period 2011–29.

The SSA has responded with a big push to move its services online, to call centers and even to remote video feeds. What choice does it have? But as we explained earlier, online tools have significant limitations. The public served by the agency does not use online tools very much and is not about to become digitally savvy anytime soon. Even if it raised its online IQ a lot, the fact remains that millions and millions of Social Security claiming decisions are too complicated to be made using online tools. So, whatever else we do about Social Security, we must improve the agency's ability to serve the public and to communicate more clearly.

THE HUBRIS OF
FORECASTING THE FUTURE

The standard for evaluating the financial soundness of Social Security and any possible reforms of the program is to evaluate their impact over the coming 75 years. There is nothing magical about 75-year time frames. This is just the one we use for Social Security. Larry and a thousand other economists have signed on to an effort to use an infinite time horizon for looking at the budget implications of Social Security and other government programs. This proposal is worth serious discussion but such debates rarely happen these days in Washington, and this one is no exception.

It turns out that the life span of the 1983 changes will, instead, be closer to 50 years than 75. Program payouts have been sweetened without compensating revenue increases. The projections of economic growth and inflation made 35 years ago have not been flawless. Projections of retirement and claiming patterns were also fallible. And then there was inflation and recession and sluggish growth and, well, you get the picture. Larry says those 1983 reforms fell far short of being an honest look at the ensuing 75 years. Today's huge pressures on old-age benefits caused by the baby boom were well known in 1983, and the reforms could have more honestly anticipated these pressures by some combination of revenue increases and benefit adjustments. But selling even limited reform was a tough task and there was no stomach for more severe changes. As Jack Nicholson famously said in *A Few Good Men,* "You can't handle the truth!"

Similar shortcomings are likely in any politically feasible Social Security reforms today that look at the 75-year window ending around 2090. But it's been known for years and years that Social Security needs adjustments in its mix of benefits and revenues to be placed again on a self-sustaining path. These changes must be gradual to avoid ruining the retirement plans and dreams of people now receiving benefits and approaching retirement age. As an example, recall that the program's Full Retirement Age will not begin rising from 66 to 67 until 2020 — a rule change made more than three decades ago. This is the biggest financial supertanker we have, and its course should not be changed abruptly. Unfortunately, the longer Congress dithers over changing Social Security, the more severe its changes will have to be to prevent the program from running out of money.

Still, there are many, many plausible scenarios for reforming Social Security without either breaking the bank or simply hiking payroll taxes on high-income earners. Higher earners should pay more but those increases shouldn't be the only or even largest source of program revenue changes. The SSA is not the IRS, nor should it be. The broad public support for the program is, in large measure, due to its near universality. Social Security benefits are already designed to be highly progressive, meaning that low-income recipients get payments that replace a much higher percentage of their pre-retirement incomes than do high-income beneficiaries. It's possible to make the program self-supporting through a broad array of benefit, timing, and payroll tax changes.

Among these, we must acknowledge the cumulative and continuing effect of longevity, but not for everyone. Extending the FRA to 68, 69, and even 70 over the next 30 to 40 years makes sense, but people with low levels of education and low incomes are not participating fully in the longevity revolution. The support we provide them at the earliest claiming age of 62 should be strengthened, not weakened. So, anything we do to "reform" Social Security must recognize that longevity gains are not being enjoyed equally.

WE NEED TO FIX 401(K) PLANS, TOO

Lastly, any effort to address the future of Social Security also must address the future of the nation's private retirement savings industry. The 401(k) and its related tax-advantaged retirement savings vehicles have not worked well. Too few people have participated, they have saved too little, and their investment decisions have been unwise. Major improvements have been made to 401(k)s in recent years, and today's plans are producing big improvements on all fronts — participation, savings rates, and investment performance. But these improved results, by and large, are limited to higher-earning employees. The people who need the help the least are thus getting the lion's share of the tax benefits of these accounts, while half of the nation's workers can't even participate in a 401(k) and many of those who could simply do not make enough money to do so.

Private retirement firms have defended their turf aggressively and there is clearly a role for these plans. However, we need to have an honest and serious debate about how we use tax dollars to promote private retirement savings.

And we need to have a *very* serious debate about increasing the role of Social Security, not decreasing it. Again, as we've noted in *Get What's Yours,* Social Security was never designed to be a provider of most of an older person's retirement income. But it has become so for most retirees. We need to recognize this reality as well as the limited success of the private retirement savings industry.

What makes more sense — an expansion of a voluntary retirement savings program that hasn't worked well, or expansion of Social Security, which has worked well, is already available to nearly all workers, is very inexpensive to administer, and offers guaranteed payments that include inflation protection?

SOCIAL SECURITY
AND YOUNGER GENERATIONS

Make no mistake. There is no free lunch here. Expanding Social Security would mean higher payroll taxes for ordinary working Americans and their employers. It would limit the growth of private savings and investment plans. It would represent further nationalization of our retirement system. All of this bothers me a lot, but not nearly as much as the prospect of millions of Americans facing longer lives with insufficient financial resources to enjoy them. And that is clearly the future we will have unless we make major improvements in our retirement programs.

It's also a future that will be felt primarily by younger generations. Paul, Larry, and I already know what our retirements will look like, at least in terms of our retirement incomes. Changing Social Security will mean very little if anything to us or to most people already in their 50s and 60s. But it will mean a lot to those who are younger. The health of Social Security is really a younger person's game, and people under 40 overwhelmingly believe it's game over for them. Opinion polls show that younger persons don't believe Social Security will be there when they retire. So, my last requirement for changing the program is to make sure that whatever we do, younger generations can once again feel confident that they can plan their lives and their retirements around a solid Social Security program.

ACKNOWLEDGMENTS

I thank our editor, Bob Bender, and agent, Alice Martell, for so adroitly and gracefully shepherding the publication of this book. And I thank Boston University for its enduring and significant support of my research and efforts to make my research of direct value to the public, the private sector, and policymakers.

— LAURENCE KOTLIKOFF

The responsibility for the contents of this book rests solely with its authors. But there are many researchers and journalists whose work has helped me immensely in understanding the issues addressed in *Get What's Yours.* Special thanks to Nancy Altman, codirector of Social Security Works and cochair of the Strengthen Social Security project; David C. John, deputy director for the Retirement Security Project at the Brookings Institution and a senior strategic

403

policy adviser with AARP's Public Policy Institute; and Eugene Steuerle at the Urban Institute. Many thanks also to the Center for Retirement Research at Boston College, directed by Alicia Munnell, which has authored an invaluable stream of research and clear analysis about Social Security and its many claiming challenges. The center, the University of Michigan Retirement Research Center, and the National Bureau of Economic Research, make up the Retirement Research Consortium, which has conducted extensive research on Social Security (much of it funded by the agency). The Employee Benefit Research Institute is a treasure trove of data and insights on retirement topics. Reports from the Congressional Budget Office and Government Accountability Office are must-reads. Morningstar is the gold standard of consumer-oriented research about retirement investments. Financial service firms regularly churn out solid research on individual retirement savings and spending habits; Fidelity and Vanguard stand out but there are many, many others doing terrific work here.

Kimberly Castro, managing editor for Money and Health at *U.S. News & World Report,* provided time and support for my own articles about Social Security from 2008 to 2013. More recently, Penelope Wang, editor-at-large at *Money,* has been equally generous and supportive of my writing there. I am thankful to them, and also appreciative of the efforts by other journalists who track important retirement and Social Security topics. There is a cadre of experienced journalists who follow these topics. With apologies for the inevitable omissions. I have been a faithful reader of Emily Brandon, *U.S. News & World Report;* Scott Burns, a longtime financial journalist and friend who later built his own asset management company, AssetBuilder; Mary Beth Franklin, *Investment News;* Michael Hiltzik, *Los Angeles Times;* Stan Hinden, AARP; Mark Miller, Reuters and Morningstar; Janet Novack, *Forbes;* Robert Powell, *MarketWatch;* and Anne Tergesen, *Wall Street Journal* (and before her, Kelly Greene, who left the *Journal* in 2014).

The Social Security Administration is, far and away, the most extensive and valuable resource for information about its programs. It has a deep and accessible website. It posts research and reports online, including its rules and its detailed Program Operating Manual System (POMS). It provides upwards of 100 forms on its website and is moving as quickly as it can to place more and more of its public communications capabilities online. Among federal bureaucracies, Social Security stands out for being transparent and accessible. Still, *Get What's Yours* would have been a more complete book had the Social Security Administration saw fit to allow me to interview its experts and managers. For reasons never provided to me, it declined to do so. Given the complexity of Social Security, there is a wealth of knowledge that officials could have imparted. Public information officer Dorothy Clark did respond dutifully to many of my questions. She also declined to respond to many other questions I posed, without explaining why. Her colleague Kia Anderson, who left the agency in 2014, was also most helpful. Thanks to them both. Despite wanting more access, I came to understand the agency's sensitivity to its public statements and its reluctance to provide comments. Nearly every American who works or has worked during the past 80 years, not to mention their family members, is affected by Social Security rules. Any public comment by an authorized representative of the agency literally can affect — and potentially confuse and alarm

— millions of people.

— PHILIP MOELLER

As for me, I'm grateful for those in the acknowledgments above, including the coauthors who wrote them, and to *PBS NewsHour* (originally *The MacNeil/Lehrer Report*), which has employed me for nearly 30 years now, giving me unparalleled encouragement — and ample time — to cover the news from an economics perspective. The program also encouraged me to initiate an online page — Making Sen$e — where Larry first posted on Social Security in the summer of 2012 and where he has generously answered viewer questions every Monday since. The Making Sen$e website, as well as our coverage over the past nine years, was made possible by the support of the Sloan Foundation. And, of course, viewers like you, though I trust you won't mind that I don't acknowledge each of you by name.

— PAUL SOLMAN

GLOSSARY

Average Indexed Monthly Earnings (AIME)
When Social Security computes an insured worker's benefit, it first adjusts or "indexes" his or her earnings to reflect the change in general wage levels that occurred during the worker's years of employment. Such indexation ensures that a worker's future benefits reflect the general rise in the standard of living that occurred during his or her working lifetime. Up to 35 years of earnings are needed to compute Average Indexed Monthly Earnings. If a worker has more than 35 covered years, Social Security chooses those years with the highest indexed earnings, sums such indexed earnings, and divides the total amount by the total number of months in those years. It then rounds the resulting average amount down to the next-lower dollar amount. The result is the AIME. If a person has fewer than 35 years of covered earnings, Social Security takes

the actual years, enters 0 for the rest, and divides by 420 (the number of months in 35 years).

Bend Point

Bend points divide your AIME into portions that contribute varying percentages to your PIA: 90 percent of the lowest portion under the first bend point, 32 percent of the middle portion between the bend points, and 15 percent of the amount above the second bend point. The dollar levels of these bend points are adjusted for inflation. In 2015, they are $826 and $4,980. A description of how bend points are used is found below in the entry for Primary Insurance Amount (PIA).

Child-in-Care Spousal Benefit

Having a child in care may allow you to claim spousal benefits if you have not yet reached 62 and may also make you eligible for mother's and father's insurance. You have a child in care if you have parental control, as defined by Social Security, over a child who is under 16 or who is 16 or older and is disabled.

Child Benefit

A child can claim child insurance benefits on a parent's record if the child is dependent on that parent as defined by Social Security and if the child is not married. The child also must either be under 18, or be no older than 19, and a full-time elementary or secondary school student. The parent on whose record the claim is based must be entitled to disability or retirement insurance. The child insurance benefit is equal to 50 percent of the insured parent's PIA if the insured parent is currently entitled to a retirement benefit.

Child Survivor Benefit

A child is eligible for a surviving child insurance on a deceased parent's record if all the conditions to receive child insurance benefits are met and the child was also dependent on the deceased parent and the deceased parent was either fully or currently insured at the time of death. The surviving child insurance benefit is equal to 75 percent of the deceased parent's PIA at the time of death.

Cost of Living Adjustment (COLA)

COLAs are applied to years after you become eligible to receive benefits in order to maintain the purchasing power of retirement benefits. They become effective in December of each year and reflect the rise in the Consumer Price Index (CPI) during the 12 months ending the previous September.

Covered Earnings

These are the maximum amount of wages on which you pay Social Security taxes. Earnings covered by Social Security are those for which you paid Social Security taxes, either by having them withheld from your paycheck or by paying Social Security taxes on earnings from self-employment. The ceiling for covered earnings rises each year to adjust for inflation. The ceiling in 2015 is $118,500.

Death Benefit

A onetime payment of $255 paid in addition to any monthly survivors benefits that are due. This benefit is paid only to a widow/widower or minor children.

Deeming

The deeming provision states that if you are eligible for both reduced retirement and reduced spouse's benefits — meaning you've filed for them before your Full

Retirement Age (FRA) — then you cannot restrict your application to just one of these types of benefits. By filing for either benefit, you are deemed by law to have filed for both types of benefits. You will collect an amount equal to or close to the greater of the two benefits.

Delayed Retirement Credit (DRC)

Between Full Retirement Age and age 70, monthly benefits will rise by 8 percent a year plus the COLA for people who defer taking their retirement benefit.

Disabled Child Insurance Benefit

A child can claim disabled child insurance benefits on a parent's record if the child meets all of the conditions to receive child insurance benefits and if he or she is 18 or older and under a disability as defined by Social Security. This disability must also have begun before the child reached age 22. The disabled child insurance benefit is equal to 50 percent of the insured parent's PIA if the insured parent is currently eligible for a retirement benefit. The benefit amount might be reduced by the Family Maximum Benefit (FMB; see below). The benefit amount also might be reduced if a disabled child is eligible for a disability or retirement insurance benefit based on his or her own record, in which case only the amount by which the child's monthly benefit rate exceeds his or her retirement or disability insurance amount is paid as the disabled child insurance benefit.

Divorced Spouse's Insurance Benefit

You can claim divorced spouse's insurance benefits if your ex-spouse is currently entitled to retirement or disability insurance benefits. You must be single and 62 or over and you must have been married to your ex-spouse for at least 10 years. Also, you cannot claim this benefit if your PIA exceeds or equals one-half of your ex-spouse's PIA and you are currently entitled to retirement or disability insurance. If your ex-spouse is not currently entitled to retirement or disability insurance benefits, but he or she has attained age 62 and is fully insured, you can become independently entitled to benefits on your ex-spouse's record if you meet all of the other requirements in the preceding paragraph and have been divorced for at least two continuous years.

Divorced Widow(er)'s Insurance Benefit

You may be eligible for divorced widow(er)'s insurance benefits if you were married to your deceased ex-spouse for at least 10 years. You must also be age 60 or over, or at least age 50 but under 60 and meet the disability requirements as defined by Social Security. Your deceased ex-spouse must also have been fully insured; you must be single; and you must not be entitled to a retirement insurance benefit equaling or exceeding your deceased ex-spouse's PIA. The same limitations as above apply to divorced widow(er)'s benefits if your deceased ex-spouse was ever entitled to reduced retirement benefits.

Early Retirement Reduction
People who claim Social Security benefits before reaching FRA are subject to a range of potentially large and permanent reductions depending on their claiming ages and the type of benefit involved. The table below illustrates the effect of early retirement for both a retired worker and the spousal benefits to which his or her spouse is eligible. For this illustration, Social Security used a $1,000 PIA.

Year of birth[a]	Normal (or full) retirement	Number of reduction months[b]	Monthly Primary Annual	Percent Reduction[c]	Monthly Spouse Amount	Percent reduction[d]
1937 or earlier	65	36	$800	20.00	$375	25.00
1938	65 and 2 months	38	791	20.83	370	25.83
1939	65 and 4 months	40	783	21.67	366	26.67
1940	65 and 6 months	42	775	22.50	362	27.50
1941	65 and 8 months	44	766	23.33	358	28.33
1942	65 and 10 months	46	758	24.17	354	29.17
1943–1954	66	48	750	25.00	350	30.00
1955	66 and 2 months	50	741	25.83	345	30.83
1956	66 and 4 months	52	733	26.67	341	31.67
1957	66 and 6 months	54	725	27.50	337	32.50
1958	66 and 8 months	56	716	28.33	333	33.33
1959	66 and 10 months	58	708	29.17	329	34.17
1960 and later	67	60	700	30.00	325	35.00

A) If you are born on January 1, use the prior year of birth. B) Applies only if you are born on the 2nd of the month; otherwise the number of reduction months is one less than the number shown. C) Reduction applied to PIA ($1,000 in this example). The percentage reduction is 5/9 of 1 percent per month for the first 36 months and 5/12 of 1 percent for each additional month. D) Reduction applied to $500, which is 50 percent of the PIA in this example. The percentage reduction is 25/36 of 1 percent per month for the first 36 months and 5/12 of 1 percent for each additional month.

Earnings Test

People collecting benefits who continue to work are subject to an Earnings Test until they've reached FRA. Social Security withholds benefits if the worker's earnings exceed a certain level, called a retirement Earnings Test exempt amount. One of two different exempt amounts apply — a lower amount in years before the year you attain FRA and a higher amount in the year you attain FRA. These exempt amounts generally increase annually with increases in the national Average Wage Index. It's important to note, however, that benefit reductions caused by the Earnings Test usually will be restored once the worker reaches FRA. At that age, his or her monthly benefit will be increased permanently to account for the months in which benefits were withheld.

For people attaining FRA after 2015, the annual exempt amount in 2015 is $15,720. For people attaining FRA in 2015, the annual exempt amount is $41,880. This higher exempt amount applies only to earnings made in months prior to the month of FRA attainment. Social Security withholds $1 in benefits for every $2 of earnings in excess of the lower exempt amount. It withholds $1 in benefits for every $3 of earnings in excess of the higher exempt amount. Earnings in or after the month the worker reaches FRA do not count toward the retirement test.

Family Maximum Benefit (FMB)
The FMB is a ceiling on the total Social Security benefits that may be collected based on a single worker's earnings record. It is not a fixed percentage but varies depending on the worker's earnings and even the kinds of benefits involved. If your PIA is very low, your FMB will be 150 percent of your PIA. With a somewhat higher PIA, the FMB rises to 187 percent of your PIA. Then the multiple drops, ending up at 175 percent of your PIA. Auxiliary benefits — those available to other family members — are subtracted from the worker's PIA and thus are 50 percent of the very-low-income worker's PIA, 87 percent of the moderate-income worker's PIA, and 75 percent of the high earner's PIA.

Second, if the worker takes her benefits early, say at 62, her retirement benefit will be reduced to 75 percent of her PIA. In this case, the most that the family, including the worker, would receive is 75 percent of her PIA (her reduced retirement benefit) plus 50 percent of her PIA — the most left over for the spouse and kids after subtracting the

PIA, not her actual benefit received from the FMB. In this case, the total amount the very-low-earner family, including the earner herself, can receive is only 125 percent of the worker's PIA.

Next, suppose the worker is a moderate earner and has a FMB equal to 187 percent of her PIA. Further assume this worker waits until 70 to collect her retirement benefit. In this case her own retirement benefit is 1.32 times her PIA and the maximum Auxiliary Benefits are 87 percent of her PIA. Hence, the largest amount the moderate earner family, including the earner herself, could receive is 219 percent of the worker's PIA.

The formula used to compute the FMB is similar to that used to compute the PIA. The formula sums four separate percentages of portions of the worker's PIA. For 2015 these portions are the first $1,056, the amount between $1,056 and $1,524, the amount between $1,524 and $1,987, and the amount exceeding $1,987. These dollar amounts are the "bend points" of the FMB formula. For the family of a worker who became age 62 or died in 2015 before attaining age 62, the total amount of benefits payable will be computed so that it does not exceed:

a. 150 percent of the first $1,056 of the worker's PIA, plus

b. 272 percent of the worker's PIA over $1,056 through $1,524, plus

c. 134 percent of the worker's PIA over $1,524 through $1,987, plus

d. 175 percent of the worker's PIA over $1,987.

Full Retirement Age (FRA)

FRA is the age at which a person may first become entitled to full or unreduced retirement benefits. The FRA for those born between 1943 and 1954 is 66. For those born before 1943, it is lower. For cohorts born after 1954, it will gradually rise to age 67 for those born in 1960 or later. (Also called Normal Retirement Age by Social Security.)

Full Retirement Benefit

This is the retirement benefit available to a worker based on his or her own work history, assuming the worker applies for a retirement benefit at their FRA. Social Security also refers to a worker's Full Retirement Benefit as their Primary Insurance Amount.

Government Pension Offset (GPO)

If you receive a pension based on your employment by the US government, state governments, or other political subdivisions not covered by Social Security, then any spouse's, divorced spouse's, widow(er)'s, divorced widow(er)'s, or deemed spouse's benefits may be reduced if you receive pension payments based on that employment. For everyone who began or will begin receipt of his or her government pension in December 1984 or later, the GPO reduces your Social Security benefit by two-thirds of the amount of your government pension.

Primary Insurance Amount (PIA)

This is a worker's full retirement benefit. It is calculated via a progressive benefits formula based on your Average Indexed Monthly Earnings. The PIA is the sum of three separate percentages of portions of the AIME (see Bend Point above for further details). For an individual who first becomes eligible for old-age insurance benefits or disability insurance benefits in 2015, his or her PIA will be the sum of:

a. 90 percent of the first bend point of $826 in AIME, plus

b. 32 percent of the second bend point for

AIME over $826 and through $4,980, plus

c. 15 percent of AIME in excess of $4,980.

Recomputation of Benefits

Social Security will automatically increase your benefit if warranted. This is most often caused by continued wage earnings after reaching age 60 that qualify to become one of your 35 highest years of earnings included in calculations to determine your AIME, on which your PIA is based. There can be other causes for recomputation but whatever they are, your PIA might be increased, but will never be decreased. The recomputation becomes effective in January of the year after the earnings were generated. For example, an increased benefit due to a recomputation based on 2015 earnings will first be applied to the payment for January 2016.

Retirement Insurance Benefit Limit (RIB-LIM)

This limit applies to widow(er) benefits claimed on the earnings of spouses who filed for their retirement benefits before reaching FRA. The RIB-LIM computation can be very complex. The benefit you can claim as a widow(er) on your deceased spouse's earnings record is limited to the higher of either 82.5 percent of their retirement benefit at his or her FRA, or the amount your deceased spouse was collecting at the time of death.

Social Security Disability Insurance (SSDI)

SSDI is the program providing monthly benefits to disabled workers and their eligible family members. It is supported by a separate disability insurance trust fund within the Old-Age, Survivors, and Disability Insurance program.

Spousal Insurance Benefit

At FRA, a spouse is eligible for the larger of his retirement benefit based on his own record or half of the retirement benefit his spouse will be eligible for at his or her FRA based on that spouse's record. (Do not feel bad if you need to read this over again — we've read it a lot!) If the retirement benefit a spouse would receive based on his own record is less than half of the retirement benefit his spouse would receive at his FRA based on that spouse's record, the excess spouse's insurance benefit at FRA is the difference between the retirement benefit a spouse is entitled to and half of the benefit his spouse would receive at FRA. The spousal benefit eligibility rule stipulates that no matter their age, a spouse is not eligible for spouse's benefits until the spouse whose earnings the claim is based on files for his or her retirement benefits. If you are eligible for both reduced retirement and reduced spouse's benefits and you file for either, you will be deemed by law to have applied for both (see Deeming above).

Supplemental Security Income (SSI)

SSI is funded by general tax revenues, not Social Security taxes, and provides monthly cash payments to aged, blind, and disabled people who have limited income and resources. It is administered by the Social Security Administration.

Widow(er)'s Insurance Benefits

If you were married to your deceased spouse at least 9 months and you are 60 or older, or if you are at least age 50 but under 60 and you meet the disability requirements as defined by Social Security, you may be eligible for widow(er)'s benefits. If divorced, you must not have remarried before age 60. Your deceased spouse or ex-spouse must have achieved fully insured status, and you must not be eligible for a retirement insurance benefit that equals or exceeds your deceased spouse's PIA. Your unreduced widow(er)'s benefit is equal to your deceased spouse's PIA at FRA plus any increases to his or her retirement insurance benefit from Delayed Retirement Credits earned by delaying receipt of retirement benefits past his or her FRA. Your widow-(er)'s benefit is limited if your deceased spouse claimed retirement benefits early before reaching FRA. (See Retirement Insurance Benefit Limit above for further details).

Windfall Elimination Provision (WEP)

You will be subject to the WEP if you earned a pension in any job not covered by Social Security and you also have enough Social Security credits for covered quarters due to other employment and are therefore eligible for Social Security retirement benefits. The WEP may reduce your Social Security benefits unless you have worked 30 or more years in covered employment (in jobs that levied Social Security payroll taxes). In 2015, the WEP cannot reduce your monthly Social Security payments by more than $413 or half of your non-covered pension, whichever amount is less.

THE BASICS*

EMPLOYMENT AND EARNINGS

Workers in Old-Age, Survivors, and Disability Insurance covered employment	163 million
Average earnings	$42,870
Earnings required in 2015 for:	
1 quarter of coverage	$1,220
Earnings Test exempt amounts for 2015:	
Under Full Retirement Age for entire year	$15,720
For months before reaching Full Retirement Age in 2015	$41,880

2013 AVERAGE MONTHLY BENEFIT

Retired workers	
Couple	$2,176
Men	$1,417
Women	$1,103
Spouses	$626
Children	$617
Survivors of deceased workers	
Nondisabled widow(er)s	$1,215
Disabled widow(er)s	$711

Widowed mothers and fathers	$900
Surviving children	$799
Parents	$1,073
Disabled workers	
Men	$1,256
Women	$993
Spouses	$304
Children	$336
Cost-of-living adjustment for 2015:	1.7 percent

NUMBER OF BENEFICIARIES

OASDI	57.5 million
Old-Age Insurance	
Total	40.8 million
Retired workers	37.9 million
Spouse	2.3 million
Child	.6 million
Survivors Insurance	
Total	6.2 million
Widows and widowers	4.1 million
Disability Insurance	
Total	11 million
Disabled workers	8.9 million

TOTAL BENEFIT PAYMENTS

Old-Age, Survivors, and Disability Insurance $812.3 billion

Old-Age and Survivors Insurance $672.1 billion

Disability Insurance $140.1 billion

TAX RATES

5.30 percent of covered payroll each for employee and employer for retirement insurance.

0.90 percent of covered payroll each for employee and employer for disability insurance.

1.45 percent of TOTAL payroll each for employee and employer for Medicare Part A (hospital) insurance. High-income households pay additional 0.9 percent Medicare tax mandated by Affordable Care Act.

Total is 15.30 percent, all of which a self-employed person must pay.

Based on current data as of November 2014.

ANNUAL TAXES PAYABLE IN 2013

Average earner: $2,779 for OASDI; $650 for Medicare

Maximum earner: $7,049 for OASDI; no

limit for Medicare

2015 payroll tax ceiling: $118,500 in annual earnings

Maximum taxable annual earnings: $113,700 in 2013; $117,000 in 2014

APPENDIX:
ACTUALLY FILING TO GET
WHAT'S YOURS

Okay. You may need a few deep breaths before tackling this next piece of advice. At some point, you actually will need to file for your own Social Security retirement benefit. We're here to help.

It will come as no surprise by this point in *Get What's Yours* that there is a seemingly endless array of reasons why you might file for some form of Social Security at many different ages. If this is the case, move with deliberate speed. Go online first and search out as much as you can.

During your online journey, you will come across articles, advice, and, of course, commercial messages from any number of groups and people who want "to help you." Use them as a guide and, when you inevitably wind up at the Social Security website, which you will, compare what these sources say with what Social Security says. Larry owns a Social Security software company that provides claiming advice; there are others as well. Check them out. But in the end, the official word, perhaps hard to find and harder still to understand, will be found somewhere at ssa.gov. So will most of the forms you will need. The agency is, after all, the Hallmark of benefits and has a form or application for every occasion (smiley faces not included).

While we regularly take Social Security to task, its website can be very helpful *if you know where to look.* You can actually file online. But if that scares you, or even if you just want someone to talk to as you go through the process, by all means call or visit your local Social Security office. Just be sure to have a copy of this book close at hand, lest a disagreement arise. We suggest bookmarking (you might consider dog-earing) any pages you hope to act on.

If you decide to defer your benefits, the odds are you will need to file for Medicare before you file for Social Security. Medicare, of course, often seems as complicated as Social Security. That's a book for another day. For now, just make sure that you file for Medicare alone and do not accidentally file for your Social Security benefit, too. Take your time. Make sure you understand ahead of time anything you sign or are asked to sign.

And while Social Security has just about every form you'll need online, we can't walk you through an online application here, given all the permutations of individual circumstances. To actually file for benefits online, you'll need to create your personalized My Social Security account and provide the agency with your personal information. Many of the forms are interactive — the information you provide on one screen will trigger the display of the next screen, taking you step-by-step through the application. We asked Social Security to provide us the text for all these screens so we could see what the agency wanted to know and whether its wording was clear. The agency declined our request.

But it did provide us the basic printed form for applications that is used if you go to a local office and apply in person. It is extensive and, while it may not ask for the information in the same way or sequence that would occur online, it provides an inventory of what you'll be expected to tell the agency when you apply for your own retirement benefit. It also provides information on filing for Medicare, some agency disclosure standards, and a list of personal events that Social Security wants you to communicate to the agency.

The form we're presenting here is called **Form SSA-1-BK**. It was last updated in February 2014. The agency regularly updates forms but the information requested here will not have changed greatly since then.

As you make your way through this form, you'll see our guidance and comments inserted in italics, centered, just like this sentence.

Ready? Here goes:

APPLICATION FOR RETIREMENT INSURANCE BENEFITS

1. (a) PRINT your name: FIRST NAME, MIDDLE INITIAL, LAST NAME
   (b) Check (X) whether you are:
       ☐ Male ☐ Female
2. Enter your Social Security number:

Answer question 3 if English is not your language preference. Otherwise, go to item 4.

3. Enter the language you prefer to: Speak Write
4. (a) Enter your date of birth: Month, Day, Year
   (b) Enter name of city and state, or foreign country where you were born.
   (c) Was a public record of your birth made before you were age 5? ☐ Yes ☐ No ☐ Unknown
   (d) Was a religious record of your birth made before you were age 5? ☐ Yes ☐ No ☐ Unknown

Shades of birthers going after President Obama? Hardly. But the agency regularly

435

encounters applicants who are not who they seem. Even people who already have a Social Security card number may be asked to provide proof of their birth and residency. And while we don't know how often the statements on these forms are aggressively checked for accuracy and truthfulness, providing false information is a strategy we would label "suboptimal."

5. (a) Are you a U.S. citizen? ☐ Yes (Go to item 7.) ☐ No (Go to item (b).)
   (b) Are you an alien lawfully present in the U.S.? ☐ Yes (Go to item (c).) ☐ No (Go to item 6.)
   (c) When were you lawfully admitted to the U.S.?
6. Enter your full name at birth if different from item 1(a): FIRST NAME, MIDDLE INITIAL, LAST NAME
7. (a) Have you used any other name(s)? ☐ Yes (Go to item (b).) ☐ No (Go to item 8.)
   (b) Other name(s) used:
8. (a) Have you used any other Social Security number(s)? ☐ Yes (Go to item (b).) ☐ No (Go to item 9.)

(b) Enter Social Security number(s) used:

Millions of people have inadvertent inconsistencies in their work records. They may be Bob on one payroll form and Robert on another. A middle initial may pop up on one W-2 and not on another from a second employer. Women who change their names upon marriage may have earnings that Social Security is not including in their benefits calculations. Helping the agency track down possible duplications makes sense.

Do not answer question 9 if you are one year past full retirement age or older; go to question 10.

9. (a) Are you, or during the past 14 months have you been, unable to work because of illnesses, injuries or conditions? ☐ Yes ☐ No

(b) If "Yes," enter the date you became unable to work: MONTH, DAY, YEAR

10. (a) Have you (or has someone on your behalf) ever filed an application for Social Security,

Supplemental Security Income, or hospital or medical insurance under Medicare? ☐ Yes (If "Yes," answer (b) and (c).) ☐ No (If "No," go to item 11.) ☐ Unknown (If "Unknown," go to item 11.)

(b) Enter name of person(s) on whose Social Security record you filed other application: FIRST NAME, MIDDLE INITIAL, LAST NAME

(c) Enter Social Security number(s) of person named in (b). (If unknown, so indicate.):

11. (a) Were you in the active military or naval service (including Reserve or National Guard active duty or active duty for training) after September 7, 1939 and before 1968? ☐ Yes (If "Yes," answer (b) and (c).) ☐ No (If "No," go to item 12.)

(b) Enter date(s) of service: From — Month, Year; To — Month, Year

(c) Have you ever been (or will you be) eligible for monthly benefits from a military or civilian Federal agency? (Include Veterans

Administration benefits only if you waived Military retirement pay.) ☐ Yes ☐ No

People who've served in the military can get wage credits that may increase their Social Security benefits. They also can receive a military pension *and* Social Security benefits. So, you should know your service record. You can find more details at http://www.ssa.gov/retire2/veterans.htm.

12. Did you or your spouse (or prior spouse) work in the railroad industry for 5 years or more? ☐ Yes ☐ No

There is a special retirement program for railroad workers, begun independently of Social Security at a time when railroads played a much larger role in the nation's economy than they do today. The program is run by the Railroad Retirement Board (https://secure.rrb.gov/). Be aware that a railroad retirement pension can be affected by a person's Social Security work history and benefits.

13. (a) Do you (or your spouse) have Social Security credits (for ex-

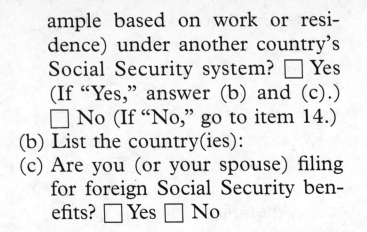

ample based on work or residence) under another country's Social Security system? ☐ Yes (If "Yes," answer (b) and (c).) ☐ No (If "No," go to item 14.)

(b) List the country(ies):

(c) Are you (or your spouse) filing for foreign Social Security benefits? ☐ Yes ☐ No

The United States has agreements with 25 other nations to help people get proper retirement credit if they've earned wages from work in multiple countries. These so-called totalization agreements are explained at http://www.ssa.gov/international/agreements_overview.html.

Answer question 14 only if you were born January 2, 1924, or later. Otherwise go on to question 15.

14. (a) Are you entitled to, or do you expect to be entitled to, a pension or annuity (or a lump sum in place of a pension or annuity) based on your work after 1956 not covered by Social Security? ☐ Yes (If "Yes." Answer (b) and (c).) ☐ No (If "No," go

on to item 15.)
    (b) I became entitled, or expect to become entitled, beginning: month/year
    (c) I became eligible, or expect to become eligible, beginning: month/year

I agree to promptly notify the Social Security Administration if I become entitled to a pension, an annuity, or a lump sum payment based on my employment not covered by Social Security, or if such pension or annuity stops.

The previous questions refer to our old friends — WEP and GPO. Check them out in Chapter 12 or in the Glossary.

15. Have you been married?
    (a) Yes. If Yes, answer Item 16.
    (b) No. If No, go to Item 17.

We have devoted much effort to talking about spousal benefits, divorce benefits, and survivor benefits. So does Social Security. The agency is gathering marital information here that could be crucial in any future benefit issues involving your spouse (present, former, or deceased) and your children. Remember the old ad campaign about it not being nice to fool Mother Nature? Well, it's even worse to try to fool Social Security. We know one thing about a program based on possibly paying benefits for the rest of your life, your present and former spouses' lives, and even the lives of your children: it has a *very* long institutional memory.

16. (a) Give the following information about your current marriage. If not currently married, write "None." Go on to item 16(b).

> Spouse's name (including maiden name)
>
> When (Month, day, year)
>
> Where (Name of City and State)
>
> How marriage ended (If still in effect, write "Not Ended.")
>
> When (Month, day, year)
>
> Where (Name of City and State)
>
> Spouse's date of birth (or age)

If spouse deceased, give date of death

Spouse's Social Security number (If none or unknown, so indicate)

(b) Enter information about any other marriage if you:
- Had a marriage that lasted at least 10 years; or
- Had a marriage that ended due to death of your spouse, regardless of duration; or
- Were divorced, remarried the same individual within the year immediately following the year of the divorce, and the combined period of marriage totaled 10 years or more.

Use the "Remarks" space to enter the additional marriage information. If none, write "None." Go on to item 16 (c) if you have a child(ren) who is under age 16 or disabled or handicapped (age 16 or over and disability began before age 22); and you are divorced from the child's other parent, who is now deceased, and the marriage lasted less than 10 years.

Spouse's name (including maiden name)

When (Month, day, year)

Where (Name of City and State)

How marriage ended

When (Month, day, year)

Where (Name of City and State)

Marriage performed by:
• Clergyman or public official
• Other (Explain in "Remarks")

Spouse's date of birth (or age)

If spouse deceased, give date of death

Spouse's Social Security number (If none or unknown, so indicate)

(c) Enter information about any marriage if you:
• Have a child(ren) who is under age 16 or disabled or handicapped (age 16 or over and disability

began before age 22); and
- Were married for less than 10 years to the child's mother or father, who is now deceased; and
- The marriage ended in divorce. If none, write "None."

To whom married

When (Month, day, year)

Where (Name of City and State)

How marriage ended

When (Month, day, year)

Where (Name of City and State)

Marriage performed by:
- Clergyman or public official
- Other (Explain in "Remarks")

Spouse's date of birth (or age)

If spouse deceased, give date of death

Spouse's Social Security number (If none or unknown, so indicate)

Use the "Remarks" space for marriage continuation or explanation.

If your claim for retirement benefits is approved, your children (including adopted children and stepchildren) or dependent grandchildren (including step grandchildren) may be eligible for benefits based on your earnings record.

17. List below FULL NAME OF ALL your children (including adopted children, and stepchildren) or dependent grandchildren (including stepgrandchildren) who are now or were in the past 6 months UN-MARRIED and:
    - UNDER AGE 18
    - AGE 18 TO 19 AND ATTENDING SECONDARY SCHOOL OR ELEMENTARY SCHOOL FULL-TIME
    - DISABLED OR HANDICAPPED (age 18 or over and disability began before age 22)

Social Security payments may be available to qualifying children and their parents if the children are young, in school, or are disabled, and became disabled before age 22.

Also list any student who is between the ages of 18 to 23 if such student was both: 1) Previously entitled to Social Security benefits on any Social Security record for August 1981; and 2) In full-time attendance at a post-secondary school.

(IF THERE ARE NO SUCH CHILDREN, WRITE "NONE" BELOW AND GO ON TO ITEM 18.)

18. (a) Did you have wages or self-employment income covered under Social Security in all years from 1978 through last year?
☐ Yes (If "Yes," go to item 19.)
☐ No (If "No," answer item (b).)

(b) List the years from 1978 through last year in which you did not have wages or self-employment income covered under Social Security:

Social Security retirement benefits normally require at least 40 quarters of earnings large enough to qualify as representing a "covered quarter" for the purposes of calculating benefit entitlements. Current information on required earnings levels may be found at http://www.ssa.gov/oact/cola/QC.html. As you know by now, unless you first opened the book to this page, the agency uses up to 35 years of covered earnings to calculate your Annual Indexed Monthly Earnings, a figure that is used to calculate your Primary Insurance Amount. If you have more than 35 years of earnings, the agency uses the highest 35 in calculating your AIME. See Chapter 3 for more details.

19. Enter below the names and addresses of all the persons, companies, or government agencies for whom you have worked this year, last year, and the year before last. IF NONE, WRITE "NONE" BELOW AND GO ON TO ITEM 20.

NAME AND ADDRESS OF EMPLOYER (If you had more than one employer, please list them in order beginning with your last (most recent) employer.)

Month Year   Month Year

(If you need more space, use "Remarks.")

20. May we ask your employers for wage information needed to process your claim? ☐ Yes ☐ No

21. THIS ITEM MUST BE COMPLETED, EVEN IF YOU ARE AN EMPLOYEE.

(a) Were you self-employed this year and/or last year? ☐ Yes (If "Yes," answer (b).) ☐ No (If "No," go to item 22.)

(b) Check the year or years in which you were self-employed: In what kind of trade or business were you self-employed? (For example, storekeeper, farmer, physician)

Were your next earnings from your business $400 or more? (Check "Yes" or "No")
☐ This year ☐ Yes ☐ No
☐ Last year ☐ Yes ☐ No

22. (a) How much were your total earnings last year? Amount: $

An accurate earnings record, including any self-employment income, is essential to

Getting What's Yours. This includes a record of months in which you did not work — information that Social Security needs to know to process your application accurately. Be aware that there's a 1–2 year lag time for the agency to gather your formal earnings records from the IRS.

(b) Place an "X" in each block for EACH MONTH of last year in which you did not earn more than *$ in wages, and did not perform substantial services in self-employment. These months are exempt months. If no months were exempt months, place an "X" in "NONE." If all months were exempt months, place an "X" in "ALL."

*Enter the appropriate monthly limit after reading the instructions, "How Work Affects Your Benefits" (http://www.ssa.gov/pubs/EN-05-10069.pdf).

☐ NONE ☐ ALL
Jan. Feb. Mar. Apr. May Jun.
Jul. Aug. Sept. Oct. Nov. Dec.

23. (a) How much do you expect your

total earnings to be this year? Amount: $

(b) Place an "X" in each block for EACH MONTH of this year in which you did not or will not earn more than *$ in wages, and did not or will not perform substantial services in self-employment. These months are exempt months. If no months are or will be exempt months, place an "X" in "NONE." If all months are or will be exempt months, place an "X" in "ALL."

*Enter the appropriate monthly limit after reading the instructions, "How Work Affects Your Benefits" (http://www.ssa.gov/pubs/EN-05-10069.pdf).

☐ NONE ☐ ALL
Jan. Feb. Mar. Apr. May Jun.
Jul. Aug. Sept. Oct. Nov. Dec.

Answer this item ONLY if you are now in the last 4 months of your taxable year (Sept., Oct., Nov., and Dec., if your taxable year is a calendar year).

24. (a) How much do you expect to earn next year? Amount: $

(b) Place an "X" in each block for EACH MONTH of next year in which you do not expect to earn more than *$ in wages, and do not expect to perform substantial services in self-employment. These months will be exempt months. If no months are expected to be exempt months, place an "X" in "NONE." If all months are expected to be exempt months, place an "X" in "ALL."

*Enter the appropriate monthly limit after reading the instructions, "How Work Affects Your Benefits" (http://www.ssa.gov/pubs/EN-05-10069.pdf).

☐ NONE ☐ ALL
Jan. Feb. Mar. Apr. May Jun.
Jul. Aug. Sept. Oct. Nov. Dec.

25. If you use a fiscal year, that is, a taxable year that does not end December 31 (with income tax return due April 15), enter here the month your fiscal year ends._____

DO NOT ANSWER ITEM 26 IF YOU ARE FULL RETIREMENT AGE AND 6

MONTHS OR OLDER; GO TO ITEM 27.
PLEASE READ CAREFULLY THE IN-
FORMATION ON THE BOTTOM OF
PAGE 8 AND ANSWER ONE OF THE
FOLLOWING ITEMS:

26. (a) I want benefits beginning with
the earliest possible month, and
will accept an age-related reduction. ☐
(b) I am full retirement age (or will
be within 12 months), and want
benefits beginning with the earliest possible month providing
there is no permanent reduction
in my ongoing monthly benefits. ☐
(c) I want benefits beginning with
(enter date). ☐

We explained how to file and suspend in
Chapter 5. If you wish to file and suspend
your benefits, you don't need to complete
this form at all. However, if you do complete it and want to file and suspend, make
sure you indicate that intention here and
that the Social Security representative
processing this form understands your
intention and confirms that this is a valid
request that complies with agency rules.

MEDICARE INFORMATION

If this claim is approved and you are still entitled to benefits at age 65, or you are within 3 months of age 65 or older you could automatically receive Medicare Part A (Hospital Insurance) and Medicare Part B (Medical Insurance) coverage at age 65. If you live in Puerto Rico or a foreign country, you are not eligible for automatic enrollment in Medicare Part B, and you will need to contact Social Security to request enrollment.

COMPLETE ITEM 27 ONLY IF YOU ARE WITHIN 3 MONTHS OF AGE 65 OR OLDER

Medicare Part B (Medical Insurance) helps cover doctor's services and outpatient care. It also covers some other services that Medicare Part A does not cover, such as some of the services of physical and occupational therapists and some home health care. If you enroll in Medicare Part B, you will have to pay a monthly premium. The amount of your premium will be determined when your coverage begins. In some cases, your premium may be higher based on information about your income we receive from the Internal Revenue Service. Your premiums will be deducted from any monthly Social Security, Railroad Retirement, or Office of Personnel Management benefits you receive. If you do not receive any of these benefits, you will get a letter explaining how to pay your premiums. You will also get a letter if there is any change in the amount of your premium.

While *Get What's Yours* is not about Medicare, we can't stress here too strongly that this program, like Social Security, can be very complicated and that you should not take decisions about it lightly or, worse, assume you don't have decisions to make. Please take the time — beginning at least several months before you sign up — to carefully explore the program and your options. In particular, use the online tools at medicare.gov to find the best insurance plans for your needs. This often involves carefully entering the specific drugs and dosages you take into Medicare's "formulary" tool to find insurance plans that will give you the best pricing deal.

You can also enroll in a Medicare prescription drug plan (Part D). To learn more about the Medicare prescription drug plans and when you can enroll, visit www.medi care.gov or call 1-800-MEDICARE (1-800-633-4227; TTY 1-877-486-2048). Medicare can also tell you about agencies in your area that can help you choose your prescription drug coverage. The amount of your premium varies based on the prescription drug plan provider. The amount you pay for Part D coverage may be higher than the listed plan premium, based on information about your income we receive from the Internal Revenue Service.

If you have limited income and resources, we encourage you to apply for the Extra Help that is available to assist you with Medicare prescription drug costs. The Extra Help can pay the monthly premiums, annual deductibles, and prescription co-payments. To learn more or apply, please visit www.socialsecurity.gov, call 1-800-772-1213 (TTY 1-800-325-0778) or visit the nearest Social Security office.

One last Medicare tip: this is not a "set and forget" program. Insurers change their coverage terms and prices every year. Most Medicare beneficiaries stick with the same plan from year to year, even after it has ceased being the best plan for them. Take advantage each fall of the annual enrollment period when you can change Medicare plans. If you find a plan that has received Medicare's highest quality rating of five stars, you will be able to switch into that plan anytime during the year. (Medicare frees top-rated plans from annual enrollment limitations.)

27. Do you want to enroll in Medicare Part B (Medical insurance)?
☐ Yes ☐ No

Filing for Medicare should not trigger a claim for Social Security benefits but make sure Social Security does not accidentally think you've filed for both (unless, of course, that's exactly what you want to do).

28. If you are within 2 months of age 65 or older, blind or Disabled, do you want to file for Supplemental Security Income? ☐ Yes ☐ No

REMARKS (USE A BLANK SHEET OR SHEETS FOR ANY EXPLANATIONS.)

I declare under penalty of perjury that I have examined all the information on this form, and on any accompanying statements or forms, and it is true and correct to the best of my knowledge. I understand that anyone who knowingly gives a false or misleading statement about a material fact in this information, or causes someone else

457

to do so, commits a crime and may be sent to prison, or face other penalties, or both.

SIGNATURE OF APPLICANT

Date (Month, day, year)

SIGNATURE (First Name, Middle Initial, Last Name) (Write in ink.)

Telephone number(s) at which you may be contacted during the day:

DIRECT DEPOSIT PAYMENT INFORMATION (FINANCIAL INSTITUTION)

Routing Transit Number: _____

Account Number: _____
☐ Checking
☐ Savings
☐ Enroll in Direct Express

Applicant's Mailing Address (Number and street, Apt No., P.O. Box, or Rural Route) (Enter Residence Address in "Remarks," if different.):

_____

City and State: _____

ZIP Code: _____

County (if any) in which you now live:

_____

Witnesses are required ONLY if this application has been signed by mark (X) above. If signed by mark (X), two witnesses who know the applicant must sign below, giving their full addresses. Also, print the applicant's name in the Signature block.

1. Signature of Witness: _____

Address (Number and Street, City, State and ZIP Code)

_____

2. Signature of Witness: _____

Address (Number and Street, City, State and ZIP Code)

_____

COLLECTION AND USE OF INFORMATION FROM YOUR APPLICATION/PRIVACY ACT NOTICE/PAPERWORK REDUCTION ACT NOTICE

Sections 202, 205, and 223 of the Social Security Act, as amended, authorize us to collect this information. We will use the information you provide to determine if you or a dependent are eligible for insurance coverage and/or monthly benefits.

The information you furnish on this form is voluntary. However, if you fail to provide all or part of the requested information it may prevent us from making an accurate and timely decision concerning your or a dependent's entitlement to benefit payments.

We rarely use the information you supply for any purpose other than determining benefit payments for you or a dependent. However, we may use it for the administration and integrity of our programs. We may also disclose information to another person or to another agency in accordance with approved routine uses, which include but are not limited to the following:

Read this privacy section carefully. Although the agency says it rarely uses your information for anything save benefit decisions, you should assume that other government agencies could see the information you've provided to Social Security.

1. To enable a third party or an agency to assist us in establishing right to Social Security benefits and/or coverage;
2. To comply with Federal laws requiring the release of information from our records (e.g., to the Government Accountability Office and Department of Veterans Affairs);
3. To make determinations for eligibility in similar health and income maintenance programs at the Federal, State, and local level; and
4. To facilitate statistical research, audit, or investigative activities necessary to assure the integrity of Social Security programs (e.g., to the Bureau of Census and to private entities under contract with us).

We may also use the information you provide in computer matching programs. Matching programs compare our records with records kept by other Federal, State, or local government agencies. Information from these matching programs can be used to establish or verify a person's eligibility for federally funded or administered benefit programs and for repayment of incorrect payments or delinquent debts under these programs.

A complete list of routine uses for this information is available in our Privacy Act Systems of Records Notices entitled, Earnings Recording and Self Employment Income System (60-0059) and Claims Folders Systems (60-0089). Additional information regarding these and other systems of records notices, are available online at www.socialsecurity.gov or at your local Social Security office.

Paperwork Reduction Act Statement — This information collection meets the requirements of 44 U.S.C. § 3507, as amended by section 2 of the Paperwork Reduction Act of 1995. You do not need to answer these questions unless we display a valid Office of Management and Budget control number. We estimate that it will take about 11 minutes to read the instructions, gather the facts, and answer the questions. **SEND OR BRING THE COMPLETED FORM TO YOUR LOCAL SOCIAL SECURITY OFFICE. You can find your local Social Security office through SSA's**

website at www.socialsecurity.gov. Offices are also listed under U.S. Government agencies in your telephone directory or you may call Social Security at 1-800-772-1213 (TTY 1-800-325-0778). You may send comments on our time estimate above to: SSA, 6401 Security Blvd, Baltimore, MD 21235-6401. Send only comments relating to our time estimate to this address, not the completed form.

CHANGES TO BE REPORTED AND HOW TO REPORT

Failure to report may result in overpayments that must be repaid, and in possible monetary penalties

- You change your mailing address for checks or residence. (To avoid delay in receipt of checks you should ALSO file a regular change of address notice with your post office.)
- Your citizenship or immigration status changes.
- You go outside the U.S.A. for 30 consecutive days or longer.
- Any beneficiary dies or becomes unable to handle benefits.
- Work Changes — On your application you told us you expect total earnings

to be $ a year.

You ☐ (are) ☐ (are not) earning wages of more than $_____ a month.

You ☐ (are) ☐ (are not) self-employed rendering substantial services in your trade or business.

(Report AT ONCE if this work pattern changes)

- You are confined to a jail, prison, penal institution or correctional facility for more than 30 continuous days for conviction of a crime, or you are confined for more than 30 continuous days to a public institution by a court order in connection with a crime.
- You have an unsatisfied warrant for more than 30 continuous days for your arrest for a crime or attempted crime that is a felony of flight to avoid prosecution or confinement, escape from custody and flight-escape. In most jurisdictions that do not classify crimes as felonies, this applies to a crime that is punishable by death or imprisonment for a term exceeding one year (regardless of the actual sentence imposed).

- You have an unsatisfied warrant for more than 30 continuous days for a violation of probation or parole under Federal or State law.

Okay. We doubt that Social Security will be on your list of pen pals if you wind up in the slammer or are fleeing from the *gendarmerie*. But other change-of-life events can, as we've stressed, have a big impact on the Social Security benefits due you and other present and even former family members. So, before informing Social Security of such changes, take a lap or two through *Get What's Yours* and make sure you understand the benefit implications of these changes, including the timing of any indicated benefit applications.

- You become entitled to a pension, an annuity, or a lump sum payment based on your employment not covered by Social Security, or if such pension or annuity stops.
- Your stepchild is entitled to benefits on your record and you and the stepchild's parent divorce. Stepchild benefits are not payable beginning with the month after the month the divorce becomes final.

- Custody Change — Report if a person for whom you are filing or who is in your care dies, leaves your care or custody, or changes address.
- Change of Marital Status — Marriage, divorce, annulment of marriage.
- If you become the parent of a child (including an adopted child) after you have filed your claim, let us know about the child so we can decide if the child is eligible for benefits. Failure to report the existence of these children may result in the loss of possible benefits to the child(ren).

HOW TO REPORT

You can make your reports online, by telephone, mail, or in person, whichever you prefer.

If you are awarded benefits, and one or more of the above change(s) occur, you should report by:

- Visiting the section "my Social Security" at our web site at www.social security.gov
- Calling us TOLL FREE at 1-800-772-1213.
- If you are deaf or hearing impaired, calling us TOLL FREE at TTY 1-800-

325-0778; or

- Calling, visiting or writing your local Social Security office at the phone number and address shown on your claim receipt.

For general information about Social Security, visit our web site at www.socialsecurity .gov.

For those under full retirement age, the law requires that a report of earnings be filed with SSA within 3 months and 15 days after the end of any taxable year in which you earn more than the annual exempt amount. You may contact SSA to file a report. Otherwise, SSA will use the earnings reported by your employer(s) and your self-employment tax return (if applicable) as the report of earnings required by law, to adjust benefits under the earnings test. It is your responsibility to ensure that the information you give concerning your earnings is correct. You must furnish additional information as needed when your benefit adjustment is not correct based on the earnings on your record.

In nearly all cases, the W-2 that your employers file with the IRS or, if you're self-employed, your tax returns, will be sufficient documentation of this reporting requirement. But we do have a problem with Social Security's statement that it's your responsibility to furnish additional information when "your benefit adjustment is not correct." How, we ask, are you going to know if it's not correct unless the agency tells you? And how would it know the information is not correct in the first place? Benefit adjustments based on the Earnings Test may not be apparent to you for years after the earnings were received and disclosed to Social Security. Our advice here (and, unlike Social Security, we do give advice) is to keep very careful records of your earnings. If you are affected by the Earnings Test, make sure any benefit reductions (which, you'll recall, are later restored to most beneficiaries) agree with your earnings records. If they don't, contact the agency right away.

PLEASE READ THE FOLLOWING INFORMATION CAREFULLY BEFORE YOU ANSWER QUESTION 27.

- If you are under full retirement age, retirement benefits cannot be payable to you for any month before the month in which you file your claim.
- If you are over full retirement age,

retirement benefits may be payable to you for some months before the month in which you file this claim.

This is a very oblique reference to the Social Security rule that most people who delay filing for benefits past full retirement age can receive a lump-sum payment equal to up to six months of their benefits. The period may be up to a year for some filers. But the entitlement period does not include periods before reaching full retirement age. So, if you filed for spousal benefits at age 66 and 4 months, your lump-sum payment would be for only four months of benefits. Check out Chapter 3 for further details and exceptions.

- If your first month of entitlement is prior to full retirement age, your benefit rate will be reduced. However, if you do not actually receive your full benefit amount for one or more months before full retirement age because benefits are withheld due to your earnings, your benefit will be increased at full retirement age to give credit for this withholding. Thus, your benefit amount at full retirement age will be reduced only if you receive one or more full benefit payments prior to the month you attain full retirement age.

With modest apologies for piling on, the *Get What's Yours* language police politely requests that the SSA rewrite the above paragraph.

RECEIPT FOR YOUR CLAIM FOR SOCIAL SECURITY RETIREMENT INSURANCE BENEFITS TO BE COMPLETED BY SOCIAL SECURITY REPRESENTATIVE

TELEPHONE NUMBER(S) TO CALL IF YOU HAVE A QUESTION OR SOMETHING TO REPORT

BEFORE YOU RECEIVE A NOTICE OF AWARD:

AFTER YOU RECEIVE A NOTICE FOF AWARD:

SSA OFFICE:

DATE CLAIM RECEIVED:

Establishing the time you filed for benefits may be crucial if any questions later occur about your eligibility for benefits or the amount of benefits due you. You can establish this time most securely by applying for benefits at a Social Security office and having the agency's representative enter the time of your application. You also can file by mail. We recommend a certified letter requiring agency acknowledgment. If you file for benefits over the phone or online, and do not receive written confirmation of your claim after a few weeks, we recommend you write a certified letter to your local SS office. You can find a ZIP code office locator at *https:// secure.ssa.gov/ICON/main.jsp.* Include the date of your claim and the details of how it was filed. If any dispute later arises, this letter can help establish a record of your actions.

Your application for Social Security benefits has been received and will be processed as quickly as possible.

You should hear from us within_____ days after you have given us all the information we requested. Some claims may take longer if additional information is needed.

In the meantime, if you change your address, or if there is some other change that may affect your claim, you — or someone for you — should report the change. The changes to be reported are listed above.

Always give us your claim number when writing or telephoning about your claim.

If you have any questions about your claim, we will be glad to help you.

CLAIMANT: _____

SOCIAL SECURITY CLAIM NUMBER: _____

NOTES

Chapter 1. Getting Paul Nearly $50,000 in Extra Benefits over Tennis

1. To be precise, it's an October-through-September inflation rate.
2. $B(a) = PIA(a) \times (1 - e(n)) \times (1 + d(n)) \times Z(a) + max((.5 \times PIA^*(a) - PIA(a) \times (1 + d(n))) \times E(a), 0) \times (1 - u(a,q,n,m)) \times D(a)$. This is the "simple" formula for the benefit, B, of a spouse at age a. There are 10 separate mathematical functions on the right-hand side. We wonder what would happen if members of Congress were asked to explain this formula to constituents.

Chapter 2. Life's Biggest Danger Isn't Dying, It's Living

1. "Framing Effects and Expected Social Security Claiming Behavior," Jeffrey R.

Brown, Aries Kapteyn, and Olivia S. Mitchell, NBER Working Paper 17018, May 2011.

2. "In particular, for most plausible real interest rates, two-earner households with average life expectancy maximize the present value of Social Security benefits when the primary earner delays claiming until age 70. Primary earners in one-earner couples can also maximize the present value of their household's benefits by delaying, though the actuarially advantageous delay period is shorter and the gains are smaller. Delaying is less attractive for secondary earners in two-earner couples, and for singles. However, at real interest rates of 1.6 percent or less, two-earner households maximize present value when secondary earners delay as well.

Single men and women benefit from at least a short delay (to age 64) for real interest rates of, respectively, 3.5 percent or less and 4.1 percent or less. "The Decision to Delay Social Security Benefits: Theory and Evidence," National Bureau of Economic Research, http://www.nber .org/papers/w17866.

3. "Social Security Consumer Study," Nationwide Financial Retirement Institute, June 2014.

4.

Exact age	MALE Life expectancy	FEMALE Life expectancy
62	19.74	22.63
63	18.99	21.81
64	18.24	20.99
65	17.51	20.19
66	16.79	19.39
67	16.08	18.61
68	15.39	17.84
69	14.70	17.08
70	14.03	16.33
71	13.37	15.59
72	12.72	14.87
73	12.09	14.16
74	11.47	13.47
75	10.87	12.79
76	10.28	12.13
77	9.71	11.48
78	9.16	10.86
79	8.62	10.24
80	8.10	9.65
81	7.60	9.07
82	7.12	8.51
83	6.66	7.97
84	6.22	7.45
85	5.80	6.95

| | **MALE** | **FEMALE** |
Exact age	Life expectancy	Life expectancy
86	5.40	6.48
87	5.02	6.03
88	4.66	5.61
89	4.33	5.22
90	4.02	4.85
91	3.73	4.50
92	3.46	4.19
93	3.22	3.89
94	3.00	3.63
95	2.81	3.39
96	2.64	3.18
97	2.49	2.98
98	2.36	2.81
99	2.24	2.65
100	2.12	2.49

Note: The period life expectancy at a given age is the average remaining number of years expected prior to death for a person at that exact age, born on January 1, using the mortality rates for 2009 over the course of his or her remaining life. Source: http://www.ssa.gov/oact/STATS/table4c6.html.

5. "Risks and Process of Retirement Survey Report," Society of Actuaries, 2012.
6. Melissa A. Z. Knoll, "Behavioral and Psychological Aspects of the Retirement

Decision," *Social Security Bulletin* 71, no. 4 (2011).

Chapter 3. Social Security — from A to Zzzzzzz

1. These steps are explained in the statement but it does not provide numerous other basic details about your benefits that we believe it should.
2. http://www.ssa.gov/policy/docs/policy briefs/pb2011-02.html.
3. Of course, a dollar received at age 100 is not as valuable as a dollar received today because you could bank the dollar received today and have more, potentially much more, money at age 100. It's even less valuable if you have to be alive to receive it. Using a reasonable 2 percent real interest rate to discount — make less of all future Social Security benefits that you might receive through age 100 — produces lifetime benefits of $556,088 from taking benefits immediately versus $712,411 from waiting till 70. This means that waiting to collect is equivalent (apart from tax issues) to finding $156,323 ($712,411 less $556,088) on the sidewalk!
4. The precise formula is the smaller of the widow(er) benefit reduction factor times

the decedent's PIA and an amount we'll call *x*. This amount *x* is the larger of a) the decedent's retirement benefit inclusive of any Delayed Retirement Credits (if the decedent suspended their retirement benefit after reaching FRA) or b) 82.5 percent of the decedent's primary insurance amount.

5. Every year, the agency and others who oversee its programs issue extensive reports. One is called the *Annual Report of the Board of Trustees of the Federal Old-Age and Survivors Insurance and Federal Disability Insurance Trust Funds.* A second is called the *Annual Statistical Supplement to the Social Security Bulletin.* Many of the tables and charts presented here are taken from the most recent versions of these documents. However, to make sure you're seeing the most current data, you might want to look up these documents in a search engine and download the current versions.

Chapter 4. Three General Rules to Maximize Your Lifetime Benefits

1. The current FRA for purposes of calculating spousal or retirement benefits is 66. That age will rise by two months begin-

ning in 2021 (for someone born in 1955) and will keep going up by two months every year until FRA reaches 67 in 2027 (for those born in 1960 and later years).

Chapter 7. The Benefits of Not Retiring

1. Not everyone will see their AIME rise if they continue working, of course. Many older persons seek part-time jobs or shift into encore careers where compensation is secondary to the appeal of the job. And for people who in the past earned near the national average wage, the end of indexing might not have much of an impact. In short, if the prospect of higher Social Security benefits is an important component of your decision to keep working, you should analyze your earnings years and see how continued work would affect your AIME.

Chapter 8. Playing Social Security's Marital Status Game

1. Same old reminder: FRA starts going up for those of you born after 1954.

Chapter 9. Married with Benefits

1. These are "plain vanilla" choices. As we've gone to great lengths to stress, claiming ages can be as early as 60 for survivors, 50 for disabled survivors, and much younger for disabled claimants and qualifying children.
2. Larry's company, Economic Security Planning, sells annual subscriptions to this online program to households ($40) and financial planners ($200) at www.maximizemysocialsecurity.com. Larry's program is top-rated by the *Wall Street Journal* and has been featured in other major media outlets. But there are other Social Security optimization programs, some of which are provided for free (as discussed in Chapter 6) and others of which are provided for a relatively small annual license fee.

Chapter 10. Gay Couples Get to Claim What's Theirs

1. The District of Columbia's sanctioning of same-sex marriage carries broad weight because Social Security claims involving people who reside outside the United States are decided based on D.C. laws.

2. Section 216(h)(1)(A)(i): "An applicant is the wife, husband, widow, or widower of a fully or currently insured individual for purposes of this title if the courts of the State in which such insured individual is domiciled at the time such applicant files an application, or, if such insured individual is dead, the courts of the State in which he was domiciled at the time of death, or, if such insured individual is or was not so domiciled in any State, the courts of the District of Columbia, would find that such applicant and such insured individual were validly married at the time such applicant files such application or, if such insured individual is dead, at the time he died." http://www.ssa.gov/OP _Home/ssact/title02/0216.htm

3. Details on spousal benefit policies can be found at https://secure.ssa.gov/apps10/ poms.nsf/lnx/0200210100.

Chapter 11. Divorced? Dark Clouds and Silver Linings

1. Recall that the excess spousal benefit is the difference between half of your spouse or ex-spouse's full retirement benefit less 100 percent of your full retirement benefit. The full retirement benefit is the PIA,

which, as we showed in Chapter 3, is calculated via a highly progressive formula.

2. If the excess spousal benefit is zero (because it was set from a negative value to zero), there is no deeming of the excess spousal benefit. So, you could, in theory, receive a nonreduced excess spousal benefit starting at your FRA were your ex to increase, via additional work, his PIA to the point that half of it exceeded 100 percent of your PIA.

3. Your total payment starting at age 70 in case A will be the sum of a) your full retirement benefit inclusive of your Delayed Retirement Credits plus b) your excess spousal benefit. Your excess spousal benefit at age 70 will be the difference between half of your ex's full retirement benefit less 100 percent of your full retirement benefit augmented by your Delayed Retirement Credits. For each dollar your own retirement benefit rises due to the Delayed Retirement Credit, your excess spousal benefit falls by one dollar *until the excess spousal benefit equals zero. At that point, having higher Delayed Retirement Credits raises your total payment. So case A can't be worse than case B and may be better.* There is a case C in which you file

for both benefits, but then suspend the collection of your retirement benefits till 70. This will reduce your spousal benefit, if it's positive, to your excess spousal benefit. But it will give you access to your Delayed Retirement Credits and give you the option of taking a lump-sum distribution of all of your suspended retirement benefits. Like case B, case C seems worse than case A.

4. Maximize My Social Security.
5. Ibid.
6. Ibid.

Chapter 12. Widowed? Why Social Security Is a Major Women's Issue

1. Widows whose husbands died before age 62 may be entitled to a slight bump-up in benefits due to a provision in the law enacted in 1983. It tried to at least partially equalize their survivor's benefits with those of women whose husbands died at later ages. This provision does so by assuming the deceased husband's benefits were calculated at a later age, using an alternative computation called Widow-(er)'s Indexing, or WINDEX for short (gotta love those clever acronym wizards at the SSA).

Chapter 13. Never Married or Divorced Too Soon

1. http://www.census.gov/hhes/families/files/ cps2013/tabA1-all.xls.

Chapter 14. Hidden Benefits for the Disabled

1. "A worker who becomes disabled before the quarter in which he or she attains age 31 satisfies the recency-of-work require-ment if credits have been earned for at least one-half of the quarters during the period beginning with the quarter after the quarter the worker attained age 21, and ending with the quarter in which the disability began. If this period contains 12 or fewer quarters — that is, if the disability begins in the quarter the worker attains age 24 or earlier — then a minimum of six credits must be earned in the 12-quarter period ending with the quarter in which the disability began."

2. www.ssa.gov/policy/docs/quickfacts/ stat_snapshot/.

3. For nondisabled workers now age 62, tak-ing benefits immediately comes at a 25 percent reduction relative to their full retirement benefit. Hence, a disabled

worker is receiving 1/(1 −.25) or 1.33 times what the nondisabled worker would receive.

4. Maximize My Social Security.

Chapter 15. Government Pensions and Windfall Penalties

1. Now, because you are an eagle-eyed reader, you probably noticed the use of the phrase "substantial earnings" in the WEP adjustment table. It turns out that you need to have earned a fair amount of covered earnings in a year for it to qualify as "substantial" under the WEP provisions. The agency defines substantial as 25 percent of each year's payroll tax ceiling. But in a trip down one of Social Security's numerous rule-making rabbit holes, it doesn't use the current law's ceiling but what the ceiling would be under laws in effect prior to 1976. You can find annual figures for substantial earnings at http://www.ssa.gov/OACT/cola/yoc.html.

Chapter 16. 50 Good-News Secrets to Higher Lifetime Benefits

1. More precisely, if 100 percent of your PIA is less than 50 percent of your

spouse's PIA.

2. Technical aficionados will find a flaw in this language. Social Security doesn't literally consider the date that you file for your retirement, i.e., the date that you walk into their office or call them on the phone and request your retirement benefit. Instead, they consider the date at which you become entitled to receive a retirement benefit. You can file for a retirement benefit up to 4 months before you are eligible to collect it and if you do so file, you become entitled to the benefit on the date at which you become eligible to collect it. You become entitled even if you suspend your benefit; hence, even though you have filed for your retirement benefit, have become eligible for it, have become entitled to receive it, you have, nonetheless, elected to suspend its receipt.

3. She would receive the smaller of a) his full PIA reduced by the survivor benefit reduction factor if the widow takes her survivor benefit early and b) an amount we'll call x. So what's x? It is the larger of c) what he was collecting when he died and d) 82.5 percent of his PIA. The earlier the deceased worker took survivor benefits, the smaller is his actual benefit entering into part c). So, up to a point, the

sooner the decedent spouse took his retirement benefit, the less his widow will collect.

Chapter 17. 25 Bad-News Gotchas That Can Reduce Your Benefits Forever

1. This is not precisely correct. What you'll get is the sum of your reduced retirement benefit plus the difference between the reduced excess spousal benefit, defined as half of your spouse's full retirement benefit minus 100 percent of your full retirement benefit augmented by any Delayed Retirement Credits. The reduction applied to the entire excess spousal benefit is based on the spousal benefit reduction factor. And because the retirement and spousal benefit reduction factors aren't identical, the total benefit is not exactly just the reduced spousal benefit.

2. Deeming does not apply to survivor benefits. You can file early for survivor benefits, and not be forced to file for retirement benefits, and vice versa. Also, there is an exemption from being deemed to file for your spousal benefit. If you file for your retirement benefit early, you can only be deemed to be filing for your spousal benefit if your spouse has filed for

their retirement benefit. So if your spouse hasn't yet filed, you are exempt and that exemption isn't revoked when your spouse does file. Thus you're free to decide when you want to file for a spousal benefit. Unless both spouses file for their early retirement benefits at the same time, one will enjoy the spousal benefit deeming exemption of Secret #36 in Chapter 16, namely, the one who files first for an early retirement benefit. Moreover, child-in-care spousal benefits do not trigger deeming.

488

ABOUT THE AUTHORS

Laurence J. Kotlikoff is a professor of economics at Boston University and president of Economic Security Planning, Inc. His company websites are ESPlanner.com and MaximizeMySocialSecurity.com.

Philip Moeller is a longtime journalist and currently a contributing writer at *Money,* where he specializes in retirement. He also is a Research Fellow at the Sloan Center on Aging & Work at Boston College, and the founder of Insure.com, a leading site for Insurance information.

Paul Solman is a Brady-Johnson Distinguished Practitioner in Grand Strategy at the International Security Studies department at Yale University. He is the business and economics correspondent for *PBS NewsHour.*